Mafia Confession

"King of Bootleggers" Murder

By Nicholas Anthony Parisi

D1718380

ISBN:
ISBN-9798860921498

Acknowledgements

I want to express my heartfelt gratitude to all my relatives, both gone and present, for the countless memories we've shared. I pay homage to all the Parisi family; the Augustino's, Bonfitto's, Dialessi's, Galarneau's, Marvici's, Selvatico's, and Viola's - and extend a special tribute to the younger generation, my beloved cousins and my three sons, Giovanni, Dominic, and Anthony. May this piece of family history be handed down for many generations to come.

I would like to express my appreciation to Dominic Parisi, my unpaid editor, who read this manuscript meticulously and provided invaluable advice that helped make it a success.

I am profoundly thankful to my cousins David, Joseph, Michael, and Peter Parisi for bestowing upon me the privilege of writing this book and for their contribution to making Joe's personal diary accessible.

Above all, I am immensely grateful to my life partner, Renee, for her love and affection. For all the sleepless nights and the break of dawns, and to keep me in my right mind throughout the past year. Thank you for being a steady supporter and encouraging me to make this book a success. But more than anything, thank you for being my best friend. I owe you everything and love you forever.

Presentazione

I told you, you 'figlio di puttana,' not to go on Water Street, or I'll kill-ya and don't try to sell booze to anyone on Water Street at all." When Carlo said that to me, I shouted, "I got no boss; I do as I like!" He turned around and reached into his hip pocket as though to draw a gun. I saw something shiny. I thought it was a gun, see. It was either his life or mine, so I fired mine first. I was so nervous I didn't know how many shots I fired. I took off and ran all the way to Park Street. I want to give myself up; I don't try to run away. I was afraid somebody would come after me from Siniscalchi's gang."

My trembling hand clutched the pen as I signed the confession at the Springfield Police Station. I muttered to the detectives, admitting to killing Carlo Siniscalchi, the "King of Bootleggers." I told them I was scared for my life and acted in self-defense - but that's not how it really went down. If Siniscalchi hadn't cheated me out of my hard-earned loot and then hired a gunman to take me out just weeks earlier, I wouldn't have felt the urge to get vengeance. With that attempt to end my life, a chain of events erupted that led our families down a devastating, bloody path of murder, corruption, and retaliation.

My name is Giuseppe Antonio Parisi. I stepped onto the docks of America in 1909, leaving my native Caraffa del Bianco, Reggio di Calabria, Italy, far behind me. I could barely contain my excitement as I watched the skyline of New York City come into view. Feeling the weight of my family's hopes and dreams on my shoulders, I was determined to make a new life for them in this new

Land. Breathing in the salty air as the boat docked and taking in the sights and sounds of my new home, I looked around at the bustling streets and people and knew this was where my family would start a new life. Settling in West Springfield, Massachusetts, we call "West Side"- home.

This gripping crime story is true.

All names, events, and conversations in this book are real and carefully documented from the newspapers of the era, reporter interviews, trial and law enforcement archives, author Nick Parisi's family conversations, and the personal diary of Giuseppe "Joseph" Parisi.

Table of Contents

Pre-Prohibition Mafia

"As is the case with all nationalities, there is a class among the Italians that has but little respect for the law and the rights of society. Having been chased out of their own country, members of this class flee to America, in proportionally greater numbers than do the peaceful citizens."

– THE SPRINGFIELD SUNDAY UNION

1

1

When I arrived in Springfield, Massachusetts, in 1909, I was immediately thrust into the chaotic violence of the South End. The Italian section of the city, known for its lawlessness and crime, was where I was to call home. Water Street, now renamed Columbus Avenue, was the city's roughest area. It was the epicenter of the Italian population, mostly Neapolitans from Napoli, becoming their own "Little Italy," providing safety and protection from strangers. We were outsiders, fighting to live in a world that seemed against us. Every day was a battle for survival. We had to be intelligent and cunning, constantly aware of lurking dangers. As we walked the streets, the smell of freshly baked bread and the sound of children playing mixed with the fear of violence and threat. We were immigrants, struggling to make it in a world that was not ours.

The Parisi family left the hustle and bustle of the South End and crossed the Connecticut River to the tree-lined streets of West Springfield. The Merrick section was heavily populated by our people, Southern Italians from Calabria, and it seemed like everyone was related by blood or marriage. The Italians had an unspoken understanding from birth that when rivals met in this new, unfamiliar land, they were instantly allies. Without a word, a simple gesture was enough to show that they would do anything for one another - as if they were long-lost cousins.

The Italian family offered us a sanctuary in our new homeland. We were never alone with family by our side; they provided comfort, help, advice, food, and money when needed. Our fathers were strict, our mothers selfless, and our grandparents loving. Within the family circle, an unspoken code of conduct extended to blood and honorary relatives, those we called aunts, uncles, and cousins but were close, intimate friends. However, outsiders were considered hostile until proven friendly or safe.

The waves of Italian immigrants began to arrive in Springfield, Massachusetts, around 1900, providing a new source of cheap labor that fueled the city's booming factories. The population of Springfield quickly rose as men and women speaking the Italian language flocked to the city. However, the state's longstanding locals, the descendants of the Puritans who had settled in Massachusetts in the 1600s, were not pleased with the changes. They openly expressed suspicion and doubt about our willingness and ability to fit into their society, and they were disgusted by our Catholic religion. The locals feared that the world they and their ancestors had built was in danger of disappearing.

On September 7, 1913, an article was published in our hometown newspaper, *The Springfield Sunday Union;*

"As is the case with all nationalities, there is a class among the Italians that has but little respect for the law and the rights of society. Having been hounded out of their own country, members of this class flee to America in proportionally greater numbers than the peaceful citizens.

"Consequently, we are led to believe, by the surface indications, that the Italians are a dreadful lot. If they are more so than other nationalities, there is a sufficient excuse for this, often stated but as often forgotten. It is in that southern part of Italy the country is infested with brigands and bandits. It is a condition similar to what existed in the western part of this country 25 years ago.

"With little or no police protection, it behooves the Italian peasants to sleep with guns near at hand and to carry weapons with them into the fields. How are they to know that in America, it is different? For generations, the peasants in Southern Italy have been protecting themselves, and it is so ingrained into their natures that it seems logical that they should carry revolvers about with them in the United States. Such a deep-seated custom cannot be uprooted by the mere sight of the Statue of Liberty or the first breath of free American air.

"Locally, Springfield has been particularly fortunate in being free from Italian rampages. There have been Italian murders and attacks, but there have also been murders in Forest Park and other sections of the city. The Italian quarter is not distinguished by its Black Hand or red record."

By the 1920s, Massachusetts was teetering on the edge of a tipping point. Ethnic and religious prejudice ran rampant, fueled by the rapid growth of the Ku Klux Klan led by Springfield Herald newspaper editor Charles Lewis. The Ku Klux Klan's staunch support of prohibition, often working with the Woman's Christian Temperance Union, saw the demonization of anything urban or ethnic in nature, particularly boxing, dancing, and liquor. When the nation declared Prohibition in 1920, the old-line purists rejoiced, while the state's many immigrants were left in despair, having no intention of giving up our beloved spirits. This created a massive demand for someone to quench the state's thirst, a demand that gave rise to the gangs that would eventually evolve into the Mafia.

Enforcing the prohibition law quickly became a joke, particularly among Springfield's heavily populated immigrant population. Liquor flowed freely, often traded in secret bars and speakeasies. The smell of cigarettes and liquor lingered in the air, and the streets echoed with laughter and music. It was a different world in which struggling settlers from the Neapolitan and Calabrian regions saw an opportunity.

As I watched my fellow Italians struggle to realize the American dream, I couldn't help but wonder how the mob had started in Springfield. In the time leading up to Prohibition, it had not yet become the well-structured criminal operation it was later to be. We were desperate; some would do anything to get money, power, and a better life. Some formed street gangs, running protection rackets on local businesses, gambling, burglary, loan sharking, brothels, and contract violence. People knew these gangs were dangerous, which was the key to their success. They weren't afraid to use violence or even take a life if they had to. It was a brutal world, but it was the only way for some.

At the turn of the century, the Albano family could be considered the first known Italian criminal gang in Springfield. The Albanos were from Bracigliano, Province of Salerno, near Napoli, often making headlines in the local newspapers for their illegal activities. The Naples area of Italy was heavily controlled by the Camorra, similar to the Sicilian Mafia and Calabrian 'Ndrangheta. It was clear the Albanos were not to be messed with. The Albanos were a law unto themselves, and the locals knew it. People were too fearful to speak out against them, and the local police seemed powerless to intervene. The Albanos were the undisputed kings of the city.

Giovanni "John" Albano is the founding father of Springfield's "Little Italy," known as the South End. His far-reaching influence was undeniable and diverse, from his extensive real estate holdings to his steamship agency and bail bonds business to his Italian bank on Water Street, which had been in operation for over two decades. He owned a sprawling estate and residence in Westfield, several large plots of land on upper State Street, and a house on William Street. Everywhere he went, he left an indelible mark on the city. His success in real estate was unparalleled, with properties popping up all over town like mushrooms after a rain. People would flock to his bank, hoping to receive a loan. His steamship agency was a reliable source of transportation for merchants and passengers alike. And his bail bonds business was a source of security in uncertain times. You could see the evidence of his ambition and hard work everywhere you looked.

John Albano was renowned as a "Padrone," a man who helped bring Italians to America to work in the factories. *The Springfield Republican* credits him with having "persuaded no less than 1,000 citizens of his native town of Bracigliano, Italy, to come to the settlement on the Connecticut River."

He made his wealth from the employers who needed low-income workers and immigrants, selling steamship tickets, renting rooms, feeding them, granting them loans until they started earning, and then holding their money in his Italian Bank. "Many a time, a man would find himself at the end of his rope or in serious trouble. His fellow's invariable advice was, "Go see John; he'll fix you up."

Albano strode confidently through the city, a leader in his own right. He founded the Mt. Carmel Society and the Patria Society more than ten years ago. Everywhere he went, his fellow members of the Foresters, Red Men, Lady of Grace Society, and Mount Carmel Church greeted him with respect and admiration. At the center of it all, Albano had become a pillar of the community. He had set up a legacy that would continue for years to come.

In 1911, the *Springfield Daily News* reported an account of the Albano family's evil doings.

The thick fog of cigar smoke filled the room of the Albano house, where four men had been playing cards for hours. The clinking of glasses and swigging of liquor could be heard as the tensions rose. Frank Albano was losing to Frank Buonomo, a guy he knew from work. Albano's face had become a flustered shade of red. Buonomo noticed the jealous gaze that Albano was giving a diamond ring on his pinky finger, and a chill of unease ran down his spine. The monster inside Albano took over, and he leaped from his chair. He lunged at Buonomo, his hands grasping for the ring. They became locked in a struggle, with Albano biting his wrist desperately, trying to get him to release the ring. Buonomo's screams cut through the air. Suddenly, Pasquale Anzololla appeared by their side with a razor and slashed at Buonomo's face, the blade glinting in the light. Buonomo felt the warm spray of his blood as he wrenched himself free from Albano's grasp and tried to run. Before he'd taken a few steps, a gunshot rang out, and he felt a searing pain in his back, his lung pierced. He fell to the ground, hearing the sound of the gun clattering to the floor as it backfired. Albano lunged for the revolver, and in a desperate attempt to take aim at Buonomo, he instead fired two shots at his cousin Carlo Sarno, hitting him in the head.

Luigi Albano frantically rushed Sarno to Mercy Hospital, where hospital staff immediately contacted the police and arrested Sarno. Pasquale Anzololla rushed to the Springfield police station to check on his friend, only to be thrown into custody himself. While Frank Buonomo lay in his Thompsonville, CT home, barely clinging to life, Frank Albano was nowhere to be found, and the police were in hot pursuit.

CONFESSION

The Albano family bolstered their illicit realm when Pasqualina Albano, John Albano's niece, married Salvatore Caroalucci "Carlo" Siniscalchi in 1912. His affiliations with the Camorra gangs in Brooklyn, where he had initially settled before moving to Springfield, helped him ascend to the top of the Albano criminal group.

In 1915, Carlo Siniscalchi and his brother Durante, accompanied by the notorious gangster Michael Fiore, descended upon an unsuspecting police officer like a wild storm.

Officer Charles Learned of the Springfield police force had been on lower Wilcox Street just before the assault and made his way to the corner of Water Street, where a large crowd had gathered. The chill of suspicion had started to spread as he pushed his way to the center of the crowd and asked Officer Champous what the trouble was all about. Learned felt two powerful arms pulling him back in the blink of an eye. It was the Siniscalchi brothers. Two others had seized Officer Champous. Suddenly, he felt a sharp slash of a razor across his right cheek. His badge was ripped off as another slash skimmed across his chest. Fortunately, the razor had grazed off Learned's badge, only slicing through his coat. Michael Fiore had slashed him twice in the face and directly over the heart.

Fiore then raced up Union Street, jumping on a beer cart and shoving the driver out of the way. He grabbed the reins, and the horses raced hard towards Main Street, where he jumped off the cart and escaped. The Siniscalchi brothers ran away, leaving the injured officer on the sidewalk, a large pool of blood quickly forming around him. Officer Champous broke free, sprinting towards the nearest police signal box and frantically calling for the police ambulance. He then rushed to Learned's aid. The officer was bleeding profusely from the wounds on his face, his condition appearing to be critical. He was rushed to the Hampden hospital, where the doctors discovered three severed arteries and suffering from the shock and loss of blood.

Later that night, Inspectors James Raiche, Frank Quilty, and Walter Henderson took Durante Siniscalchi into custody for assault with the intention of murder. He was discharged soon after his apprehension upon a bail bond of $10,000. The police are now searching for Michael Fiore and Carlo Siniscalchi.

The day before, Carlo Siniscalchi had been arrested and convicted for owning a vicious dog, and authorities believed that this was the motive for the assault. Just weeks prior, police had been alerted that Siniscalchi's dog had terrorized pedestrians on Wilcox and Water Streets, and an order was issued for him to rid himself of the animal. He did not comply and faced charges in police court, where he was found guilty and given a fine. Siniscalchi stepped back and surveyed his handiwork. His plan had been a success, and he was satisfied. He smiled with satisfaction, knowing his message had been heard loud and clear.

Nine months later, in 1916, the Siniscalchi brothers and Michael Fiore were being prosecuted for the assault. Springfield District Attorney Joseph Ely commanded the room, pointing a finger at Michael Fiore, Durante Siniscalchi, and Carlo Siniscalchi. "You three, stand up!" Patrolmen Charles Learned and Fred Champous looked the three men up and down, each nodding in recognition, positively identifying the attackers. Officer Learned's voice was heavy with disdain as he recounted the attack in vivid detail. Officer Champous testified that shortly before the attack, Carlo Siniscalchi had said, "God Damn Learner make trouble for me; I fix him!"

Fiore's gaze shifted to Officer Learned, his expression tight with rage. "You had some trouble with me before the attack," he accused.

CONFESSION

The officer's cheeks flushed with anger, and his eyebrows narrowed. "I just made a remark about two young women passing by, and you pushed me into the street!" The room was thick with tension as Learned and Fiore locked eyes.

Carlo Siniscalchi's face was red with rage, and his veins bulged as the judge announced the guilty verdict. The jury had been out for only an hour, and the three men were sentenced to three years in the House of Correction. Carlo sprang to his feet; his finger pointed accusingly at the officers. "I'm going to get you!" he snarled before court officers wrestled him to the ground and dragged him from the courthouse. His screams echoed down the hall until the heavy door slammed shut.

Michael Fiore's brother, Vincenzo, a notorious gangster linked to the powerful Albano family, was arrested in 1917 for a vicious attack on a man on Water Street. Vincenzo's menacing presence was felt in the streets as his reputation for violence and power preceded him.

A man named Madranco was strolling down the dimly lit Water Street when Vincenzo Fiore and a mysterious figure blocked his path. Fiore demanded the stranger attack Madranco, and the assailant obeyed, brandishing a weapon and slicing Madranco just inches from his windpipe. Madranco fell to the ground, his blood spilling from the deep wound that stretched several inches long. The police soon arrived, and Madranco reported the name of his attacker. They searched the Italian colony, eventually finding Vincenzo Fiore, but the unknown assailant was nowhere to be seen. Arrested for his part in the assault, Fiore's brother was taken away in handcuffs.

A week later in court, Madranco, who had initially identified Fiore as the man who had commanded a stranger to slash him, dramatically reversed his testimony, his heart pounding and his

11

body trembling with fear. With no evidence to back up the charge of assault with a dangerous weapon, the judge had no choice but to drop the case. Fiore let out a whoop of joy, his face breaking into a wide grin. His eyes sparkled with relief as his legs, heavy with anxiety, suddenly filled with an energy he had not felt for weeks. He leaped up and down, his smile stretching from ear to ear.

John Albano and his son Felix were savvy entrepreneurs, owning a successful wholesale liquor distribution business on the corner of Lombard and Main Street. John Albano died in 1915 at the age of seventy-one, and Felix passed away from pneumonia in 1917. His legacy lived on through his niece, Pasqualina Albano, and her husband, Carlo Siniscalchi, who took over the family's liquor business, ensuring that the Albano name would remain an integral part of the Springfield underworld for many years to come.

It was painfully clear that the Albano family were untouchable, their criminal empire sprawling and their reach expanding. Messing with them was a surefire way to invite trouble, and those who did so were rarely seen again.

Three years later, on January 16, 1920, prohibition became effective at midnight. From 12:01 am, the "manufacture, sale, or transportation of intoxicating liquors within, the importation therefore into, or the exportation there of the United States and all the territories subject to the jurisdiction thereof, for beverage purposes" is prohibited by the 18th amendment to the constitution.

The roaring twenties in Springfield were a time of wild indulgence despite the 18th Amendment outlawing the sale of intoxicating liquors. The liquor industry went underground, with homemade batches of moonshine being brewed and distilled in back-alley stills. Barroom doors were shuttered, replaced with the more clandestine speakeasies, where the tangy scent of illicit alcohol hung in the air. Talks whispered as patrons discussed where to find the next round, while the clink of glasses and boisterous laughter filled the smoke-filled rooms as the pool rooms, all-night restaurants, and soda shops stayed open and poured on the sly. The era of Prohibition was a lawless time in Springfield, yet the citizens continued to enjoy a good drink - no matter the cost.

The police and federal agents were always one step behind, finding liquor in the strangest of places: candy shops, fruit stands, auto garages, gas stations, shoe repair shops, barber shops, office buildings, and even funeral parlors. But the party seemed to go on forever, no matter how hard law enforcement tried to keep up.

A shockwave of surprise swept through Springfield six months later when thirty-eight federal agents of the Department of Internal Revenue descended upon Springfield, their mission to crack down on the rising issue of drunkenness. As they dug deeper, it became clear that obtaining liquor was not a difficult task. It was common knowledge that one could easily find it in many places around the city. Without warning, the agents raided forty establishments and made eleven arrests for illegal possession and sale of liquor. The bar owners, along with local police, were left baffled and unaware of the operation until the men were brought in for booking. The surprise raids were the first sign of the new Prohibition laws being enforced, and the consequences were clear for all to see.

The agents entered places that had been under surveillance for weeks, ready to make arrests and seize liquor. However, the bartenders and owners had been tipped off; as soon as the agents appeared, they sprang into action. Bottles rattled as they were hastily dumped, and voices echoed as the owners barked orders. The agents watched in disbelief as the evidence of their investigation was washed away in seconds.

Like most cities across America, Prohibition brought a new wave of illicit activity to Springfield. Carlo and Pasqualina Albano-

Siniscalchi saw this as the perfect opportunity to make their mark on the city. The couple quickly rose to the top of the bootlegging game, earning Carlo Siniscalchi the nickname "King of the Bootleggers" from the local newspapers. His newfound success was visible to all. They moved from the South End's Water Street to a lavish house on Chestnut Street. He traveled around town in a chauffeur-driven limousine; the countless eyes of the city watched his movements. The Albano-Siniscalchi's reign over the Springfield bootlegging scene was undeniable, and nothing seemed to stop them.

Regarding Siniscalchi's illegal liquor running activities, *The Springfield Republican* reported a box truck packed with genuine "Old Crow" whiskey came barreling through the fence on Pecousic Avenue hill near Forest Park's Barney estate.

Detective Lieutenant Joseph Murphy arrived just in time to see a flurry of activity as spectators rushed to the trolley car, arms full of bottles. When he started to investigate, all that remained were eight bottles of the liquor. A touring car with a New York license plate had already whisked away the driver and most of the liquor before police arrived. As Prohibition agents continued to investigate the case, Carlo Siniscalchi, owner of the truck, showed up at police headquarters determined to reclaim his property. But the federal authorities refused to allow him to take it. After huffing and puffing in frustration, Carlo slammed the door behind him as he stormed out. Carlo Siniscalchi had earned the reputation, as the *Springfield Daily News* put it, "as the recognized leader of the Italian district, and his word is more or less law in that quarter."

Siniscalchi found himself in more hot water a month later. The vice squad raided several of his Water Street locations and was met with an intimidating warning. Siniscalchi had vowed to "get" the officers, who, familiar with his reputation, were unwilling to take any chances. Consequently, he was promptly apprehended and taken into custody.

But when Carlo arrived in court, the judge's powerful voice echoed off the walls as he declared the patrolmen liars. The police would not testify against Siniscalchi. The air was still and heavy, as if all the onlookers were holding their collective breath. Even the judge's gaze seemed to penetrate every corner of the room, determined to uncover the truth. The patrolmen shifted uncomfortably in their seats, their faces pale in the stark light of the courtroom.

His words were damning; "I am confident the police testified dishonestly; I think the testimony of the uniformed officers to be utterly unworthy of any credit. They appeared as witnesses deaf and blind to anything against the defendant." Siniscalchi's expression shifted from smug satisfaction to an audacious grin that stretched from ear to ear. The officers' faces grew redder with each passing moment, hinting at the truth behind the judge's words. Clearly, the police had either been paid off or were too scared to testify. The accusation hung heavy in the air, a tangible reminder of the corruption of the law. The room was so still that Siniscalchi's grin seemed to echo off the walls. He had won, and he knew it. The judge's words had sealed his fate, and the triumph on his face was unmistakable. He was clearly above the law.

Across the river in West Springfield, the Parisi and Pugliano families kept a watchful eye on Carlo Siniscalchi's every move. Hailing from Calabria, a region in the south of Italy, not unlike the Sicilian Mafia, Calabria was home to the notorious 'Ndrangheta. Carlo had gained many allies in the police station, allowing him to operate in Springfield as he wished. But in the bootleg world, he soon made many enemies, and with his empire less than a year old in 1921, Carlo Siniscalchi made a fatal mistake: crossing the wrong men, the "Boys" from West Side.

SINISCALCHIS AND FIORE ON TRIAL FOR ALLEGED SLASHING ATTACK ON OFFICER LEARNED

Champous Testifies That One of the Siniscalchis Had Threatened to "Fix" Learned Because of Trouble Over Dog; Complainant Denies Making Derogatory Remarks About Young Woman Which Were Resented by Fiore; Story of Murderous Assault Is Rehearsed

FIORE A FREE MAN

Madranco, Who Once Said Fiore Directed a Gangster to Stab Him, Changes His Tone and Prisoner Goes Free

PROHIBITION IN EFFECT TO-NIGHT

Great National Drouth Will Settle Down Upon Springfield Without Hubbub

FEW "PARTIES" WERE NOTICEABLE

Many Famous Saloons Are Leaving Stores, Bible Missions and New Buildings in Their Wakes

Killing the "King of Bootleggers"

> "I had to make a decision that no one should ever have to make. It was his life or mine. I could see him reaching for his gun, and I knew what I had to do. I drew my own and fired. In that moment, my life and the lives of two families changed forever, and the brutal war that resulted had no end in sight. I had done what I had to do, what any man in my position would do. But I felt no satisfaction, no relief, only sorrow that it had come to this."

-GIUSEPPE "JOSEPH" PARISI

Seconda Parte

2

Salvatore Coroalucci "Carlo" Siniscalchi was born in Quindice, a town in the Province of Avellino in Italy. In 1895, he voyaged to America, landing at the Port of New York City, and then set up himself in Brooklyn. Initially, he worked as a laborer before taking up the role of a saloon keeper.

When in Brooklyn, Siniscalchi was in and out of trouble with the police. He became a frequent target of Captain Michael Fiaschetti, the world-famous Italian detective of New York City. Fiaschetti was a handpicked member of the five-man unit, the "Italian Squad." They dealt with specific cases involving Italian Americans and Black Hand bombings and extortion. During his career, Fiaschetti often dealt with organized crime figures and criminals in New York's Little Italy and throughout the city, such as the Black Hand kidnap-murder of five-year-old Giuseppe Varotta.

Carlo, eventually driven out of New York by Fiaschetti, escaped to Springfield, Massachusetts, in search of refuge. He opened a pool hall on Water Street in the South End of Springfield around 1912. That same year, he married John Albano's niece, Pasqualina Albano, and moved to Wilcox Street, just off Water Street. Together, they have five children.

I met Carlo Siniscalchi about six months after I moved to West Springfield, maybe eight or nine years ago. We had shared many evenings of laughter and wine with friends and family, but this particular night was special. A small group of us had gathered around Carlo, and tales of prowess poured from the drunk man, boasting about his great skill as a shooter. His gold-plated pistol dangled dangerously in the air as his deep, basso voice - hardened from years of smoking, drinking, and yelling - announced his challenge. "See that bottle?" he slurred, pointing to a bottle on the table, "I can put a bullet right through the neck without breaking the sides." Our laughter died in our throats as he squinted through one eye and carefully lined up his shot. We all ducked for cover, but it was too late. "Bang!" he roared, letting the gun recoil and kick back against his shoulder. He quickly holstered the gun, where he carried it at all times, and a nervous laugh broke out as we returned to our drinking and stories.

Carlo Siniscalchi was a known troublemaker in Springfield, just like in his hometown of New York. In the past couple of years, he had made a sizable fortune by running gin joints and bootlegging and had become the feared leader of the Italians in the South End. The police had been after him for a while, but it was not until a few years back that he had sparked their attention more severely. During a knife fight on Water Street, an officer had been slashed across his face and neck - and Siniscalchi spent time in Concord Penitentiary as a result. Once Siniscalchi was released from the big house, he sent a man to meet me. Then, I realized the extent of his influence - and how feared he was.

As the small bell jingled above the door, a stranger entered my store; the stale stench of his cheap cigar encircled him as he approached me. "Giuseppe Parisi? I'm a friend of Carlo Siniscalchi." His eyes glinted with an underlying meaning.

I stood up, my hand just inches away from the bean shooter beneath the counter, just in case I needed it for this goon. "I'm Giuseppe. What do you need?"

"Carlo's out of jail and having a party at the Italian-American club in Agawam. It's a fundraiser to help him get back in business."

"Back in business?" I tried not to laugh but could feel my mouth's corners rise. "When is this 'fundraiser' party?"

The corner of his lip twitched as he said, "Next Sunday."

I shook my head softly, "I'm busy on Sundays."

His firm, dark eyebrows furrowed together, giving his face an oddly menacing look. "Well, Carlo will be upset if you don't come." His voice was firm, and his gaze held me captive.

I inhaled deeply, my words as bracing as a slap in the face. "You tell him I'm busy at my market on Sundays, but I will buy a ticket anyway."

His jaw clenched as he looked away. I reluctantly handed the man twenty dollars for the ticket, my palms sweaty with anxiety. The windows rattled as the door slammed shut behind him, the sound rumbling through me like a shockwave. I knew if I didn't donate, it would look bad on me if I wanted to keep my reputation.

Not long afterward, Carlo was back in front of a judge. He had been found guilty of threatening to harm some police officers violently and was sentenced to four months in jail - suspended. The officers had been conducting a liquor raid at the store of his sister's son, Theodore Vona.

The courtroom was so silent that a pin drop would have been heard. Carlo was shaking from head to toe, his throat tight and heavy. He could smell the tension in the air. Theodore Vona was in the audience, looking somberly at Carlo. Vona said to the judge, "I know my uncle; he wouldn't do something like this. Please, let him go." The judge, after a long moment of silence, shook his head and said, "He is still guilty. However, in light of his family's plea, I will suspend the sentence." A collective sigh of relief washed over the courtroom as Carlo was released.

I can't remember exactly when, in October sometime, when I was at his house, Carlo and I talked about doing some business together. I know I had considered it before, but I didn't want to make a bad decision.

Carlo's smile spread wide, revealing large, yellowing teeth. "Giuseppe, come down, and I'll fix you up with a supply of whiskey," he said.

I rubbed my hands together. "Lately, my supply in West Springfield has been unreliable, so maybe we can make a deal."

He nodded, "I can sell you a 50-gallon barrel of alcohol at $15 a gallon for $750."

I paused. "I'll take it if you haul it to my house in West Springfield on Sprague Street. West Side Chief of Police Marshall Belmer has been watching my comings and goings."

Carlo's eyes narrowed. "We have a deal, Giuseppe." We shook hands, his long, slender fingers cold against mine. I returned to the party, a sense of satisfaction washing over me.

A few days later, the sunshine pierced through the window shade, dazzling my eyes as I woke up to the sound of a ringing telephone. Groggily, I glanced at the clock, the hands reading 7:00 am. I sat up and stared at the phone on the wall, the shrill ringing echoing around the room. I wondered who was calling at this hour. I groaned as I stretched and tried to wake, feeling the grumble of Carlo's words as I stirred. "You come down and get that barrel tonight once it's dark," Carlo said, his voice taking on a sharp edge.

I pressed the phone to my ear, my voice rising as I asked, "The deal was that the liquor would be sent to my shop, no?" The background hum of percolating coffee filled my ears, a sense of anticipation hanging in the air. I shifted my weight from one foot to the other, my fingers tapping anxiously against the kitchen counter. I waited for a reaction, eager to hear his response.

"If you want it," Carlo continued, "you must come get it now. I've got the Police Chief of West Side in my pocket; you won't have any trouble." He spat the words out like bullets, emphasizing his point.

The night I was to buy the barrel, I had about $600 stashed at my house and withdrew another $200 from the bank. I drove my brother Francesco's new Hudson to his garage, arriving around 7:30 pm. The darkness had settled in, and the only light was the moon, illuminating his home on Wilcox Street. The leaves crunched under my feet as I approached the door, and a dog barked in the distance. I gave the screen door a few knocks, and the porch light came alive. His wife, a young gal named Pasqualina, appeared in the doorway wearing an apron. The sweet scent of pumpkin and cinnamon wafted out from the house.

I huddled into my coat, shivering in the cold fall night as I stood on the porch. "I'm here to see Carlo," I said.

"My husband says he will be right out." Suddenly, the door slammed shut, causing a splinter of wood to fall to the floor. The minutes seemed to stretch endlessly as I waited.

Then, Carlo burst out of the door and waved his hand impatiently, indicating I should follow him. I hurried after him, my breath fogging in the chill air. "Giuseppe, amico mio, come with me across the street; I have everything you need in the garage."

He bounded down the front steps, scrambling to keep pace. The street was dark and silent, void of light, and I followed him to a neighbor's house. We crept down the driveway and stepped into the garage. He shut the door behind us, and I took a deep breath, my heart racing as I counted out the notes, totaling $750.

One hundred, two hundred, three," he cut me off mid-count. His cheeks flushed as he narrowed his eyebrows and outstretched his right hand for the money. "Give it to me; I'll count it later." He pocketed the cash without waiting for an answer.

I adjusted my fedora, angling it back on my head as I tried to make sense of the situation. "Where's the barrel?" I asked, my confusion intense. The smile left his face, and out of nowhere, he raised his hand and gave me a slap in the face. His eyes spark with fire, and his nostrils widen; he says, "Get out, and don't come back here again."

My fists were like iron, knuckles white with rage. I spat out my words, the anger searing through my core. I glanced down, and there it was - a gun in his hand. My pulse raced, and my legs quivered as I stumbled back, my eyes darting around for an escape. Carlo followed me, a menacing glint in his eyes, and commanded, "If you tell the police, I will kill you." The icy chill of his words sent a shiver down my spine, and I knew I was in serious trouble.

He double-crossed me and swiped my hard-earned loot, but this was not the time to deal with it. Right then, he had the gun and the upper hand on me. There had been no quarrel over the price, so I don't know why he does this. He wanted to have everything for himself and not let others have a piece of the pie. I knew he was a powerful man, and his influence had spread far and wide to the point where even the police feared him. Everyone was intimidated by him, especially West Side Chief Belmer and Patrolman Lyons, who had been rumored to have taken bribes to overlook Siniscalchi's shady business dealings.

Thinking of ways to get my dough back, my mind raced. I began to hatch a plan. I would need to be calculated and smart if I wanted to see that cash again.

Not long after, I stood behind the counter at my store on School Street, counting the day's earnings, when Michael Piemontese walked in. His tall frame cast a long shadow, and his wingtips tramped on the wooden floor. His face was set in a defined expression. "Come to pay off the debt I owe ya," he said, his voice gruff from months away fighting in the war.

I remembered when Michael had stayed at my parents' house on Sprague Street in West Springfield. We had become friends fast; before he'd left to join the army, I had loaned him some cash.

Mike stepped up to the counter, his face showing signs of a man who had seen too much in his recent travels. I looked up and smiled, relief flooding my face. "You made it back in one piece, Mike."

Mike nodded, his voice heavy. "Yes, I was lucky. Others I was with overseas didn't make it."

I picked up the old bottle of whiskey and poured two fingers into two glasses, inspected the level, and then poured some more. "Here, have a glass with me."

Mike shook his head, not looking up. "Giuseppe, I'm not here for a social call."

My face softened. "Mike, we've been friends for a long time. What's bothering you?"

Michael nervously rubbed the back of his neck, head still down. "Carlo Siniscalchi."

"I see, what about Siniscalchi?" The name tasted like a mouthful of food gone bad. I stepped closer to Michael, my fists clenched. His throat went dry, and his palms moistened, but he didn't dare reach in his pocket for his handkerchief. Instead, he wiped them on his pants.

"He hired me to kill you," he said, his voice strained.

"What?" I asked, my voice intensifying.

He raised his hands, palms out, trying to assure me that he was no threat. "No, Giuseppe, I would never hurt you."

I narrowed my eyes and took another step forward. "What did you tell Carlo then?"

Michael sighed. "Parisi is a dead man."

Carlo Siniscalchi had ordered him to gun me down and pressed the cold metal of a pistol into his hands. Michael was terrified of Carlo, so he reluctantly agreed, though he had sworn to me he never would since he liked me and my parents gave him a place to call home. As we finished our drinks, he reluctantly said goodbye and walked out.

Three or four days later, on a Friday night, I was driving my car down Water Street in Springfield when I saw two figures lurking in the shadows.

"This is the time to shoot him!" shouted Siniscalchi, pointing at me and urging Michael off the curb.

Before I had time to react, four shots exploded. I ducked down and slammed my foot on the accelerator, narrowly avoiding a collision with a parked car. I glanced up over the dashboard just in time to straighten the wheel. The sound of the shots still ringing in my ears, I drove away with my heart pounding. I continued straight to the Memorial Bridge, my heart pounding in my chest. Michael was an exceptional marksman in the army, a master shot, so when he opened fire on my car, I held my breath. But he kept his word, and his bullets sang an eerie song as they ricocheted off the ground near my floorboards, not a single shot finding its mark. I got home, my hands shaking, and immediately searched for bullet marks, but to my immense relief, there was not a trace of what had just happened. Michael had kept his word.

A patrolman heard the distinct sound of four gunshots echo through the streets of Water and Williams. He sprinted towards the source and saw Piemontese, gun in hand, running away. Adrenaline surging through his veins, the patrolman lunged at him and, after a brief struggle, managed to wrestle the pistol away.

The steel doors of the paddy wagon slammed shut, locking Michael Piemontese inside. He felt an icy chill as it wheeled away, taking him to police headquarters. Upon arriving, he was escorted into a small, dimly lit room and told to sit. The officers began their interrogation, peppering him with questions as he sat in uncomfortable silence. For the next hour, he was grilled, feeling the intensity of their gaze as if it were a physical force. He could smell the sweat and hear the clock ticking, counting the moments until his release.

When asked what the shooting was all about, he just closed his eyes and raised his chin to the side, responding, "I'm no stool pigeon."

One cop muttered, "Fuck this WOP and these stale doughnuts. Why bother leaving this box here from the morning shift?"

Tired of Piemontese being a mute, he was placed under arrest and charged with carrying a loaded gun without a permit. Later in the evening, Carlo sent his cousin, Frankie Albano, to bail Michael out of jail, and he was back on the street before dinner was cold.

Two goons swaggered into my store the next day, and one seized me by the arm. In the corner, my brother-in-law Joe Dialessi sprang up, shoving his chair back, its legs scraping against the wooden floor with a shriek that made them wince. He reached inside his jacket breast pocket, pulling out his gun with lightning speed. The stranger's grip on my arm loosened, and he stumbled back in alarm. Joe Dialessi had an eerie stillness as he stood tall, his weapon drawn and ready.

"Carlo Siniscalchi wants to see you."

"Let him come here," I growled in a thunderous voice. "I'm too busy today."

My reply was met with a pair of uneasy glances. "Okay, Joe," one of them replied. "We'll give him the message, but he won't be pleased."

The air crackled with tension as I slammed my fist on the counter. Coffee cups rattled, and my face flushed red; I leaned across the counter, my voice sharp like a blade. "I don't care if he's happy or not. Now get out of my store."

The shrill sound of the phone pierced the air just an hour later. On the other end, it was Siniscalchi. He says he wants to sort things out. Carlo's voice, sharp and authoritative, echoed through the phone. "If the cops ask you anything about the shooting, tell them that you know nothing about it," he said.

"I ain't no snitch," I growled, "but I'll see you soon." The tension in the air was intense. Siniscalchi was silent on the other end, and it is evident that he understood.

The next day, Sunday, I went to Carlo's home for a sit-down. All my people knew I was going, and a few of the boys were ready, some of them packing heat just in case protection was needed. Siniscalchi came out in his pajamas and slippers and sat across from me. A bottle of whiskey was sitting on the table between us. He poured each of us a cup, and I went ahead with caution, keeping a close eye on him as he swallowed his first sip. I wanted to make sure the booze wasn't laced. I took my cup and sipped slowly, ready for whatever was to come.

Siniscalchi tried to convince me that Piemontese had not shot at me but at somebody else. "Michael was shooting at someone on the sidewalk, and you happened to drive into the line of fire," he says, "He's not a good shot."

I don't believe a single word that escaped that crook's lips - Piemontese had warned me, and I was well aware of his ability with a weapon from his years in the military. But I acted none the wiser. My eyes darted around the room, noting the tense atmosphere filled with distrust and apprehension.

Carlo tells me, "The man who did the shooting will come in shortly and say he is sorry, and the two of you will shake hands."

I shook my head, refusing to budge. "That won't fix our problem," I said, waving away the offer of the alcohol we had been negotiating. My voice left no room for negotiation. "No, I won't shake hands with your crony, and you can keep your booze. I am through with this matter." Carlo was shaking, red-faced, and visibly angry. He couldn't stand it that I had thumbed my nose at him. I got up and left with my crew.

Later in the week, I saw Carlo in front of Goldstein's clothing store on Elm Street. He again mentioned the alcohol, and again I refused it. I demanded my money back. "Giuseppe, how about I give you $500 and I keep $250?"

My eyes were sparking fire, and my nostrils were wide. My mouth opened, and my teeth glared at him. My knuckles were white. "That's not gonna work, Carlo," I said, "I want it all, $750."

Carlo met my gaze with an unreadable expression. He knew I meant business. "Fine," he said slowly, "come to my house later, and we'll take care of it." The air between us sizzled with tension, and I held my stance until he finally broke eye contact.

I go there an hour later for my money, my stomach in knots. Sweat beaded on my forehead as my thoughts raced, imagining the worst possible outcome. "Carlo is unable to see you," they tell me.

Pacing back and forth, I could feel my heart pounding in my chest as my mind kept spinning out of control. "What could go wrong? How bad could the consequences be?" I muttered to myself.

That same week, Michael Piemontese stood before the judge, his hands trembling as he spoke. He tells the judge, "Parisi is a member of a Black Hand gang, and I heard he was going to kill me."

The courtroom fell silent as Michael continued, his voice quivering with fear. He could feel the judge's eyes upon him, demanding an explanation. He was desperate to evoke a shred of pity. He pleaded with the judge, trying every excuse he could, but the judge's stern face remained unmoved. The gavel fell, and the sentence was announced   fifteen months at Concord Prison. The courtroom fell silent, the gravity of the situation weighing heavily on all present. Mihael hung his head low, knowing his actions had brought him here.

While locked up, a guy from New York stepped up behind him and whispered into his ear in the chow line. The words sent a chill up Mike's spine - "Before you get out of this place, somebody else will have already killed Parisi." An ominous sense of dread descended over Mike as the prison walls seemed to close in. The news of the plan quickly spread, and Piemontese got word to a friend of mine of the plan.

Siniscalchi recklessly underestimated me, not grasping the full scope of my capabilities. His miscalculation was an egregious error, one he will regret deeply. He should have had the guts to clip me himself rather than getting a button man like Piemontese to do his dirty work. I wouldn't give him another chance, so I immediately decided to be on guard for him the next time; see? I went to O.C. Alderman's on Worthington Street, across from the Victoria Hotel, and bought a Smith & Wesson .32 caliber revolver. I kept my gun close, never leaving its side, always within reach, whether in my car or pocket. I was on high alert, ready to unleash the power of my weapon at a moment's notice.

Less than two months later, on December 20, 1921, the news of the great "King of Little Italy's" fate blazed across every newspaper within a thousand miles. It was a shock to all, and the words on the front page of every paper left a deep impression on the hearts and minds of all.

On Tuesday afternoon, I made my way up the street from my house on Sprague Street to Edward Parisi's barber shop on Main Street in West Springfield. As I arrived, the pungent smell of hair and aftershave hit me like a wave, and I saw Edward sweeping the floor of freshly cut hair from his last victim. Another man sat in the waiting area. Edward's razor-sharp scissors glinted in the dimly lit shop, and the sound of the clippers filled the air like a buzzing beehive.

"Buongiorno, Ed," I greeted him.

"Ciao, Giuseppe, what can I do you for?" Ed replied in his cheerful, inviting tone.

"I'm here for a trim and shave," I said eagerly.

Ed glanced over at the man reading the newspaper, who had patiently waited his turn. "This gentleman is just about to get a haircut, Giuseppe," he said with a nod.

"Ok, no problem," I replied, giving a polite nod of deference. "I will just come back later."

"Good, my pal," Ed said with a smile. "I will see you later."

So, I left the clip joint and headed over to Springfield. I had been running a store over on School Street in West Springfield with my brother, Francesco, for about seven or eight months. I needed to stock up on a few things and headed towards the town common, around the rotary, and over the North End bridge towards Springfield. I go to Max Wolk's on Lyman Street for supplies.

Lyman Street is in the North End, the wholesale produce district where all grocery merchants get their provisions. The pungent smell of sharp provolone assailed my senses as I opened the door. My eyes widened in delight at seeing huge blocks of imported prosciutto, mortadella, and sopressatta neatly stacked and waiting to be sliced. Loaves of crusty bread were perched on the shelves, and the cutting snap of broccoli rabe filled the air. I could see a feast everywhere I looked - pastas, peppers, olives, and more. I could hardly contain my excitement. "What a delight!" I said out loud. I couldn't help but feel like I had stepped into heaven.

After placing an order for delivery to my store, I left Lyman Street and made my way down Bridge Street towards Adams & Crockett's Jewelry shop. The narrow walking aisles are lined with glass cases that sparkle in the sunlight, reflecting the silver and crystal like a million tiny mirrors. Above me, chandeliers and lamps dangle, glittering in the light. I pause for a moment, admiring the sight of the sparkling displays. I step up to the counter, inhaling the salesgirl's faint smell of perfume that wafted through the air. "I'm here for a couple of Christmas presents," I said, glancing around the store at the festive decorations.

"Very nice," she replied, "and who are these gifts for?" Her eyes sparkled with the same cheer that seemed to be everywhere, and a smile tugged at the corners of her lips.

I smiled back, feeling the holiday spirit all around me. "My wife, Raffaela, and something for her mother," I said. "It's always so much fun to find the perfect gifts for them."

The young salesgirl gently guided me through the aisles full of glistening trinkets. I could feel my heart skip a beat as I saw a beautiful chain and locket shimmering in the light of the display case for Raffaela. For the chain, I pay $28, and I buy a set of looking glass and a brush for her mother for $11. I could feel the thrill of giving them something so special and valuable.

With a sense of excitement, I then go to Ware Pratt Men's Clothiers, next to the new post office on the corner of Worthington and Main Streets. My gaze falls on a shiny silk shirt glimmering in the store lights. I reach for the price tag. "$6.95 plus 40 cents war tax," I mutter. After a few calculations, I hand the clerk $7.35. A Christmas gift for my brother Giovanni.

I go next to visit my mother-in-law, Francesca Mazzarino, on Water Street in the South End. After knocking on the door for a few minutes, I saw nobody there, so I returned to my car, drove up Freemont Street, and went onto Main Street. Crossing Main, I turn down William Street, parking near Our Lady of Mount Carmel, the Italian church. I want to see my sister-in-law, Mary Mazzarino, my wife's sister, but she was not home either, so I left my car near Mary's house, just beside the gelato store, near the corner of the church, see.

With my scarf pulled up around my neck, and my hands tucked deep in my pockets, I brave the cold winter wind and walk up Main Street. I want to go over to the corner of Wilcox Street to see a pal of mine, a shoemaker named Joe Luvern. To avoid the traffic, I left my car parked on William Street. After my errand, I plan to visit my sister-in-law's house. On the way to the shoemaker, I take a detour up the opposite side of Main Street to the Italian Bank to read the exchange rate bulletin outside. I was in the habit of sending money to Italy, you see. From $1 American, we get $3 of Italian money. The rate on Italian money, I don't remember now. I think it is twenty-six and a little more on a dollar. As I stroll along Main Street, my gaze lingering on the festive holiday decorations in the shop windows, the smooth, cold metal of the gun in my pocket pressing against my palm. I carry it wherever I go since the

Piemontese shooting on Water Street. I can feel its weight as a reminder of the danger lurking around every corner.

While this was happening, the owner of a South End cigar store on Cross Street was catching a ride with Siniscalchi. Carlo picked him up on the corner and dropped him off at the Third National Bank building on Main Street, near the big clock. Siniscalchi was headed to an appointment with his dentist on Main, and it was on his way. After dropping him off, Carlo came to the office at 3 pm, but he was met with a delay. The dentist was still occupied with another patient and asked if he could come back a little later. Carlo stepped out of the building and headed on his way, his shoes tapping lightly against the pavement. He glanced back at the office one last time before turning the corner. "I guess I'll have to come back at 4," he spoke to himself, his voice muffled in the busy street.

At this time, I was strolling leisurely along Main Street with the chain and locket tucked safely in my coat pocket. It was a few days before Christmas, and I was musing about my family as they unwrapped all the presents I had given them. I imagined my children's expressions when they saw what Babbo Natale left for them beneath the tree. But I don't see Siniscalchi when I walk up. Keeping my head low to shield it from the winter air, I don't see anybody when I get there. But I do notice Siniscalchi's Lincoln limousine parked outside Felix Delizia's store. Siniscalchi had stepped inside to talk some business with Felix Delizia, the owner of the jewelry and music shop. When their discussion had ended, Felix saw him to the door, wishing each other a Buon Natale before walking to the back of his store.

While admiring the festive displays in the store windows, I heard somebody knocking on glass. "Rap, rap, rap." I started to turn around and squinted against the sun reflecting off the snow. Carlo's beckoning gestures were so frequent it seemed like he was fanning himself. My heart told me not to go there. I turn back as though I don't know he's trying to get my attention.

"Rap, rap, rap," hit my ears from behind, accelerating the already rampant pounding of my heart. I was worried it would look bad if I did not go. I went over to his car, and Carlo slid over to the middle of the seat, leaning closer to me. My heart is beating faster. I put one foot on the running board of his car, my other foot still on the curb. I had both hands in my pockets as I leaned toward the car. I thought he was going to pay me back my money. Carlo's limo driver was not with him today. And although it was the middle of the day, he was attired like he was going out for a luxurious evening. Silk shirt, tie, blazer, waistcoat, cashmere overcoat, and fedora. He cast a disdainful glance at me. Maybe he felt he was superior to me because of how he dressed.

Things go bad very fast. He isn't looking to pay me my money. Instead, Siniscalchi threatened me with some bad Italian words and glared at me through narrowed eyes. His fury was tangible in the air, and I felt like I was being suffocated. I could feel the tension, my heart pounding. He was getting angrier and angrier, and I knew I had to act fast if I wanted to get out of there unscathed.

Carlo's eyes flashed with rage as he jabbed his finger towards me. "I told you, figlio di puttana, not to go on Water Street or I'll kill you, and don't try to sell any alcohol to anybody on Water Street at all!" he growled in a deep voice.

I stared at him, my face unreadable. I refused to be bullied. "I got no boss," I said, my voice level and calm. "I do as I like." I felt my gun tighten in my hand as I uttered the words to the man known as the "King of Little Italy."

His eyes grew wide with surprise, his wrinkles deepening across his forehead. Siniscalchi spat, "O you bucchina," a phrase only used in Napoli that I couldn't translate. But I could tell from the tone that it was an insult.

He spun around, his hand darting to his back hip pocket as if he were going for a gun. I caught a glint of something shiny; I was sure it was a gun, one with a magazine. Colts, what do you call it, an automatic? It was a matter of his life or mine, and when I saw Siniscalchi reach for a gun, I acted swiftly, yanking my own and pulling the trigger. I heard the click of my gun and saw Siniscalchi's eyes widen in shock. The gun was cold in my hands, its weight heavy, and I could feel the fear radiating from Siniscalchi. He was still, like a statue, and I could see the terror in his eyes. His mouth was open as if he were about to say something, but no words came out. He was frozen in place.

I felt the mighty blasts of hot gas as the powder in the cartridges exploded, sending the barrel of the gun straight back against my shoulder with each pull of the trigger. The bullets shot out with a sharp crack, echoing through the air. I could feel the heat of the gun against my skin and smell the acrid scent of gunpowder. I can't remember. I kept pulling the trigger, and I was so nervous I didn't know how many shots I got off. I won't say because I do not recall. I thought I was dead. I fire in the direction of the car. I don't know if he was shooting at me or I was shooting him. I didn't see the direction of the shots.

My finger was still pulling the trigger, yet all that emerged was a click. A deep pool of scarlet spread out from his neck, staining the seats with its peculiar paisley pattern. I saw his eyes bulging with horror, his mouth agape in a silent scream as his lifeblood drained away. The smell of gunpowder filled the air. I heard the faint thud of his body as it slumped into the seat, a sound that echoed through the car.

Screams of panic filled the air as shoppers dove for cover, packages tumbling to the ground. The scene was chaotic; people pushing and shoving each other out of the way in a desperate attempt to escape. Main Street was busy with Christmas shoppers, and a wild bullet struck a woman on a passing trolley. She cried something in French, but I didn't understand. A streetcar conductor, who had stopped at the corner of Main and Union Streets to allow a passenger to get off, looked me straight in the eye as I looked up from the door of Siniscalchi's car. His trolley car had stopped so that the rear door was nearly opposite the hood of the Siniscalchi limousine.

I escape down Park Street, and some man says, "Don't run, Giuseppe, just walk." But I kept running in case Siniscalchi's gang was coming for me. I should have listened and blended into the thick crowd.

A patrolman was going to his beat in Forest Park on another trolley car when he saw the limousine at the curb with a crowd gathered around. The officer quickly jumped off the car and took in the situation, seeing Siniscalchi slouching inside, his limp, lifeless body lying against the blood-covered front seat. "There goes the shooter; he just ran up the street!" a woman screamed, her voice shrill and desperate. "Get down!" shouted a man, diving for a nearby shop doorway. People were frantically ducking and dodging, trying to escape the danger. The atmosphere was thick with fear and confusion as chaos reigned in the street.

He saw me fleeing and gave chase. I felt his eyes on me as I took off, my feet pounding against the pavement. I could hear my heart thumping like a steam train as I raced along Main Street and then down Park Street, desperately dodging left and right. The footsteps behind me grew louder, and I almost felt the fear seeping through my veins. My breath came in shallow gasps, and I could taste the sweat on my lips. I could feel the chill of the night air against my skin, a stark contrast to the heat radiating from my body as I ran. My pursuer's footsteps seemed to echo through the empty street, and I could feel the tension in the air. I looked back over my shoulder, searching for a sign of the police officer, and all I could see were dark shapes moving in my direction. I knew I had to keep going, so I pushed on, my mind flooding with adrenaline.

The police officer's hand trembled as he drew his gun. He steadied his arm, taking careful aim at my back. The click of his thumb pulling back the hammer echoed through the street, but he froze at seeing a group of small boys playing nearby. They laughed, oblivious to the danger of their situation. My heart pounded in my chest as I watched the officer's expression change from determination to hesitation. He slowly lowered his gun, the sound of the boys' laughter still ringing in the air.

My heart raced as I sprinted down Hubbard Avenue, quickly turning onto Willow Street and then Park Street. My feet felt like they were made of lead as I forced them to slow to a stop, every muscle in my body trembling with fear of the Siniscalchi crew coming after me.

On Park Street, a fellow in plain clothes grabbed me. "I'm a special officer; you're under arrest," he said. I was unable to move, my heart pounding so hard that I could hear it.

"All right, I'm done running," I said, submitting myself to the situation. He pushed me into a garage near the Electric Trolley company and held me there. He wasn't an undercover, as he said, but a chauffeur driving along Main Street near Park who saw the crowd following me.

We were standing in the garage doorway when the police officer finally caught up to me. He had me covered with his gun, and it was all over. Both hands were in my coat pockets as the officer approached me. "Get your hands up," he commanded. My fingers trembled as they inched closer to the depths of my pocket. I could still feel the weight of my revolver; its cold metal reminded me of what I had just done. Taking a deep breath, I slowly withdrew my hand, revealing the emptiness of my palms. An intense sense of relief swept over me as the chase had finally come to an end.

The icy air stung my nose, yet I was drenched in sweat. The man frisked me and found my Smith & Wesson revolver with six spent shells, still carrying the acrid scent of gunpowder. In my pocket, he discovered a handful of fresh ammo. He clamped the handcuffs around my wrists and asked a woman from the nearby office to telephone police headquarters. An angry crowd was quickly growing, their murmurs rapidly escalating into a roar, their faces twisted with rage as they surged ever closer. I glanced at my captor, whose face was ashen. Suddenly, a rock flew through the air and smashed through the window above us, shards of glass raining down. The patrol car arrived just in time, their sirens slicing through the air. They moved quickly, ushering us out of the danger before it escalated further. I could feel the mob's heated breath on my neck as we moved, and I knew that if we had stayed any longer, it would have been too late.

While all this was happening, a doctor was inside the Springfield Drug Company when he heard a man burst into the store, shouting about a shooting. Without hesitation, the doctor followed the man outside to find Siniscalchi slumped behind the wheel of his car, his head resting on his chest and Carlo's limp, bloody body sprawled on the seat. One of the men climbed over his body and into the car. The atmosphere was thick with shock and tension, the air heavy with the pungent smell of gunpowder. The doctor could feel the tragedy in the air, his hands trembling as the men tried to revive Siniscalchi. He roared down the street in the Siniscalchi car, the doctor desperately clutching Carlo in his arms, the door swinging open with alarming ferocity as they raced to the hospital. Carlo's blood pooled on the front seat, smeared across the two men's clothing, a vivid reminder of the urgency of their mission. The wind howled around them, and the sky seemed to darken as if even the heavens were mourning Carlo's peril.

As the flashing sirens of the police car approached Wesson Memorial Hospital, I nervously glanced from the backseat. I had been arrested for shooting Siniscalchi, and the officers were already interrogating me about the incident. "Why did you shoot Siniscalchi?" one of them growled.

"I did it because Carlo had done me out of $750," I replied, my voice trembling.

"You shot him over some money?" the other one piped in.

"I thought I saw him reaching for a gun in his hip pocket when I shot him," I said, my hands shaking.

We arrived at the hospital, with the officers still questioning me. I was rattled, and my heart pounded as I exited the car. As I followed the officers inside, I could feel the cold air of the hospital rush past me, the smell of antiseptic stinging my nose. All I could think of was the fear of what was about to come.

The orderly sped down the corridor with his cart of medical supplies, straining to reach the Italian. Carlo's body was taken into the operating room, and he was stripped of his bloody clothes. Doctors swarmed the bed, feverishly working on him to stop the bleeding and to get a pulse, racing to bring him back from the dead. A bullet had passed through both of his lungs, severing the "vena cava," or central vein. A nurse wiped the blood from the surgeon's face. Another put more towels on the floor where the blood was accumulating, the first ones long since saturated. The battle continued: more stitches, more swabs, more tension, more failure.

It was time to stop. The surgeon left the operating table, ripping off his bloody gown and slamming it into a bin. The door to the scrub room slammed shut. A pause of silence momentarily blanketed the room. It was over. They pulled a white sheet over his face and declared the "King of Little Italy" dead.

Relatives and friends of Siniscalchi were constantly about the table where Carlo was laid to rest and patted his body while uttering prayers in broken Italian. Clutching rosary beads in their trembling fingers, they began the Lord's prayer, "Nostro padre che e in heaven…" News of the shooting spread like wildfire through the Italian South End, and friends of the dead man swarmed the hospital by the score. Mrs. Pasqualina Siniscalchi, her sister Anna Albano-Fiore, and brother-in-law Vincenzo Fiore arrived shortly afterward and immediately broke down under the excitement.

The police arrived with me for identification, unaware Siniscalchi had already passed. As soon as Pasqualina saw me in the hallway, she let out a deep scream and charged towards me with arms stretched out and tears streaming down her face. I could feel the force of her rage as she clutched onto my arms, shrieking and sobbing, desperate to get to me. The hallway seemed to close in around us, the air thickening with the moment's intensity.

I watched in shock as the hospital attendants desperately tried to keep Mrs. Siniscalchi back and pacify the hysterical woman. The scene only intensified when I was brought outside, and I was confronted with a threatening mob of Italians shouting and threatening to take my life. I could feel the tension in the air, and the police had no hesitation in rushing me back to the safety of police headquarters in fear of an attack. That's when I learned Carlo Siniscalchi had taken his last gasp.

In the meantime, the woman who was struck by the wild bullet was rushed to Mercy Hospital. She had been slightly hurt by the stray bullet with only a tiny mark, which did not produce much blood, found on her left arm. The district attorney was immediately notified and went to Mercy Hospital to get a statement from the woman. Since Carlo was dead, I was also taken there to be identified by her, but because she only spoke French and was too shaken up from her experience, she was unable to give a positive account of the shooting.

The *Springfield Republican's* headline blared across the front page with big, bold letters that demanded attention. "Carlo Siniscalchi Fatally Shot." Every word seemed to have an extra emphasis, and the story was written so that the readers could almost feel the impact of the news.

"Carlo Siniscalchi, widely known amongst Italians over many whom he wielded great power and influence in Springfield, received four of six shots fired from the revolver of Giuseppe 'Joseph' Parisi as Siniscalchi was seated in his luxury limousine on the corner of Main and Union Street at 4:15 pm. He died shortly after from hemorrhages in the care of Dr. Charles Furcolo.

"Parisi, equally as prominent in West Springfield Italian circles as Siniscalchi was in Springfield, was caught within 15 minutes by Reserve Officer Thomas Dowling, a young policeman who has been on the force for only seven weeks.

"Later, Parisi furnished Detective Captain Frank Quilty with a written confession in which he said he felt obliged to shoot because he feared a similar move on the part of his victim."

The chilly Vermont air carried the news from the *Brattleboro Daily Reformer* as it lined the newsstands. People stopped in their tracks, eagerly taking in every word, eager to learn the latest information.

"Carlo Siniscalchi, the most powerful and best-known Italian leader in Springfield, was murdered in Main Street late yesterday afternoon when Joseph Parisi, said to be a member of the Camorra mafia of West Springfield, jumped on the running board of Siniscalchi's automobile and emptied his revolver at him."

The evening sky glowed a dull orange as District Attorney Wright strode confidently into the conference room. All eyes watched intently for the DA's response. "Do you have any comment about the murder?" a journalist asked. The room was silent; the only sound was the hum of the microphone and the rustling of the journalists' papers.

Wright cleared his throat and stepped forward. His voice echoed throughout the room. "This adds one more criminal homicide to the already large number of criminal homicides about which I have very recently commented."

"What about your private meetings with Siniscalchi's wife and other known criminals?"

A tense silence filled the room as the district attorney refused to answer, his expression hardening as he replied with a single word, "No comment."

The reporter's gaze narrowed as he noted the man's refusal, the air around them thick with suspicion. "What about a motive for the shooting?"

"The prosecution might try to prove that revenge was the motive for the shooting."

"What did Siniscalchi's widow have to say?"

"Mrs. Pasqualina Siniscalchi was exhausted when I saw her last night and was in no condition to say much."

"Are you associating this shooting with any former cases?"

"I don't care to say so or go into any details. According to Parisi's deposition, he was threatened by Siniscalchi, who warned him amid a flow of indecent language not to sell alcohol on Water Street on the threat of death. When Parisi replied he would do as he pleased, Siniscalchi reached towards his pocket, which caused Parisi to shoot."

"And Officer Dowling appeared on the scene of the shooting almost immediately after it happened?"

"Yes, and he was highly commended by Captain Quilty for his mighty good work."

The district attorney had called for a special investigation of the shooting. Last night, he called Colonel Foote for help from the State Police. State Inspectors Manning, Fleming, Blighe, and Daly from Boston and Pittsfield were assigned to the case.

The reporter's voice rose in pitch as he inquired, "Do you usually summon the State Police for situations like this?"

"It was always done when circumstances seemed to call for it. The summoning of these officers to act beyond the confines of powers vested in the police department follows the plan to sift through the matter to the bottom." District Attorney Wright called an end to the questions and left for his office, swinging the door closed behind him.

Immediately after roll call the following day, I was taken into a room in the basement. The ceiling is turning yellow where the rusty pipes leaked through. The ceiling fan squeaks loudly as it spins and blurs out the chipped, flaking paint. My mugshot was taken in front of a whiteboard, holding a placard with my name and booking number. A lieutenant presses my fingers into the ink pad, carefully rolling them one at a time for my prints, then records my measurements in the mug book.

The lieutenant's gaze fixated on me as he asked, "Are you sorry you shot Siniscalchi?"

My tired eyes darted around the room as if searching for an escape. "No," I replied, my voice hoarse from the lack of sleep. "If I didn't, he would have killed me."

The lieutenant saw my worn-out appearance. "Didn't you sleep last night? You look shot."

Later that day, after a short deliberation, the grand jury returned a true bill of indictment charging me with murder in the first degree of Carlo Siniscalchi.

The next day, the courtroom was crammed to capacity with people spilling out into the hallway and throughout the building, desperate to catch a glimpse of "the man who shot down the famous Siniscalchi." Tensions were at an all-time high, and the atmosphere was hostile. Extra officers were stationed in the courtroom, and detectives lurked in the crowd, wary of a possible riot. Due to reports that Carlo Siniscalchi's friends had sworn vengeance, I wasn't brought into the prisoner's dock until my case was called. The onlooker's voices were angry, and jeers and insults were shouted at me. People surged forward, pressing closer and closer to me until the police officers had to step in to keep them at bay. The judge slammed his gavel on the desk, and the courtroom fell silent.

He gestured to the officers to bring in the accused, and the room filled with anticipation as I stepped inside, flanked by two officers. I surveyed the scene with a solemn expression as the judge read out the charges against me. The crowd erupted into a frenzy, and the police had to form a barrier between me and the angry crowd, their faces grim with determination as they worked to keep the peace. Although a heavy steel cage separated me from the crowd, I observed every man, anticipating a gun to be aimed at me any second.

The Commonwealth's evidence was brought over to the courthouse. It included my signed statement admitting I shot Siniscalchi and did so in self-defense. The blood-stained clothing Carlo was wearing, the gun found in my pocket, and the empty shells were also taken over. The police, with the medical examiner who performed the autopsy last night, and the doctor who attended to Siniscalchi were the only witnesses revealed. The detective bureau scrambled to gather more witnesses and evidence for my trial. The street bustled with shoppers that day, but the Italian community stayed tight-lipped, refusing to speak up. The police pleaded for anyone who had seen the shooting to come forward, but their pleas fell on deaf ears. The shoppers were silent, their eyes wide and fearful as they stared in the direction of the crime scene. No one dared to come forward and provide a statement. The detective bureau was desperate for details, but the only thing they could find was the lingering smell of gunpowder.

I was arraigned before Judge Wallace Heady in district court and charged with murder in the first degree. If proven, I face life behind bars or, worse, the electric chair. Since I was without an attorney, no response was asked to the clerk's formal question, "Guilty or not guilty?" and a plea of not guilty was entered for me. I'm being held at York Street Jail until a date for trial is set.

In the *Daily Kennebec Journal* in Augusta, Maine, I was lauded as "one of the best-known men in the city with friends outside his own people where his following was the biggest of the Italian colony."

The streets of Springfield and West Springfield were already rife with tension between the Italians, but with the murder of Carlo Siniscalchi, the atmosphere grew even more charged. His many friends and associates respected and feared him, and a sense of rage and dread lingered in the air as if retribution were inevitable. No one wanted to speak of it, but the promise of revenge was evident in every hushed conversation and every meaningful glance. The bad blood between the two cities had caused trouble in the past, and now it seemed that the tragedy of Siniscalchi would be no exception.

CONFESSION

Retaliation is not just a concern; it is expected.

Springfield Daily News | EXTRA

SPRINGFIELD, MASS., TUESDAY EVENING, DECEMBER 22, 1931 — ONE CENT

CARLO SINISCALCHI FATALLY SHOT

CARLOS SINISCALCHI
Italian Leader Slain by Parisi

GUISEPPE PARISI
Held for First-Degree Murder of Siniscalchi

Luxurious Limousine in Which Carlos Siniscalchi was Murdered Showing Glass Broken by Parisi's Bullet

The Weather
FAIR TONIGHT AND THURSDAY

Springfield Daily News

5 o'Clock Edition LATE NEWS

VOL. YEAR, NO. 193   SPRINGFIELD, MASS. WEDNESDAY EVENING, DECEMBER 22, 1926   ONE CENT

PARISI INDICTED FOR KILLING SINISCALCHI

Joseph Parisi, Arrested For Murder of Carlo Siniscalchi, and His Captors at Headquarters

Detective Lieutenant James T. Raiche, Parisi, and Patrolman Thomas Dowling
[Photo by The Republican Staff Photographer]

LIQUOR DEAL ENDS IN MURDER

Confessed Springfield Slayer Jumps on Motor in Main Street—Empties Gun

STRAY BULLET HITS WOMAN ON TROLLEY

Funerals and Corruption

"We must show a spirit of reparation in this particular instance. We must think more carefully before committing a crime, particularly murder - the willful taking of another's life." The priest's words seemed to linger in the air long after his sermon ended, a reminder of the dire consequences of evil actions on earth and in the world to come."

– FATHER ALFREDO BATESTRAZZI, LADY OF MT. CARMEL

3

The guard dropped off a small stack of newspapers to my cell and gave me a sly grin of approval. Carlo Siniscalchi's funeral was today, but the guards seemed more pleased than saddened that the "King of Bootleggers" was dead. Is it because he has threatened to "get" the cops and even slashed one of them with a razor in the past?

I picked up the Friday, December 23, 1921, edition of *The Springfield Republican* first. Carefully unfolding the paper, I read it in perfect sequence, the first section first and the second section next, making sure to savor every word, folded back knife-sharp when I'm done. God forbid someone should mess with the paper before me!

"Interest in the murder case of Carlo Siniscalchi, fatally shot by Giuseppe Parisi while in his automobile near the corner of Main and Union Streets, late Tuesday afternoon, will center on the funeral of the dead Italian at home at 76 Wilcox Street at eight this morning. The authorities will give the services careful attention against any undue excitement or incidents bearing on the prosecution."

I slump back onto my bunk, savoring the smell of the jailhouse percolating coffee. I pull the *Springfield Daily Newspaper* up into focus, continuing my morning ritual. They report the scene of the funeral;

"With a display of pomp and ceremony uncommon at most funerals, fully 2,000 friends and family paid final tribute to Carlo Siniscalchi, "King of Little Italy."

The harsh smell of death was unmistakable as Carlo Siniscalchi's body lay in wake at his Wilcox Street home. The air, a toxic blend of sweet strawberries and sharp garlic, hung heavy and thick with sadness. Mourners, dressed in traditional black, filled the room, a somber crowd of countrymen from the South End of Springfield and beyond standing in silent reverence. The air was thick with the aroma of flowers and grief. Floral tributes were piled about the coffin, a staggering sight of beauty amid sorrow.

District Attorney Charles Wright stood tall and imposing on the sidewalk near the entrance to the Siniscalchi house. His dark eyes were cold and penetrating, like a sharp blade slicing through the air. His chiseled jaw jutted out, and his hands were planted firmly on his hips as if he had just won a long-fought battle. The crowd around him parted to make way for the funeral procession, yet he remained unmoved, like a stone statue. What was the purpose of his presence there? Was he there to pay his respects, or was something else going on? His presence was like a bad omen, casting a dark shadow over the gathering. He stood out among the mourners like a black cloud on a sunny day.

Pasquale Mondaro, the infamous "star" witness at the heart of the Police Chief Belmer-Patrolman Lyons bribery case of West Springfield, was also there. At the time of the Lyons case, Mondaro was employed by Siniscalchi as a chauffeur. His presence was like a heavy, dense fog full of tension and anticipation. People whispered his name in hushed tones as if the fear of even saying it out loud might cause his madness to be unleashed.

The mourners solemnly shuffled out of the house, the notes of Gennaro Zaggero's 35-piece band gently accompanying their steps. The members of the immediate family and relatives of the deceased man were the first to leave, followed by his close friends. Cars loaded with floral tributes began the procession, leading the way up Wilcox Street, Main, and William Street to Our Lady of Mount Carmel church. A funeral march was played as Siniscalchi's own Stutz touring car led the line of eighty vehicles carrying the mourners, flowers, and the casket. All along the route, delegates of the Italian Catholic societies marched in full regalia, a sad reminder of the gravity of the occasion.

As the funeral procession arrived at the church, a low murmur spread among the first to arrive that bombs and other explosives had been planted inside. Everyone in the building quickly evacuated and was investigated by detectives, yet there was no proof of this. The parish priests dismissed the gossip, only to be interrupted by the janitor who had found a lady's purse beneath one of the seats. Even in this solemn atmosphere, one couldn't help but experience relief that the rumor had been baseless.

Our Lady of Mount Carmel on William Street was bursting at the seams as hundreds crammed into the church. As the funeral procession approached, there was hardly any space available for the mourners and friends who occupied the long line of vehicles in the procession. As more people filed in, the church began to feel suffocating. By the time the high mass of requiem had gotten underway, the church was filled to capacity, and no standing room could be found. In addition to many members of the Italian societies and the 20th Regiment band, more than one hundred people waited outside for the finish of the service, huddled in hushed conversations, their breath forming puffs of fog in the chilly air.

The six pallbearers stood in perfect formation, three pairs lined up shoulder to shoulder. Robert Mari and Samuel Mazzarro stepped forward; their hands outstretched to grasp the handles of the hearse. They hoisted the heavy, solid bronze casket onto their shoulders with one heave. Robert and Albert Santaniello and Ludovico and Dominic Cipriano followed suit and solemnly walked through the church doors. The casket was a weighty burden, and the bearers shuffled carefully as it swayed, creaking with each step. The church was deathly still, the only sound the gentle thud of the pallbearer's feet on the marble floor.

American flags and those representing various Italian societies were solemnly paraded down the center aisle and placed around the casket, standing to attention. The altar was draped in black, solemnly adhering to the Catholic church's tradition. Despite the subdued atmosphere, everything was eerily calm.

The widow, Pasqualina Siniscalchi, remained seated throughout the service, her face veiled from sight.

Father Alfredo Batestrazzi, an assistant to Father Anthony Dalla Porta, head of Mount Carmel Church, celebrated the requiem mass at 10 o'clock after the mass was delayed by one hour due to the large gathering. The priest turned to the people, his face grave and solemn, and began to preach in the Italian language. Heavy with condemnation, his words echoed throughout the colony for the great evils that had been committed recently, specifically, the slaying of Siniscalchi. His plea to have crime corrected in the Italian district was emphatic. "We must be more attentive to God and pray to manifest the confidence of God," Father Batestrazzi declared. He pointed to the death of Siniscalchi as an example of the crime being committed in the city.

"We must show a spirit of reparation in this particular instance. We must think more carefully before committing a crime, particularly murder - the willful taking of another's life." The priest's words seemed to linger in the air long after his sermon ended, a reminder of the dire consequences of evil actions on this earth and in the world to come.

Sergeant Charles Geary led a police unit, standing vigilantly in anticipation of any potential outbreak of violence. Their presence was complemented by detectives from the Springfield Detective Bureau and private investigators, who had infiltrated the gathering of the Italian community in an effort to prevent any demonstration that might follow in the wake of Siniscalchi's death at the hands of a murderer. The atmosphere felt heavy and tense, with the officers standing by with their hands on their holsters and the detectives scouring the crowd for any sign of unrest. People murmured amongst themselves, exchanging fearful glances, and although the officers were ready to step in at a moment's notice, the crowd remained peaceful.

At 11:30, the procession slowly moved along William Street and westward to Water Street. The widow rose to her feet, and with each heavy, labored step, her heart ached as she walked alongside her husband's body. Taking a deep breath, she slowly lifted her veil and gazed into the sea of faces staring back at her. Her eyes were swollen and red, and her cheeks were stained with the tracks of her tears. The solemn atmosphere was thick with emotion as the widow's grief filled the air. The procession eventually arrived at St. Michael's cemetery, where the widow's husband was laid to rest.

The widow, Pasqualina, felt the snowflakes on her face as she saw the procession of members of the various organizations and the band marching along the road toward the cemetery. Despite the bad weather conditions, the last rites of the Catholic church were given by Father Batestrazzi at the cemetery. Francesco Marinaro, editor of L'Eco Coloniale, the local Italian newspaper, eulogized

Siniscalchi with a heartfelt speech, and Alessandro Genosi, president of the Sons of Italy, spoke on behalf of the members of that society. The Mount Carmel Society, Our Lady of Grace Society, and the Protective Sons of Italy all paid their respects to Siniscalchi. Pasqualina stood at the grave's edge, her feet sinking into the soft soil. Her hands trembled as she grasped a handful of dirt, watching as the coffin was lowered into the ground. She heard the shovels ringing in the distance, a solemn reminder of the finality of death. As she walked back to the car, she couldn't help but feel the overwhelming sadness that had settled over the cemetery.

The Springfield Daily News solemnly reported his passing; a heavy silence hung in the air, the kind that only death can bring.

"Carlo Siniscalchi was born in Quindici, province of Avellino, Italy, in 1884. He came to this country in 1906 and lived in New York City for three years. Later, he came to Springfield, where he had lived since. Prominent in local Italian affairs, Mr. Siniscalchi was only initiated into Bersaglieri Lodge, Order of the Sons of Italy, last week. Besides his widow, he leaves two sons, Carlo, eight, and Teodoro, three, and three daughters, Angelina, seven, Rosina, five, and Gloria, two months."

At a press conference, the cold air was filled with the foggy breath of a dozen reporters as they fired questions at the three men leading the media circus. Sergeant Anton Stipek, who had charge of the squad of West Springfield officers who had conducted the liquor raid with Federal Agent Harold Harvey, remembered me threatening him after the raid. He said I threatened to do something so Stipek would lose his job.

The reporter posed his question to Sergeant Stipek, his pen perched above his notepad. "What do you know about Parisi?"

The Sergeant cleared his throat before responding. "Joseph Parisi is rated as the 'King of the Italians' in West Springfield, just like Siniscalchi was rated the 'king' among his countrymen in Springfield."

"What about his family?"

The Sergeant leaned back. "The Parisi family occupy all four apartments in a four-tenement house at 52 Sprague Street, West Springfield. Antonio Parisi, the father, is the hierarchical head of the family. Joseph has two brothers, Frank and John, and a brother-in-law, Joseph Dialessi, who occupy apartments in the same house."

The reporter scribbled down the details before looking up. "What was his reputation in West Springfield?"

"Joseph Parisi has the reputation of being a good family man and very fond of his children," the Sergeant replied.

"Did the West Side police know he was involved in bootlegging?"

"It was commonly known that Parisi was dealing extensively in illicit liquor trafficking."

Federal Agent Harvey's steely eyes surveyed the reporters, his voice a low growl. "I will follow up the Siniscalchi case to uncover evidence and bring prosecutions against men in this section who violate the Volstead Act as information from the murder case develops."

District Attorney Charles Wright stepped forward, the determination in his voice. He refused to take questions and made the statement, "I am on the trail of the 'big fellows' in the liquor running traffic in this section and will smoke out some of those who have made thousands of dollars through the illicit traffic of liquor." His gaze swept the room, and a tense silence fell. "And I won't rest until I do," he added.

The district attorney's voice echoed through the room as he spoke, his open palm slamming on the podium for emphasis. "The investigation into wholesale bootlegging will be made along with the probe of the motive in the murder of Carlo Siniscalchi Tuesday. I am convinced that Giuseppe Parisi, who was indicted by the grand jury yesterday for murder, did not tell the whole truth in his confession to the police. Parisi said he killed Siniscalchi out of fear of the Italian leader, who had threatened him."

The atmosphere in the room was tense, everyone holding their breath to hear the DA's next words. With a heavy sigh, he continued, "When the axe falls, someone is sure to feel its edge. Just how far the investigation will go is still unknown."

It's been four days since they lowered Carlo Siniscalchi into the ground. Last night, I had a long discussion with my new lawyer, Joseph B. Ely of Westfield. The former district attorney of Springfield, Massachusetts, was taking his first steps to become Governor of Massachusetts.

Attorney Ely stepped out of the jail to meet the reporters, his face confident and unreadable. He spoke in a low tone, his words carrying the weight of authority. "I have nothing to say about this case," he said, "but I wish to announce that Attorney Joseph Carmody will remain with the defense."

District Attorney Wright addressed the reporters with a stern expression, his voice rising as he declared, "We are determined to uncover the truth behind this shooting. Parisi's confession does not tell us the whole story, and we intend to dig deep and get to the bottom of it." He paused for a moment, then continued, "Dr. Furcolo was called to the conference and added his knowledge to the case." His gaze swept the crowd as he finished, "This is a matter of great importance, and we will not rest until the truth is found."

The palatial limousine of the murdered Carlo Siniscalchi was a work of art. My brother, John Parisi, an expert welder, and other men helped build the special automobile body, including the plan for the secret compartments- a large tank in the doors for carrying liquor and pockets in the seats to hold weapons. John had warned me of the secret spot where Siniscalchi hid his gun. I allegedly confronted the unarmed Siniscalchi and let off a series of shots. Yet, witnesses recalled an Italian entering the car after the shooting and retrieving the revolver, casting it away into the crowd before police arrived. It is believed that Siniscalchi didn't dare go armed with a gun due to the suspended sentence levied against him for threatening a police officer, as any violation of the law would have resulted in a prison sentence. My remark after the shooting leads to the conclusion of self-defense-- that, indeed, Siniscalchi was armed at the time.

A few days later, Attorney Frank Hinckley, candidate for selectman in West Springfield, stood with conviction before Chairman Charles Palmer. His voice booming in the room, he vigorously contested the Chairman's denial that Carlo Siniscalchi had been granted permission to carry a gun. The temperature in the room seemed to drop as the two men locked eyes, neither one willing to back down. He gestured emphatically towards the board of selectmen's meeting records from June 5, 1920, and exclaimed, "It's right there, on page 108!"

The attorney then detailed that Siniscalchi had been released from jail in Springfield mere weeks prior after serving a sentence for assaulting a police officer. "Yet, despite his criminal history," Hinckley continued, "the West Springfield Board of Selectmen still voted to give him a permit." Hinckley held up the records and demanded that Palmer prove otherwise, his voice tight with accusation.

Palmer remained stoic, and when pressed for an answer, he merely shook his head and responded, "I know nothing about Siniscalchi getting permission to carry a gun."

The following week, the courtroom for my arraignment was packed as the bailiff firmly refused admittance to any additional spectators. "Sorry, you can read about it in the paper." I was led in, my wrists and ankles bound in metal, and the officer helped me to my seat in the dock. I sat still, my foot tapping a steady rhythm to an Enrico Caruso song playing in my head like time had come to a standstill.

The judge, black-robed and firm, surveyed the scene from his polished wood bench, his thin white hair framing a face etched with deep age lines and sunken eyes. My attorney, Joseph Ely, entered the courtroom carrying his briefcase, and after setting a file down on the table, he took his seat. District Attorney Charles Wright and Assistant District Attorney Rufus Eton were present to represent the Commonwealth. When my case was called, Attorney Ely rose and announced to the transfixed crowd that I fully understood English. He cast me a reassuring glance, and I felt my heart race as I jumped to my feet and proclaimed a resounding "Not Guilty" to the charge.

The courtroom was deathly quiet as Judge Heady rose and presented the inquest report on the death of Carlo Siniscalchi. Every person in attendance held their breath as the Judge flipped through the pages, his fingers trembling against the paper. The only sound heard was the rustle of the papers as the Judge searched for the two crucial statements.

Outside in the hall, whispers of shock and disbelief could be heard as people processed the information. In the courtroom, I stood with my head up, my hands clenched tightly in front of me, as the harsh reality of what he had done sunk in. The judge spoke into the stillness, his voice heavy with sorrow. "The evidence speaks for itself. Carlo Siniscalchi was unarmed and had not moved when his life was so callously taken. Additionally, Giuseppe Parisi, the perpetrator of Siniscalchi's death, had acted alone."

As the judge concluded, the courtroom was filled with a deep, heated chatter. In that moment, the tragedy of Carlo Siniscalchi's death sunk in. The judge's gavel thudded against the wooden bench as I was asked to step down from the dock. I felt a firm grip on my elbow from the bailiff, guiding me away from the courtroom and back towards the cold, grey walls of York Street jail. The clang of the barred gate echoed in my ears as I was locked away, awaiting the trial that would decide my future.

Four months had passed since my attorney had spoken a single word to reporters- until last night, Friday, May 19, 1922. Former District Attorney Joseph B. Ely, democratic aspirant for State Governor, was asked to comment on District Attorney Wright's microphone installation at the Hampden County Jail on York Street. Rumors had circulated that the district attorney used the device to gather evidence against the jail inmates.

Attorney Ely declared, "Joseph Parisi, confessed killer of Carlo Siniscalchi, has but one story to tell- the one he told police." Ely's gaze was heavy, unrelenting, and his words hung like a chill. The room was eerily silent, all eyes on the man, searching for answers in the darkness. What secrets did Parisi hold? What really happened to Carlo Siniscalchi?

Ely's face tightened, eyes narrowing. He clenched his jaw, clearly stating he did not favor the district attorney's actions. "This is a clear violation of my client's rights," he said firmly. The jail was silent and dank, the walls lined with cells where inmates were held. Ely glanced around the premises, a disgusted expression on his face. He had no intention of standing by while the DA's misconduct continued. "It's appalling that the District Attorney would resort to such tactics," Ely growled. He peered intently at the recording device, shaking his head in frustration. "This must be stopped."

Wright stared blankly at the reporters gathered in front of York Street Jail, saying nothing in response to their inquiries about the microphone. When pressed further, he refused point-blank to discuss it for publication.

Sheriff Embury Clark admitted that a microphone had been installed at the jail on order of the district attorney, the device having been put in three weeks prior. As the news spread, local lawyers were up in arms, their faces of disapproval and disappointment clearly visible, words of condemnation like "unethical" and "violation" washing over the group. The microphone had no place at the jail, and Wright's silence spoke volumes.

While this was going on in West Springfield, Attorney Paul Connor fiercely interrogated West Side Police Chief Marshall Belmer during his testimony at the local district court on charges of bribery. He posed a long list of searing questions. The queries raised questions about the unbecoming conduct of members of the police force and alleged vice conditions in the town, involving many bootleggers.

Connor's voice thundered through the chamber as he spoke to the legislators. "These questions must be answered in full! They must be addressed for the sake of the citizens of West Springfield and Springfield!" The atmosphere in the room crackled with the pressure, and all eyes were on the Chief. But Belmer remained silent, knowing that the answers he gave would decide his future as West Side Chief of Police.

The tension rose as Connor's questions flew rapidly, Belmer's face increasingly flushed. Connor's voice echoed off the court walls, each word delivered with an intensity that reverberated throughout the hushed chamber. Belmer tried to keep his composure, but it was clear that he was struggling to answer the barrage of questions. Connor glared at Chief Belmer, his jaw clenched. "The questionnaire is in the public files of the legislature. Anyone can see it," he said. "It's about time you gave an answer. I know the Springfield newspapers don't want the questions published, so they're trying to hide the issue. But I won't be scammed out of it."

He paused, taking in the reporters of the Springfield newspapers with Chief Belmer and the list of questions that included many prominent West Springfield men and town officials. "I have the highest regard for the people of West Springfield, and I'm always ready to do anything that will add to their protection and that of their children," Connor exclaimed with conviction.

Chief Belmer was then met with a series of probing questions. He stared into the crowd, his gaze lingering on each face in the audience, searching for signs of judgment. His brow furrowed as he listened to each inquiry, considering his answers carefully. His lips pursed as he struggled to find the right words, his hands fidgeting in an attempt to quell his nerves. His voice wavered as he spoke, the uncertainty evident in his tone. He knew that every word carried weight.

"What is your relationship with Siniscalchi, who was recently murdered by West Springfield booze runner Joseph Parisi?"

"No comment."

"What is your relationship with Hunky Finn? Is he not the bouncer for Cumming's ice cream stand?"

"No comment."

Daniel "Hunky" Finn slung scoops from an ice cream stand on an otherwise dull street corner. He had a reputation for selling far more than just ice cream, and it was no secret that the police had been called there repeatedly. But each time, the charges were mysteriously discharged. Hunky smirked as he handed each customer their order. He knew he was getting away with something and would enjoy it while he could. "You want a cone?" he said, a glint in his eye. "I might be able to hook you up with something else too."

"Does he not act as police chief, sitting in your chair, when you are away?

"No comment."

Though he wasn't an officer, Finn had been known to step in and act as West Side police chief when Belmer was away. He commanded the respect of the officers and the citizens, and his presence created a strong sense of security in the neighborhood.

"Do you always carry a bottle of liquor in your car? Where do you replenish the liquor when the supply gets low? What is your relationship with Joe Coster, and don't you have dinner with him?"

"No comment."

Joe Coster, a convicted bootlegger, lurked the streets of Springfield and West Springfield, a breeding ground for the murderous feud between the two gangs. His name had been linked to the notorious Joseph Parisi, fueling the fire. A witness account claimed to have seen Coster stashing away crates of illegal alcohol, a sure sign of his involvement in the Parisi criminal enterprise. Coster had done time for his crimes, but still, the war between the two gangs raged on.

"Do you remember the fake raid at the Dante Club?"

"No comment."

The police department swarmed into West Springfield's Marconi and Dante clubs, ready to execute the raids. Bottles of liquor clinked and clattered as they were seized from the Marconi club, a total of 120. But at the Dante club, nothing was found. It was almost as if someone had tipped them off. A chill descended over the scene as the officers exchanged knowing glances, and the proprietors of the Dante club smiled smugly.

"Do you know Negrucci very well? Is he now the chairman of the board of public health of West Springfield?"

"No comment."

Giordano Negrucci was the first Italian-born citizen to hold public office in West Springfield.

"How much salary do you get as chief of police? How much do you get from your bootlegger friends? Did you enter into negotiations with District Attorney Wright on a recent drive to Pittsfield? Are you not friendly with Remington of West Springfield? Do you know he had a key to your office?"

West Side Police Chief Belmer remained silent, stony-faced and unmoving. His lips pressed tightly together as his eyes stared straight ahead, refusing to meet Attorney Paul Connor's gaze. The atmosphere was heavy with anticipation as Connor waited for his response, but it soon became clear that the Chief was not going to give any answers. His silence spoke volumes, and Connor knew further questioning would be futile.

*Solid Bronze Casket Containing Body of Carlos
Siniscalchi Being Borne Into Mt Carmel Church*

Siniscalchi's Pet Auto
Said to Contain Tank for
Liquor, Pockets for Guns

Specially Designed Body of Luxurious Limousine Said to Have Been Built in West-Side Shop; Authorities to Overhaul Car

Retaliation Against the Family

"You think you can get away with this? You think you can do whatever you want without consequence?" He spat, his voice ringing with challenge. "Think again." He stepped closer to the mirror, his gaze unwavering as he met his opponent's glare. "Retaliation," he said, his voice low and deliberate, "it works both ways."

-GIUSEPPE "JOSEPH" PARISI

4

The air in the jail cell was stifling, and I paced back and forth, awaiting my trial date. As I sat there, I couldn't help but think of my family and the Pugliano's, their pockets lined with money from the sale of illegal booze. I could almost hear the clinking of their glasses and smell the sickly sweet scent of the alcohol wafting through the air. I clenched my fists, feeling the anger and frustration swell inside me. But I knew there was nothing I could do but wait.

Tomorrow is the Fourth of July, but the celebration is behind bars for me. The hum of voices in the prison cells fills every corner of this York Street Jail, and I've been here for over seven months, waiting for justice. Outside, I can hear the crackle of fireworks, but the only display I'll see is my cell's bars. I can almost taste the freedom I'm missing out on, but all I have is the cold steel of my cell door. I try to keep my chin up, but whenever I hear a guard's footsteps echoing down the hallway, I feel my heart sink slightly.

"You're still here, huh?" a guard says, passing my door.

I can only nod in reply. I know I'm not the only one here, but sometimes it feels like I am. I'm determined to keep my head up and wait for the day I can finally walk out of this place. Until then, I'll have to make the best of my Fourth of July in jail.

I had a pleasant visit with my wife, Raffaela, and my extended family - my brother-in-law Joe Dialessi, who's married to my sister Lucia, brother-in-law Joe Marvici, married to my sister Agata, and their four-year-old son, Pasquale Marvici. We were also joined by William Giles, one of my attorneys. A lively conversation filled the visitor's room as we discussed topics ranging from current events to our favorite restaurants. We all shared stories and laughed until tears filled our eyes. Joe Dialessi shared a funny joke, and William Giles responded with a witty remark. Pasquale Marvici excitedly spoke about his recent school trip to the zoo, his eyes sparkling with joy. Raffaela beamed with pride as she watched our family come together, each person's unique personality bringing life to the room. We all shared hugs and said our goodbyes, looking forward to the next time we could all be together.

Seeing my family really takes my mind off of things inside of this place. Pasquale, my four-year-old nephew, was beaming with excitement for the fireworks display the town of West Springfield was putting on from the Memorial Bridge. The recently completed bridge connected Springfield to West Springfield, and the city was buzzing with anticipation. "Pasquale, can you believe it?" I asked. His eyes sparkled with delight as he nodded in agreement. His little fingers pointed eagerly out the barred windows towards the bridge as if he was ready to take off and join the celebration. I took a deep breath and savored the moment. I imagined the display of lights in the sky and the sound of the fireworks echoing in the night. The thought of the upcoming fireworks display was enough to take my mind off the walls of this place. I felt a sense of freedom and was grateful for the chance to celebrate this special day with my family.

The clock struck 1 pm, and my family had to go. I watched them disappear, feeling helpless and sad. Soon after they left, a guard came to my cell. "Giuseppe, I have some bad news to tell you," he said, his voice heavy.

"What is it?" I replied, my heart sinking.

"Gunmen ambushed your family from another car."

My fists clenched in rage. "Is everyone okay?" I asked, my voice cold and hard.

"The little boy was shot in the arm," he said, his face grim.

"Cowards!" I spat. "Why would they hurt a woman and a little boy? If they have a problem with me, let them come face me!" My chest tightened as my hands balled into fists, blue veins popping up on my forearms. I tried to keep my voice down as I spoke. "What happened? Tell me everything."

"A touring car, carrying two or more men, drove down Water Street and let off a barrage of bullets into your brother-in-law Joe Dialessi's car."

My knuckles turned white as I clenched my fists harder, my voice strained and tight. "Do they know who was involved?"

"No, but I'm told the car is registered to Felix Santaniello of Wilcox Street and believed to be owned by Pasqualina Siniscalchi, widow of the man you murdered."

I stepped back, my jaw clenched tight and my hands raking through my hair. My breath came out in short bursts, and my heart rate steadily increased. In my mind, I heard a faint voice, "Calm down, Giuseppe. Everything will be okay." I slowed my breathing, trying to make sense of the chaos.

My family and Attorney Giles were viciously attacked, a result of the longstanding feud between Italian families that began seven months ago - when Carlo Siniscalchi was murdered. The threats of violence and the smell of fear lingered in the air. The dispute that led to this attack had been brewing for months, and it seemed no one was willing to back down. It was a battle of honor and pride, and it had claimed the life of Carlo Siniscalchi. Now, it threatened the lives of my family and Attorney Giles.

The guards allow me to call my home in West Springfield. On the other end of the line, my brother-in-law's voice echoed through the receiver. "This is Joe Dialessi."

"Joe," I asked, my voice trembling, "is Raffaela alright?"

"Yes," he replied, a hint of worry in his voice. "But she's very shaken up. The other women are with her."

"What happened?" I asked, my chest tightening with dread.

"We were returning home to West Springfield when a Stutz touring car roared beside us. Gunfire suddenly exploded, bullets whizzing overhead and ricocheting off the asphalt. The car was going so fast that the aim of the gunmen was poor, and all of the shots went wild. Miraculously, none of the shots struck our car."

"I see; then how was the Marvici boy hurt?

"After the Stutz had passed some distance, the gunmen turned around and headed back towards our car and when, alongside again, fired point blank at us. I felt a sharp tug on my arm as I pushed Pasquale down, shielding him from the gunfire. Through the thick smoke, I saw his shirt ripped by a bullet, the fabric shaking in the breeze.

"They shot Joe Marvici's boy. Did anyone else take a hit?"

"Luckily not, another bullet lodged in the front seat directly behind Attorney Giles, who was seated next to me. He would have been hit if he hadn't been ducked down low."

"That was close. Did any other bullets hit your car?"

"I found a third bullet on the exterior of the door, just below the window where I was seated. Things could have been much worse had those bullets been slightly more on target. My foot stomped the accelerator as I raced to police headquarters. I burst through the doors, ready to report the shooting. Attorney Giles followed close behind me. "I couldn't get the number of the car," he said. "It all happened so fast. The shots came out of nowhere."

"That's ok, we know who owns the car."

"Who was it, Giuseppe?"

I felt the tension in my jaw as I clenched it tight, my eyes narrowing as I spoke her name. "That bitch Pasqualina," I growled, the words rolling off my tongue like a thundercloud. "She was behind this attempt on your lives." I could feel the hatred in my voice, my hands shaking with rage. No one should ever threaten those I love.

"I'll give the information to Joe Marvici, and we'll take it from there."

"No more talk on the phone," I sternly interrupted.

The room was still; the only sound was the ticking of the clock. "I understand, Giuseppe. We'll see you in a few days."

I slammed the phone down, my fists balling up in rage as I glared at the warden. The guards standing in the doorway stepped back, keeping their distance as I stormed past them, my fury unmistakable. I heard them murmur something about keeping me informed of the investigation, but my mind was elsewhere, consumed with the need for justice. I trudged out of the office, my heavy footfalls echoing through the corridors and blood boiling in my veins. All I wanted was to find out who the shooters were and make them pay.

Captain of Detectives Frank Quilty straightened up abruptly, coming to an immediate alert when he heard the news. He dispatched a team of detectives at once, and they got information from two eyewitnesses. They reported to him that they saw a Stutz touring car, matching the description of the gunmen's car, whizzing down Water Street at a great clip. Another witness saw the vehicle enter Mrs. Pasqualina Siniscalchi's garage. Quilty was determined to get to the bottom of this case and find out who these gunmen were.

The detectives rushed up the steps and pounded on the door. Pasqualina's heart raced as she stood motionless in the hallway. She heard the creak of the door opening and the steely voices of the detectives demanding entrance. "We need to ask you some questions," one detective bellowed.

Pasqualina stepped aside to let them in, and they took their positions in the living room. The detectives then began to interrogate her, their voices full of intensity. She fidgeted, her gaze darting around the room, her hands shaking as she nervously tried to answer their questions. The detectives looked around the room, taking in every detail. They were relentless in their questioning, pushing Pasqualina for more information. She felt exposed and vulnerable, with nowhere to hide. "Pasqualina, we are confident you own the vehicle used in the attack on Parisi's family," the police inform her.

She smirked, "Yes, it is my car, but it was stolen from my garage this afternoon."

"We know the vehicle was not in the garage during the time of the shooting, but it was back in the building a half-hour after the time when the shooting took place."

"Well, I don't have any knowledge of the shooting whatsoever," she tells the police.

Finally, after what seemed like an eternity, the detectives stood up, cynically thanked Pasqualina, and left. She exhaled deeply, relieved that it was over. Without sufficient evidence, the police needed to track down more witnesses.

Captain Quilty addressed the crowd of reporters, his serious expression conveying the gravity of the situation. "I believe the attack on Mr. Parisi's family was a continuation of the clash existing for some time between the Springfield and West Springfield groups of Italians. Following the shooting of Siniscalchi, it is claimed his relatives swore to avenge his death."

The air around them seemed to still as the reporters hung on Quilty's words. One reporter in the back spoke up, his voice quivering, "How did it come to this?"

"Unfortunately," Quilty sighed, "these clashes have been inevitable. The animosity between the two groups has been brewing for far too long."

Later that evening, I awoke with a jump as I felt the cold bars of my cell rattle with the force of the nightstick against them. Blinking away the sleep, I forced my eyes to focus on the guard standing beside my bed. "What time is it?" I croaked, my throat dry from the late hour.

The guard's face was cast in shadow, but his lips curled into a smirk. "It's 1 am," he replied. "I've got some news for you."

My heart thudded in my chest as I waited for him to continue, my mind racing with the possibilities of what the news could be. "What is it?" I asked, my voice barely a whisper.

"I just got word that nineteen-year-old Theodore Vona, who lives at the home of his aunt, Pasqualina Siniscalchi, and twenty-year-old Salvatore Guerriero, were arrested by police shortly before midnight."

My heart sank, and I asked, "Did they do the shooting on my family?"

The guard stayed silent, but his grim face said it all. They were taking the two of them to the police headquarters for questioning in connection with the attempt to murder my family.

Despite the lack of rain, the two young men rapidly walked by Margaret and Water Streets, an umbrella held down to cover their faces. Three patrolmen, suspicious of their actions, promptly tried to question them. "Hold up there!" One of the officers called out. The two men glanced back before trying to break into a run. But it was too late. In a matter of seconds, they were both in handcuffs. The officers could tell something was up. It wasn't raining - so why were they hiding their faces? What were they trying to hide?

The two men, Salvatore Guerriero and Theodore Vona, were dragged into headquarters and interrogated relentlessly by the detectives. The police accused Salvatore of driving the Stutz touring car, from which nine shots were fired at the vehicle carrying my family. The police claim Theodore fired the shots. The two denied knowledge of the incident despite a full hour of questioning. When asked where they were at the time of the shooting, around 1:30 pm, they merely shrugged their shoulders and muttered they were "around the city." Lieutenant Daly then ordered the men locked up.

The morning of the Fourth of July was a tense one as reporters of all sorts crowded into the conference room. The police chief stepped forward, his shoes echoing off the walls. His face was stern as he declared, "We believe an attempt was made to murder Mrs. Raffaela Parisi because of the murder of Siniscalchi, who was the leader of the Springfield Italian south end. Joseph Parisi was the head of the Italian group in West Springfield."

The reporters shifted in their seats, their heartbeats quickening as the chief continued. "Charges of assault with attempt to kill and of driving an automobile to endanger the lives and safety of the public have been made against Vona. No charge has been placed against Guerriero, who is being held as a suspect. The assistant clerk of courts demanded their bonds of $20,000 each at the suggestion of detectives. Thirteen persons pooled their interests today to obtain sufficient bail to free the two men."

The room filled with murmurs, whispers of disbelief and shock. The chief's voice boomed out, silencing the room. "It is believed by police the real intent of the gunmen was to either kill Mrs. Parisi or her brother-in-law, Giuseppe Marvici, or both. The shooting was the most daring that has been attempted in Springfield in some time. The police are still investigating the case, and more arrests will likely be made."

The next day, Vona and Guerriero strode into the imposing District Court, their steps echoing off the marble floors. Associate Judge Edwin Lyford regarded them icily from the bench, his gavel poised. "Not guilty," Vona declared, his voice ringing through the courtroom. Guerriero echoed the same a half-second later, his deep baritone voice reverberating off the walls. Every gaze in the chamber was fixed on the two men, the attorneys and the judge, all motionless in anticipation.

"The case will be heard on the 25th of July, 1922." Lyford's gavel finally slammed down, breaking the tense silence.

District Attorney Charles Wright stepped up to the podium that evening, his face set in a determined expression. The crowd of onlookers held their breath in anticipation as he declared his intention to take on the Water Street shooting case immediately. He paused momentarily, his gaze sweeping across the crowd, and continued. "In all probability, I will cause an investigation to be made, but how long the probe might take is unknown. I want to know the facts of the shooting Monday because of its close relation to the killing of Siniscalchi," he said, his voice ringing with authority. He was ready to do whatever it took to ensure justice was served.

Two months later, the crisp air of the early September morning hung heavy in the courtroom as Vona and Guerriero took their seats to face their trial. Delayed twice already, the jury and witnesses alike were eager to see justice served.

The Italian's code of honor is unwavering - not even the evilest of villains could break it. When those dirty gangsters tried to put my family and attorney's lives at risk, I knew I had to act fast. I directed them all to remain silent and told them that any justice must be handled by the family. I could feel the tension in the air, the tightness of my fists as I ensured my voice carried the gravity of the situation. Even in the face of danger, I knew snitching would never be an option for any honorable Italian.

"No see." "No see." "No can tell." "I don't know!" These words were used by my family as the Commonwealth's witnesses against Theodore Vona in district court today before Judge Heady.

Attorney William Giles walked into the courtroom as the first witness called, his steps echoing off the walls. He began to testify, his voice steady, "I visited Joseph Parisi on the noon of July 3rd in the company of Rafaella Parisi, Joseph Dialessi, and Joseph Marvici- along with his four-year-old son, Pasquale Marvici." The presence of the small boy was evident in the courtroom, his bright eyes wide with curiosity as he peered around the room.

"Mr. Giles, tell the court what occurred on July 3 after you left the York Street jail," asked Prosecutor John Madden.

"We left the jail at around 1:30 pm and were heading north on Water Street when I heard shots behind me. An instant later, a big touring car passed at tremendous speed. Two or three more shots sounded from ahead, but I paid no particular attention, thinking it was probably part of the Fourth celebration," Giles responded.

Madden's eyes widened in disbelief as he asked, "You didn't hear the gunshots? The sharp sound of metal piercing the air, echoing off the car body? You didn't feel the fear that comes with knowing someone is shooting at you?" He shook his head. "How could you not know?"

"I did not realize we had been the target at the time and did not know any bullets had struck the car until we arrived at police headquarters. Then one bullet was found lodged in the left front door, a second had torn the upholstery in the rear, and the shirt of Marvici's little boy had been pierced."

"Did you see who was in the other car?

"I saw only one man in the car. I did not see the driver and couldn't describe the man I did see."

Under cross-examination;

Attorney Thomas Moriarty paced the courtroom, his piercing gaze scrutinizing the witness as he stopped before him. "Giles," he began, his voice low and even. "did you see a gun in the hand of the second man or see any of the shots you heard?"

Giles shook his head slowly, his hands clenched nervously in his lap. "No," he replied, his voice barely a whisper. "I did not see a gun."

Vona stood before the courtroom, his hands trembling as he awaited his fate. He could feel the eyes of the judge and jury bearing down on him, and the room's silence was deafening. The prosecutor stepped forward and directed a question at the witness, Mr. Giles. "Is this the man who shot at you?"

Mr. Giles glanced at Vona for a moment before averting his gaze. "I cannot identify him," he said quietly.

The courtroom fell silent as the judge called out, "Mrs. Raffaela Parisi!" All eyes turned to Mrs. Parisi, her mother's hand gently squeezing her shoulder in support. She slowly rose, her steps echoing through the silent chamber as she made her way to the witness stand. It was time to testify.

"Mrs. Parisi, tell the court what you know about the shooting," asked Prosecutor John Madden.

"We visit my Giuseppe in jail, and I hear shots before and after some big car had passed us at a great speed. Two men were in the car," she responded.

"Would you know either of the men?" asked Prosecutor Madden.

"No can tell," was her answer.

"Did you see any gun?"

"No see."

"Did you think the shots were being fired at you?" asked Madden.

"Yes," she replied, "the boy's shirt was torn, and a bullet went through the automobile."

As instructed, she shook her head; no recognition, no sign of who these men might be. With a sigh of resignation, she declared she had no idea who they were.

She was excused, and Madden recalled Giles;

"Did you see the car a second time?"

"We left Water Street after the shooting and drove to Main Street. There, Joe Marvici called my attention to the car that had just passed us at high speed. I only caught a glimpse and thought it looked like the first car but was unsure and did not see the occupants."

Prosecutor Madden turned his gaze to Joe Dialessi, the third witness. "Mr. Dialessi, what can you tell us about the shooting that day? he asked, his voice ringing out in the courtroom.

Joe shifted in his seat, his eyes darting around the room. "I heard some shots, sir," he said, his voice barely a whisper, "then a car sped past us so fast I couldn't get a look at it."

The courtroom was silent, except for the clock ticking away in the corner.

Prosecutor Madden cleared his throat with a hint of disappointment as he said, "I see. So, you can't tell us anything then?"

Joe shook his head and looked away, unable to meet the prosecutor's gaze. "No, I didn't see anything," he said, his voice heavy with regret.

Madden probed the witness, Dialessi, relentlessly for more information, but the latter held firm, insisting that he had no recollection of any car passing them on Main Street. The dimly lit courtroom seemed to suck away Dialessi's voice, his words echoing off the walls and slowly dissipating into the air. He nervously shifted his weight from one side to the other as he spoke, never once locking eyes with the prosecutor. Madden's face tightened with frustration as he watched the witness, his questions becoming more and more pointed to unearth anything that could move the case forward. But it was not meant to be, and eventually, Madden had to concede defeat.

Patrolmen Michael Curley and John McDonald were the following witnesses. Both testified to seeing Vona drive north on Water Street at about 1:30 on July 3rd at high speed. They estimated the rate at 50 miles an hour. The car bore the registration, "Mass. 127-027." Both officers were positive Vona was driving it. A second man was seated in the back. They did not recognize him.

Officer McDonald stated, "We looked up the registration number and found Mrs. Pasqualina Siniscalchi owned the car."

Attorney Moriarty rose to his feet and thumped his fist on the desk. His objection echoed around the courtroom, reverberating off the walls like a clap of thunder. The judge glanced up from his papers, his expression stern. He paused for a moment before nodding his head in agreement. The attorney smiled, triumphant, as the other lawyers in the room shifted uncomfortably in their seats.

Officer Owen Sloan was the last Commonwealth witness. He testified at being at Main and York Streets very shortly after 1:30 and seeing Vona pass in a big car. He was driving very fast. Sloan tried to stop him for speeding, but Vona disregarded his signal. Sloan took the car's number. It was Massachusetts 127-027. He reported it for speeding. He had no knowledge of the shooting at the time. There were two men in it. He did not recognize the second.

Joe Marvici and Pasquale, his young son, slumped in their seats as the Commonwealth rested its case. Their witnesses had failed to supply the evidence they desperately needed and said they "didn't see anything." Dismay and frustration flooded the courtroom, and the judge's gavel banged loudly against the desk, ending the proceedings. Marvici and Pasquale glanced at each other with a sigh of relief; neither called to the stand.

The courtroom was filled with hostility as Theodore Vona was accused of assault with an attempt to kill and drive an automobile to endanger the lives and safety of the public. The jury returned with their verdict: Not guilty on the first charge and guilty on the second. Vona was fined $100 for the second charge. Mrs. Pasqualina Siniscalchi watched quietly from the sidelines, her eyes focused on Vona. She stepped forward and, without a word, pulled out a hundred-dollar bill to pay his fine. The courtroom was filled with an awkward silence as Vona stared at the woman with a look of relief. Mrs. Siniscalchi simply gave him a small, knowing smile before turning away.

Vona and Pasqualina strutted out of the courtroom, smugly believing that they had gotten away with attacking my family. As they went, my brother, John Parisi, muttered faintly, "Italians don't snitch; we handle problems ourselves." Pasqualina suddenly stopped in her tracks, her face pale. She knew that her husband, Carlo, had paid the price for his misdeeds with the Parisi family a year ago and that the same fate awaited her. John gave her a knowing glance, a reminder that he was not afraid to take matters into his own hands.

John's threat took no time to come to fruition. The news made its way to me in the morning's edition of *The Springfield Republican*, where it was emblazoned across the front page in bold print. "Italian Shot, Seriously Hurt, May Lose Life."

The paper reported, "Durante Siniscalchi's life took an unexpected turn yesterday afternoon as he found himself on the receiving end of an unknown assailant's bullet near the corner of Wilcox and Water Streets. His brother's unfortunate fate from the December before, Carlos Siniscalchi, still hanging like a dreary fog over the family, Durante felt the sickening thud of the bullet as it tore through the air and pierced his body."

The patrolman sprinted down Water Street, gun drawn, in pursuit of the gunman. He raced around the corner and was met with a grisly sight - three deep pools of blood on the sidewalk in the fading sunlight. He called out to the storekeepers and witnesses, but no one could tell him where the wounded man had gone. Minutes later, when other officers arrived, the pools of blood had vanished, replaced with nothing more than puddles of water. Now more confused than ever, the patrolman looked around for answers, but all he could find was a lingering air of mystery.

Three shootings have rocked the Siniscalchi family since December. It all began with the notorious Carlo Siniscalchi, who was gunned down while sitting in his luxurious limousine on Main Street. Frank Albano, a cousin, was then mysteriously hit with two bullets in his legs a short while later. The detectives were unable to find any witnesses or make any arrests, as the victim had kept silent about who was responsible. And just recently, his brother, Durante, was shot in the streets of the South End.

The Chief of Police stepped up to the podium, his voice ringing out through the crowd. "The police of this city and West Springfield are keeping a close watch on both sides of the river for possible further outbreaks in the feud in which the Siniscalchi and Parisi families are thought to be involved," he said, his gaze sweeping across the audience.

He paused momentarily, letting the weight of his words sink in. "We're doing our best to ensure no further outbreaks occur."

Back in his jail cell, Joseph Parisi glared into the mirror, raising his voice. "You think you can get away with this? You think you can do whatever you want without consequence?" He spat, his voice ringing with challenge. "Think again."

He stepped closer, his gaze unwavering as he met his opponent's glare. "Retaliation," he said, his voice low and deliberate, "It works both ways."

SINISCALCHI'S NEPHEW HELD IN CONNECTION WITH MURDER ATTEMPT

Revenge for Killing of Italian Leader Last December Believed Incentive of Yesterday's Outbreak—Gunmen Used Car Owned by Widow of Murdered Man—Attorney Giles in Machine Fired Upon

BELIEVE SHOOTING WAS DONE FROM SINISCALCHI CAR

Police Expect Arrests Soon on Attempt to Murder Relatives of Parisi

PARTY WAS RETURNING FROM VISIT TO PRISONER

Wife of Murdered Italian Leader Claims Automobile Was Taken From Garage Without Her Consent

ITALIAN SHOT SERIOUSLY HURT, MAY LOSE LIFE

Duranti Siniscalchi, Target For Seven Bullets, Three Taking Effect

BROTHER OF MURDERED CARLOS SINISCALCHI

Murder of Joseph Marvici

For months, rival gangs of Springfield, West Springfield, and Connecticut towns have engaged in competition. Several shootings have occurred, and many more stabbing affrays with two or three robberies. In each instance, little headway was made by the police in tracing the guilty. All parties apparently preferred to fight it out and would give no assistance to the authorities.

-THE SPRINGFIELD DAILY NEWS

5

Only a few days had passed since Vona, Pasqualina Siniscalchi's nephew, was released, and the charges of attempted murder were dropped due to "uncooperative" witnesses – but I knew that Siniscalchi would continue with equal intensity and continue this way of handling things. I feared for my brother-in-law and business partner, Giuseppe "Joe" Marvici, the husband of my youngest sister, Agata Caterina. After the attack on Carlo's brother, Durante, I was sure they would come for him next.

On September 11, 1922, Joe Marvici and John Musolino lingered outside the York Street Jail in Springfield, their intense faces revealing the seriousness of the issues they had to discuss. The old folks on the street talked in whispers, pointing out the two men as they walked by. They made their way inside, where I waited in the dimly lit visitors' room. James Mosca, of Bridgeport, Connecticut, and a member of the West Side rum-running gang, was recently shot and killed by Springfield gunmen. We huddled together, our voices tense but hushed, trying to decide what to do now that one of our own had been attacked. I could feel the rage bubbling in my veins as I frantically searched for a way to strike back without making things worse. Everyone else seemed equally determined, their eyes darting around the room, desperately seeking something—anything—that could be used to our advantage.

"We have to do something," one of our guys said, his voice tight with anger.

"But what?" another replied. The clock ticked on, the only sound in the room as we weighed our options. Finally, after what seemed like an eternity, we devised a plan. We would take swift and decisive action against the culprits. We would not let this go unpunished. We were united in this and would ensure everyone knew it.

After an hour of heated debate, the two men were back on the street, heading to my home in West Springfield.

Siniscalchi's gang had been watching the York Street Jail daily for several weeks. Marvici and Musolino's recent visit to the jail and the news of their presence in the city quickly spread throughout the South End like wildfire. Everyone knew that Siniscalchi's crew was on the prowl, and the atmosphere was thick with tension.

As the sun set, they left my home and drove south, searching for Dominic Parati, a notorious bootlegger from Connecticut who had been mixed up in several bootlegging scrapes in the Nutmeg state over the past year. The crisp autumn air was a refreshing change from the muggy heat of the day, but the chill was a reminder of the danger they were about to face. The night was quiet, the stars twinkling through the darkness as they drove toward Westville. The occasional streetlamps served as beacons, guiding their path to the small town.

"Do you think he'll be at the bar like Joe Parisi said?" one of them asked, breaking the silence.

The other nodded. "It's worth a shot. Parati's been mixed up in some shady business and likely holed up there."

Musolino's eyes darted around nervously as he exclaimed, his voice trembling, "I-I'm sure of it. That black car was definitely following us since we left West Springfield!" He glanced out the window as if expecting the tail to appear at any moment. He could feel the tension in the air and the fear that something sinister was afoot.

John Musolino and Joe Marvici were nearly out of North Haven on the deserted highway when a big, black touring car pulled up alongside them. It was as if it had come out of nowhere. Before either of them could react, the air was filled with an ear-splitting crack. Shots were being fired from the car, and the gun battle began.

Marvici's hand darted to his hip pocket, but it was too late. He gritted his teeth and cursed under his breath. His fingers closed around the cold metal of his gun, but it didn't have a chance to clear the pocket. He felt the tension in the air and the beads of sweat sliding down his back like icy fingers. His body jerked as four bullets from a .45 caliber revolver ripped through his flesh, one through his right eye, sending a shockwave of agony through his brain that ended his life in an instant. A second bullet struck his left forearm, while a third pierced an inch away from his heart in his left chest area. The fourth hit him in the neck, causing a violent spurt of blood to erupt and stain the air around him. The sound of the gunshots echoed through the air, hanging there like a silent scream. The smell of gunpowder and the sight of the spilled blood created a gruesome scene that would be forever burned in the memories of those who saw it. Marvici's body lay still, his life taken in a matter of seconds. The shock from the bullets was too much to bear, and he was gone in a blink of an eye.

Musolino's stomach dropped as he watched in shock. His eyes widened, glued to the sight of Marvici slumped over, still and lifeless. Time seemed to stand still as he tried to understand what had just happened. A hoarse voice broke the silence, Marvici's last words echoing through the car. "I'm sorry, I didn't see the car pull up on us." Joseph Marvici was dead.

As their car was riddled with bullet holes, the sound of gunfire echoed through the air as Musolino fired off three shots from his .32 caliber pistol toward the assailants. He was shot through the left ear. He felt a sharp pain as he fell back, the warm blood scattering from his ear into his eyes. With a new determination, he grabbed the wheel and steered it into a sand bank, the grains of sand crunching beneath the tires. He gritted his teeth as he held the wheel tightly, determined to make it to safety. Through the silence, he heard a voice break the stillness. "We're almost there; keep going!" he thought to himself, knowing that if he could just make it a little further, they would be safe.

Musolino felt a surge of anger and sadness. He wanted to scream, to rage against what had happened. But his body was frozen, unable to move or speak. His world grew dim as he slipped into unconsciousness.

The other car roared away in a southernly direction, its tires screeching as it blasted off into the distance. The sound of its engine lingered in the air for a few moments before fading into the night. The driver peered through the rearview mirror, watching as the street lights blurred past, each passing in a flash. His grip on the steering wheel tightened as he pushed the car to its limits, desperate to escape.

The Springfield Republican reported, "The murder of Marvici yesterday is believed to be another chapter in the feud between certain rum-running and bootlegging interests on both sides of the Connecticut River. The ill feeling started, it is claimed, when bootleggers from West Springfield, where Joseph Parisi was a power for some time, started to broaden out to this city and aroused the ire of certain interests with headquarters on Water Street."

The Bridgeport Times spread the news of the murder. Reports of the gruesome event were splashed across the front page, detailing the scene with a sense of alarm and grief. In the corner, an article revealed the tragedy – the murder – and the depth of the crime. "Rigid Probe Into Rum and Murder at North Haven." People gathered to read the story, their faces reflecting the horror of the situation. Voices were hushed, whispers carried, and the atmosphere was tense. Even the air seemed to be waiting for justice. "Control of the bootleg traffic in parts of Massachusetts and this state is said to be at the bottom of the feud."

The headline in *The Brattleboro Daily Reformer* made waves throughout Vermont, drawing people in with its captivating details and powerful impact. "One Man Killed In Running Fight." People were eager to learn what had caused such a stir, and the article quickly spread from person to person. Conversations were filled with speculation and excitement as people discussed the news, and the atmosphere was electric with anticipation.

The Connecticut State Police were called into the case immediately, and Captain Frank Nichols and Inspector Anthony Buddus came to Springfield last night. Nichols and Buddus talked with my wife, Rafaella Parisi, and some friends at my home on Sprague Street in West Springfield. Interrupting each other and punctuating their words with pointed fingers, they discussed the situation at hand with intense focus. Rafaella's eyes darted between the men; her brow furrowed as if she were trying to make sense of the conversation.

My friends huddled around the officers, their fists clenched so tightly that their knuckles turned white. Their faces had heated to a burning red, eyes wide with fury as they, without a word, conveyed their rage through deep glares. The tension was evident; every ounce of air seemed to vibrate with their seething emotions. Hushed whispers and sporadic shouts constrained exchanges, the group's hostility and distrust of the officers clear in their every movement.

One of them spoke up, their voice shaking with rage. "This isn't right!"

Another one chimed in, their voice dripping with disdain. "We have to do something about this!" The group nodded in agreement, ready to fight.

The police left and began to probe the area, their eyes drawn to a parked vehicle. Its windows were fogged with dried droplets of crimson, evidence that a violent act had occurred.

"That car," one of the officers said, pointing to the West Springfield automobile. "That's the murder car."

Members of the Connecticut State Police who hurried here last evening after the murder in North Haven, Connecticut, discovered that the car was followed from the time it left my home in West Springfield until the shooting occurred in Connecticut.

Detective Captain Frank Quilty raced down the street, his men following close behind. He had been called in to aid the Connecticut officers, but as they arrived on the scene, the mystery only deepened. The car was abandoned, and no one seemed to know who it belonged to or who had been inside. With a heavy sigh, Captain Quilty turned to his men and shook his head, indicating that they should go out and look for any clues. The officers spread out, examining the car from all angles. They took in every detail - the vehicle's make, the burn marks on the frame, the broken window - and then began scouring the surrounding area. But, despite their best efforts, no one could answer the question of who owned the car or what men were in it. As Captain Quilty looked on, he couldn't help but feel disappointed. He had been called in to help, yet he could not give any information.

His men had also combed through the entire Italian South End of Springfield, scouring every inch for any trace of the occupants of the death car. "We've searched the local Italian district completely," he declared, "and we can confidently say the death car is not from around here. We've been keeping tabs on the York Street Jail – noting who visits."

The air around me was thick with vengeance and regret as I thought about Joe Marvici's lifeless body. His death was a result of my own actions, a direct consequence of my taking the life of Carlos Siniscalchi. Bootlegging may have fueled the fire, but revenge was the driving force that brought us to this point. I could not shake the guilt that came with the knowledge that I had caused this. Every sound, smell, and sight reminded me of the tragedy I had caused. I wanted to turn back time, to erase the fateful events of the past. But it was too late. This was the result of my actions.

The Springfield Daily News clattered onto doorsteps, headlines shouting news of the latest developments. The paper rustled as its readers flipped through the pages, coming to rest on an article detailing the area's newest tragedy. The words jumped off the page, vividly depicting the events unfolding. Conversations filled with disbelief and questions echoed through the streets as people discussed their reactions and opinions. Rumors flew like fireflies in the night, each more fascinating than the last. All eyes were on the *Daily News*, eagerly awaiting the next update.

An article read, "The shooting is considered another chapter in the bootlegger's feud. For months, rival gangs of Springfield, West Springfield, and Connecticut towns have engaged in competition. Several shootings have occurred, and many more stabbing affrays with two or three robberies. In each instance, little headway was made by the police in tracing the guilty. All parties apparently preferred to fight it out and would give no help to the authorities."

A daunting team of investigators interrogated Theodore Vona, Carlos Siniscalchi's nephew, and Salvatore Guerriero. Captain Frank Nichols and Inspector Anthony Buddus of the Connecticut State Police, along with members of the local detective bureau, descended upon the scene with questions about the murder of Joseph Marvici and the wounding of our cousin, John Musolino. Vona sat in the interrogation room, surrounded by harsh incandescent light and the smell of stale coffee. He squirmed in his chair, eyes darting around the room as the questions began to fly.

Captain Nichols leaned in, his voice stern, and asked, "Where were you the day of the ambush? Theodore felt his throat tighten as he tried to find the right words, but the silence hung like a heavy fog.

Suddenly, Inspector Buddus slammed his hand on the desk and shouted, "Answer the question!" His words echoed off the walls.

Theodore gulped and arrogantly replied, "I was around town."

Vona and Guerriero's conversation with the police felt like an eternity. The officers remained tight-lipped as the two hours dragged on, refusing to divulge their discussion's exact content or outcomes. People on the street wondered if they had uncovered any clues that could lead to the capture of the men who had fired on Marvici and Musolino.

John Musolino was also interrogated closely, his denials ringing hollow as the police pressed further. He was held without bail by the Connecticut State Police, the air of the precinct heavy with the intent to uncover the truth. The officers firmly believed he knew the other vehicle's occupants, their questions increasingly pointed as they looked to break through his defenses.

John sat in a hard chair, the room's silence bearing down on him like a physical weight as he nervously ran his fingers through his hair. "Please," he begged, "I'm telling you the truth. I don't know who they are." The police continued to press, refusing to accept his words as fact. He could only sit and wait as they continued searching for answers he would not give them.

The Connecticut State Police believed it was the work of two Brooklyn, New York, professional gunmen hired by local gangsters with orders to take out Marvici. The Springfield crew was thought to be at the heart of the crime. The investigators worked tirelessly, piecing together the clues that pointed to the murderers. They examined bullet casings and interviewed witnesses, creating a picture of the cold-blooded killers who had been sent to commit the crime. The detectives felt a chill as they walked the deserted highway where the shooting had taken place. The atmosphere was heavy with the knowledge that professional gunmen had been hired to take a life. The investigators spoke to the locals, trying to glean any information that could lead them to the culprits.

The past two days had revealed an unsettling truth - several men with unsavory reputations in Brooklyn had been spotted in Springfield prior to the shooting. It was a tight-knit neighborhood, and news of their arrival had spread quickly. As word spread, the locals glanced over their shoulders, their uneasiness clear.

Musolino, held captive by Connecticut authorities, described the chaotic scene— "the first shot fired from the murder car struck Marvici in the head, and three others lodged in his body, while I was shot in the ear." According to the police, "Only expert shots could have done such effective firing, as both vehicles were traveling at a high rate of speed." This led them to conclude that professional gunmen did the shooting. The police are convinced, however, that the shooting had its instigation in the Springfield underworld.

While this was happening, a political campaign got nasty between incumbent District Attorney Charles H. Wright and his opponent Richard J. Talbot. Talbot has been criticizing Wright's actions in the recent police probe, charging him with undue friendliness with Italian gunmen and specifically the Siniscalchi family.

Pasqualina Siniscalchi, the widow of Carlo Siniscalchi, felt her blood boil when she heard Richard Talbot's speech during the political campaign. With a voice laced with venom, Talbot had accused Wright of "fraternizing with the underworld, mainly gangsters Siniscalchi and Mondaro." Pasqualina marched into Talbot's office the following day, her heels clicking on the marble floor with each determined step. She threw the door open with a bang and glared at Talbot with steely eyes; her hands balled into fists at her sides.

"How dare you accuse District Attorney Wright of consorting with Carlo and Mondaro!" she spat. "What do you have to say for yourself?" Mrs. Siniscalchi was visibly agitated and kept fumbling beneath her clothing. She demanded Talbot prove her deceased husband was a member of the Black Hand.

Talbot replied, "I do not care to discuss such a subject."

"You can't prove it," she countered. "You have no proof that he was with the Black Hand."

From that, she launched into a tirade of mixed Italian and English. Both men tried to quiet her. The enraged woman's voice rose to a screech as she yelled, "Damn you, I came here to do it!" She grew more excited and suddenly picked Talbot's hat from his desk and hurled it at him, screaming in Italian. Talbot dodged the hat, and as he did so, her arm whipped out, and her hand clamped around the ten-pound steel check protector from Talbot's desk. She hurled it at him with all her might, and it connected with his right shoulder with a sickening crunch, the handle shattering on impact. The air in the small office seemed to thicken with tension as if the walls were holding their collective breath.

She sprang to her feet with a single bound, her eyes blazing with rage. Across the room, she flew, her steps echoing off the office walls. Talbot was swaying, desperately trying to regain his balance, when Major John Canfield jumped between them. The two of them grappled fiercely, their fists slamming against each other with a thunderous force. Desks and chairs were overturned in the chaos, and papers flew around the room like a storm of snowflakes.

"Stop!" Canfield shouted as he held them apart. "This is not the way to sort things out!" His voice was calm, but his eyes were blazing with the same intensity that had ignited the fight. The two of them stood there, panting and exhausted, as the office slowly returned to its original state.

Realizing what she had done, Mrs. Siniscalchi froze, her body trembling with shock. She stumbled backward until she sunk into a chair, her eyes wide with fear. Her mouth moved quickly as she muttered Italian prayers under her breath. The room was eerily silent, apart from the muffled sound of her voice. The air was thick with tension, and her face looked drained of color. She was in a state of shock, barely able to process what had happened.

The clamor of the commotion reverberated through the offices, causing those nearby to rush in, alarmed. Talbot stood tall and composed, his voice steady and reassuring as he waved them off. "It's all under control," he said, his gaze fixed on the woman before him.

"Leave," he commanded, his voice unwavering, and the woman quickly scuttled away, her hurried footsteps echoing in her wake.

Detective Lieutenants Daniel McCarthy and Matthew Meade arrived at Mrs. Siniscalchi's home to find her waiting for their arrival. Her expressionless face revealed no emotion as she silently accompanied them out of the doorway and into the waiting police car. She was arrested on a warrant charging assault with intent to kill. They reached the station, and the booking process began - her stillness and lack of response to the questions thrown her way was deafening. Bail was set at $10,000 and furnished by Lorenzo Sylvester, Mrs. Rose Santaniello, and Vincent Fiore.

Attorney Talbot's eyes hardened with determination as he spoke to reporters. "Well, it shows pretty well on whose side the underworld forces are. Mr. Wright has declared they support me, but it seems they come to his defense mighty promptly." He pounded his fist on the table and declared, "This won't frighten me a bit. I'm going on, for the right will finally prevail. For my safety, I shall ask the court to place this woman under bonds to keep the peace."

In reply to Richard Talbot's comments, District Attorney Charles Wright stood before journalists. His booming voice echoed throughout the room as he vehemently declared, "Talbot, for some time past, has issued public statements that are false, which I would not have troubled to answer. Mostly, they have not seemed to me worthy of an answer. One false statement by Talbot is, 'When Mr. Wright wanted information on the police, he went to Carlo Siniscalchi, a jailbird. And who drove this pair, Siniscalchi and the district attorney? Why, Mondaro? And Mondaro met Mr. Wright in the Nayasset club.'

"Carlo Siniscalchi first called upon me at the Nayasset club, and once only. When he came, I did not know he was coming to see me or who he was until he was brought into my room by an American friend, whom I will not name now. I have never ridden in an automobile with either Mondaro or Siniscalchi. I should be perfectly willing to ride with either at any time if I believe that by doing so, I will aid the ends of justice. After meeting me at the club, I met Siniscalchi on two other occasions, once at the courthouse and once in the private office of a very prominent businessman in Springfield and in the presence of a high city official. At my last meeting with him, he made an appointment with me to meet again. He was shot on the main street of Springfield on the day that he had the appointment to meet me."

He finished his statement with a powerful conclusion, "Talbot further said that the police department is a 'splendid body of men.' Why does he not boldly say this in his published statement? Does he want to speak around the street corner to curry favor with this department while saying, as he has in the press, that he would investigate them? He says anything that he thinks will get him a vote." It was clear that District Attorney Wright's words had made a lasting impression.

Joseph B. Ely, my attorney from Westfield, stood in front of me, face grim, on the first day of the new year - January 1, 1923. He informed me that the Parisi-Siniscalchi murder case, which had been postponed several times, would not come up until after the January superior court term in Pittsfield. He paused for a moment, letting the news sink in. I felt a sense of dread in my stomach, knowing that the trial was being pushed back again. I struggled to keep my composure, and I asked him if there was anything else he could do. He shook his head and told me that I had to be patient. I nodded silently, the weight of the situation heavy on my shoulders.

I make sure I use my time wisely. My attorney suggested that I take classes while I'm in jail so that it will be beneficial for me when I'm up for sentencing. I enrolled in Justice Webster Thayer's course on social justice, and I'm one of the prisoners in the Hampden

County Jail system who stepped up to defend the institution in the face of allegations by Stanley Lamonte and Hannibal Cummings, who were recently sentenced for breaking and entering. Every day, I attend classes, taking in all the information and understanding the importance of the topic I'm learning about. I sit there with the other inmates, listening to the lectures and participating in group discussions. We all focus on the material and how it can help us in the future. I feel empowered by the knowledge I'm gaining, and I'm confident it will help me when it's time for my sentencing.

As the morning light spilled through the window, I grabbed my newspaper and settled into my bunk. *The Springfield Republican* was filled with stories of District Attorney Wright and Pasqualina's involvement with several shady Prohibition agents. I raised an eyebrow at the headline, not sure what to expect.

On a crisp January morning in Boston on January 23, 1923, the federal trial of United States v. J. Albert Tomlin and J. Raymond "Red" Daniels began. The former prohibition agents both faced charges of theft of government property. The courtroom buzzed with anticipation, the air thick with the sound of murmured conversations as citizens shuffled into the gallery, eager to see the proceedings. J. Albert Tomlin and J. Raymond Daniels, dressed in their finest suits, were led to the dock, heads held high but eyes downcast. The judge entered the court, and the bailiff cried, "All rise!" The courtroom rose in unison, all eyes on the judge as he took his seat. He banged the gavel with authority, and the trial began.

Attorney William A. Tirrall strode into the courtroom, his voice booming as he spoke of the connection between District Attorney Charles H. Wright, Prohibition Agent Warren S. Fielding, and Mrs. Pasqualina Siniscalchi. The bustling courtroom hushed as he revealed that Mrs. Siniscalchi had taken over the duties of her husband, Carlo and that Fielding had the use of her car. A wave of whispers swept through the room, and all eyes turned to the defendant.

The three individuals were grilled relentlessly, the prosecution unrelenting in their questioning. Had District Attorney Wright and Prohibition Agent Fielding "wined" at the Siniscalchi home? Was there a secret meeting between the two, the intent of which was to get a federal appointment for Fielding? The atmosphere was tense, the air thick with unspoken accusations. Every detail, every murmur was scrutinized, the slightest gesture noted. A drop of sweat trickled down Wright's forehead; Pasqualina shifted her stance, her gaze averted. In the end, the questions remained unanswered, the truth elusive.

Witnesses testified seeing a government truck, filled with confiscated barrels of alcohol, back into Mrs. Siniscalchi's garage. Agents Daniels and Fielding were there, unloading the truck. Wright stood by, offering to supply whatever information he could on police activities, insisting he'd do anything to help.

Tomlin queried Daniels about the Parisi family of West Springfield, stressing the importance of Mrs. Siniscalchi, as he figured "she would do anything she could to help because it was a member of the Parisi family who had been implicated as killing her husband." The room was silent, and the tension tense as his words hung in the air, a sense of dread permeating the atmosphere.

District Attorney Wright's face grew serious as he was questioned about his involvement in the police investigation and his meetings with Mrs. Siniscalchi. His brow furrowed as he declared, his voice ringing out in the courtroom, "I have been active in clearing up a bad condition of crime in the city where certain members of the police department were implicated." The impact of his words was felt throughout the room, the tension unmistakable in the air.

Wright had first seen Siniscalchi just a short while before he was shot and met with him the day before his murder when he had scheduled a meeting with him for the following day. With his heart pounding, Wright arrived at the appointed place and time, only to find Siniscalchi had been shot and killed.

He had gone down to the Siniscalchi home the day of the shooting to pay his respects to Mrs. Siniscalchi. Rumors of her husband's appointment with him weighed heavy on his mind, and he wondered if it had something to do with his death. From then on, his conferences with Mrs. Siniscalchi were in regard to prosecutions in connection with the murder.

The proceedings were suddenly halted as Edward Williams, Director of Prohibition Enforcement, burst into the room with a thunderous expression. His fists were clenched tightly, his face red with rage, and his eyes blazing with fury. Everyone shrank back in fear, the air thick with tension. "What is the meaning of this?" the Judge bellowed, his voice echoing around the courtroom. The courtroom was silent, no one daring to answer his question.

His resignation letter slammed down onto the desk, the words of discontent and betrayal searing his mind. He resigned due to extreme disgust with the conduct of Warren Fielding and the corruption within the entire Prohibition agency. His ideals and plans had been pushed aside and trampled upon, his hard work and toil disregarded. He could no longer stand the sight of the man, so he had made his decision. "I can't take this anymore," he muttered under his breath. He had made his decision, and he was going to stick to it. Edward Williams glared around him, rage simmering in his veins, before he finally turned and stormed out of the courtroom.

The jury's verdict was announced in a solemn silence, their faces somber. J. Albert Tomlin's expression was one of shock and disbelief, the jury finding him "guilty" of larceny of government-seized wine. J. Raymond Daniels wore a mask of relief and joy, deemed "not guilty." Daniels is still a principal in a bribery case, and the investigation is still being made. The courtroom was filled with a tense atmosphere as the clerk read out the judgment. The sound of the gavel reverberated as the judge declared the case closed. Mrs. Siniscalchi heaved a sigh of relief as the verdict was read while Wright looked on with a sense of trepidation. The jury had spoken, and the decision was final.

Strangely, no charges were made against Wright or Mrs. Siniscalchi for their involvement.

A week later, my cellmate Eugenio Bonavita and I anxiously awaited the news that would decide our fate. We had been awaiting our trials for over a year.

Journalists from all over the city gathered in front of the courthouse on January 30, 1923, buzzing with anticipation. In the center of the steps, Wright stood at the top, his voice unwavering. "This trial is a symbol of justice," he declared. "Giuseppe Parisi is accused of committing a heinous act on the afternoon of December 20, 1921. It is our duty to ensure that he is held accountable for his actions." The audience watched as Wright's words echoed throughout the court. When he finished, a pin could be heard dropping in the silence that followed. All eyes were on Wright as he concluded his statement. "Let us make sure justice is served," he said.

The impact of his words hit us like a punch in the gut. Our lives and freedom were in the hands of the court. We exchanged nervous glances, knowing our lives were now out of our hands.

ONE MAN KILLED
ONE BADLY HURT
IN RUNNING DUEL

Had Visited Joseph Parisi In
Springfield Jail an Hour
Before

JOSEPH MARVICI FALLS
DEAD IN SPEEDING CAR

John Musalino, Shot and
Seriously Wounded, Steers
Auto. Into Sand Bank—
Assailants Escape

Giuseppe "Joseph" Marvici

La Mia Famiglia

"I wrote to my father and mother asking them to come to America with my three sisters and my brother Francesco to join us. They came all, and I was so glad to see them that tears ran down from my eyes."

-GIUSEPPE "JOSEPH" PARISI

6

Eugenio leaned over from the top bunk and peered at the notebook. "What are you writing, Giuseppe?" he asked.

I sighed and set down my pencil. "It's my diary," I said, tapping the page. "A way to clear my head of all my troubles." I paused, my eyes distant, recalling the memories of my past. "I write about my home in Calabria. Growing up with my famiglia, and how I met my beautiful wife, Raffaela. The joy of raising our children together." I smiled, letting the warmth of the memories fill the room.

I lay in my bunk every night, the lumpy mattress creaking beneath me, and wrote in my diary. My thoughts swelled with memories of life before my imprisonment: my beloved Calabria, Italy, known as the "toe of the Italian boot" for its prominent peninsula. I could almost see the majestic mountains dropping off into the crystal clear blue ocean separating the Tyrrhenian and Ionian seas, the sound of the waves crashing against the shoreline. Tears of longing welled up in my eyes.

My fifteen months of confinement in the York Street Jail in Springfield, Massachusetts, felt like an eternity since I had been indicted for the murder of Carlo Siniscalchi, the notorious "Bootleg King of Springfield."

Each day, I would stare blankly at the dank walls of my cell, counting the hours until my trial. The musty air clung to me like a second skin, and the only sound that filled the oppressive silence was the occasional clang of the guard's keys as he made his rounds. I felt my spirit slowly slipping away with each passing day. I would often try to distract myself, but nothing seemed to ease my misery. Time seemed to stand still as I agonized over the fate that awaited me. The only thing that kept me going was the hope that I might be found innocent. Still, I couldn't help but dread the long days ahead. With every passing moment, my anxiety grew. I felt like I was walking a tightrope that stretched into infinity, desperately searching for a way out of this never-ending nightmare.

My cellmate is Eugenio Scibelli. In 1921, he made the mistake of running away with Antonio Bonavita's wife. One day, as he walked down the street, he saw Bonavita and knew he was in for a fight. His heart thumped in his chest like a drum as he reached for his revolver, ready to defend himself. But before he could draw, Bonavita had already pulled out his gun. Scibelli watched as the weapon jammed, and he seized the moment. He fired his own revolver, and Bonavita fell to the ground, dead. Scibelli was charged with Bonavita's murder and is now awaiting trial.

My voice rose excitedly as I asked Eugenio, "Did you hear the good news? My lawyer says my trial starts tomorrow and thinks I have a good chance of being acquitted."

Eugenio shook his head sadly and replied, "That's good news for you, amico mio, but I don't have the scratch for big-shot lawyers like that."

"What are you going to do?" I asked.

A desperation filled the air as Eugenio sighed, "I just don't know. I want to get out of here; this place drives me crazy. The district attorney says he'll make me a good deal if I plead guilty."

I couldn't believe what I was hearing. "Are you an idiota?" I exclaimed. "They'll send you to the electric chair!"

"But the district attorney said he'd help me, no?" Eugenio's voice was filled with desperate hope.

Scibelli paced back and forth, the stale air of our cramped cell suffocating him. His desperate need to be reunited with his new wife ached in his heart, the promise of freedom frustratingly distant. Sweat beaded on his forehead as he clenched and unclenched his fists, tears stinging his eyes. He mumbled a prayer for help, hoping for some miracle, a brief moment of comfort coming from the thought of her. He dug deep, determined to make it through his sentence, knowing that one day soon, they would be reunited.

The dingy cells of York Street jail were not fit for even a dog. The oppressive stench of overcrowding and disease hung in the air, making one want to gag with disgust. Voices echoed off the walls of the prison, carrying the misery of the inmates who were locked away in the dank cells. The air was thick with the fear of those facing impending death sentences. It was a place of dread and despair, where even the bravest of souls faltered. In this very place, back in 1898, the last legal hanging in Massachusetts was carried out. Now, those convicted of first-degree murder are sent to the electric chair - if they survive the horrors of York Street.

Eugenio and I worked in a cramped chamber, shoulder-to-shoulder with a hundred men, weaving cane-chair seats in the oppressive heat. With 144 cells to house 175 men and twenty-seven women, forty-four were stuffed into several makeshift rooms, and fourteen were shuffled into a tiny 250-square-foot attic with one small window and no ventilation. In the jail's hospital, healthy and diseased inmates slept side-by-side in close quarters. Once a week, we get to take a bath, but there are only two bathtubs for the entire joint, and two men - sometimes even four - have to go through the same filthy water before it is changed out. Each morning, we'd march down the hall to the cellar, buckets of excrement in hand. We'd dump the contents into a funnel, which fed straight into the city's sewer. The heavy iron doors of the hatchway could not contain the stench of the room, and its vileness added to the already foul air, suffocating us with its intensity.

A man worked tirelessly, his brush dipping in and out of the whitewash paint bucket, desperately trying to mask the deplorable living conditions. But even the law requiring access to the open air couldn't help us here - there was no escape from the cramped, rat infested quarters. The women had a pit open only to the sky, barely wide enough to stretch out their hands. Inmates' clothes that they had washed and hung to dry were hung around it. The smell of soap and sweat mingled in the air, a grim reminder of our helplessness.

This is not the America I dreamt of or the beautiful tree-lined streets of West Springfield where my family settled. Every time I crossed the bridge to Springfield, I felt my hand instinctively reach into my pocket to clasp the handle of my pistol. How did it come to this?

At the turn of the century, Water Street – recently renamed Columbus Avenue – was a place of fear in Springfield. Known as the South End, "Little Italy," it was a slum populated by immigrants who had fled poverty and persecution in Southern Italy and found only more of the same in their new home. The streets were a treacherous place where violence was a daily occurrence. Murder, stabbings, robberies, extortion – even police corruption – were all part of life in the South End. The desperate cries of the victims echoed through the alleys while the perpetrators lurked in the shadows, their faces hidden by darkness. On the corner of Water and Union, the corner boys lounged in the lamplight, talking and laughing, while a few feet away, a lone figure hurried past, clutching her purse and looking over her shoulder – just in case.

We lived across the newly built Memorial Bridge, over the Connecticut River, in West Springfield, with the other Southern Italians who came to America. It was a short distance between our societies, and peering over that bridge, you could almost see one another. But that river was a dividing line amongst families, mafia families.

My padre, Antonio Parisi, was born in the quaint village of Staiti, while my madre, Maria Cecelia Battaglia, hailed from Caraffa del Bianco. Growing up during the Risorgimento, the unification of Italy, was no easy feat. The legendary Giuseppe Garibaldi, an Italian soldier and patriot, commanded the guerrilla "Redshirts," leading them in the country's unification. Our padre told us stories of his bravery, of battles won with the power of his courage and tenacity. He remembered the sense of pride that filled the air, of a nation reborn and a people with the courage to fight for what was rightfully theirs.

But the joy of my parents and their countrymen was short-lived. The Italian south was hit hard by an economic depression, soon followed by the eruption of Mt. Vesuvius, a flu pandemic, and a malarial outbreak. My father had a secure job with the government, but most of the Calabrians were farmers, living off of the land they worked, which was seen as "latifundia": large estates with small plots of land for the peasants. They struggled to make a living, growing grains and olives and raising sheep and goats. Taxes were high, and wages were low, making the region one of the poorest in Italy. As my parents toiled through the hard times, their hope for a better future slowly faded.

In the 1860s, Calabrian villages were plagued by a surge of organized crime, marking the rise of the 'Ndrangheta in the prison system. As the 1880s brought about a surge of violence due to mass politics in Italy, granting my father and other adult males the right to vote, local politicians resorted to fear tactics and strong-arming to ensure their candidate was victorious. The air was thick with apprehension as my father set off to the ballot box, my family gripped by fear of the ensuing violence. The 'Ndrangheta emerged to set up its authoritarian control in Southern Calabria, a rule that remains today. Amidst the turmoil, the 'Ndrangheta quickly cemented its influence, leaving Calabrians to suffer under its oppressive regime.

Amidst the chaos and anarchy of the time, Antonio Parisi and Maria Cecelia declared their love for one another in the breathtaking town of Caraffa del Bianco, Reggio di Calabria, in 1886. Together, they created our family, becoming the proud parents of seven children in the span of 14 years: three bambinos and four bambinas. Maria Angela, my eldest sorella, was first born, followed by Mary Caterina, then Giovanni, my first fratello. I came next to my younger fratelli, Francesco and Lucia Carmella, and my youngest sister, Agata Caterina. Every single one of us was born in the same place, the stunning Calabria, Italy.

I impulsively scribbled my thoughts into my diary, my pencil flying across the page as I tried to capture the emotions swirling through my head. The moonlight shone through the barred window, filling the room with a tranquil aura. I could feel my heart racing as I struggled to make sense of my feelings. I felt a little more in control with every stroke of my pencil. The words I wrote stood for my thoughts and brought to life the sensory details surrounding me. I could practically smell the crispness of the air and hear the birds singing outside. I could almost feel the warmth of the sun on my skin. My emotions were slowly being replaced with clarity as I wrote.

"I went to the public school in Caraffa until I was 12 years old. Then, my father and mother sent me to Siderno Marina, where I worked in the house of Ingegnere Bruno Romeo. They were very good people. Romeo was a very good man, but his wife, Signora Francesca Mezzatesta, was not as good as he was. After three years, I went back to my people, and I went to a private school. After a year of hard studies, I went to Siderno to get my diploma of maturity."

The salty breeze from the Ionian Sea caressed Siderno Marina, a small town nestled along the coast of Calabria in Italy. Its sun-kissed streets and picturesque harbor were home to the powerful 'Ndrangheta. The Commisso 'Ndrina, one of the most influential clans, controlled the town's inhabitants with an iron fist. The sun shone brightly, glinting off the shimmering waves of the sea, and the fishermen and their families bustled through the streets, speaking in whispers of the Commisso 'Ndrina's influence. They had heard tales of the clan's brutality, and none dared to challenge their authority. The town's shops and restaurants buzzed with activity as the locals went about their daily lives, but in the shadows lurked the unseen presence of the 'Ndrangheta. A hush of silence and fear hung heavy in the air as the mafia's presence loomed ever closer.

"In 1908, my parents sent me to Messina, Sicily, to work and to study. I worked in the house of a professor at the University. His name was Salomone; he was single and kept a "governaut," an estate manager, to take care of his house. His old father was living with him. Every morning

the governaut gave me the money and a list, and I went to the market to buy the food. It cost me four cents to go and come back with the Tramway.

"I had a beautiful room to sleep in, the palace of the professor. It was there I saw my first telephone. Many times, I spoke with the professor and with some other people of his. The governaut was a young lady of about 25 years old, she was born in Northern Italy, and she was a very beautiful woman. I slept on the third floor, and she slept on the fourth floor.

"Every morning, she came down to my room and woke me up. She would call me "Beppo," Italian for young Giuseppe. I slept soundly every morning, so she opened the door of my room and came near my bed; sometimes, she opened my eyes, and sometimes she pulled my nose to wake me up. She played all kinds of tricks on me, but she gave me to eat anything that I wanted and also let me drink some wine.

"One day, the professor and the governaut had an argument, and he became so violent that he took the governaut into his arms and threw her from the dining room into the kitchen. When I saw it, I opened the door to run away for my safety, but the professor called me and said, 'Do not fear, she is the servant, and if she does not treat you alright, let me know.' The professor left for Palermo, and the governaut told me that his mind does not work alright sometimes as he has been insane once."

I slam my diary shut and hug it as the guards bellow, "LIGHTS OUT!" My room is plunged into darkness, and the only sound left is the sound of my breathing. I'm surrounded by the familiar musty smell of the prison walls, my only company at night. I lay my head down, my thoughts still racing, and try to close my eyes and drift off to sleep.

The streets were filled with grief-stricken faces as millions of Italians of the southern provinces, known as the 'Mezzogiorno,' bid farewells to their homeland during the Calabrian diaspora. Clutching their belongings, they set off on their journey, searching for a new life that was their only choice. The determination in their eyes was enough to break the hearts of those left behind. With hope in their hearts, they took their first steps away from home towards an unknown future. The sky was filled with their weeping as they left the only home they had ever known. They refused to let the tears dim their determination and courage and pushed forward into the unknown, filled with the hope of a new life.

The deep bond I shared with my oldest sister, Maria Angela, was undeniable. I remember the day she married Vincenzo Violi in Reggio di Calabria, where their daughter Maria Eufemia was born in Caraffa in 1908. They were the first to leave Italy for America and settle outside Worcester, Massachusetts, in Fitchburg. I longed to have them and my "nipoti di zii," niece, near me. Although I miss them dearly, I know I will be reunited with them someday.

Soon afterward, my oldest brother made the journey to America, and I was left with a heavy heart and a longing to follow in his footsteps.

Three months after my brother Giovanni left for America, the sky darkened, and a rumble shook the ground beneath our feet for twenty seconds. I furiously wrote down the devastation I saw in my diary, taking in every last detail. Reggio di Calabria and dozens of coastal towns were reduced to rubble.

"The next day, while the professor was about, I left Messina and went back to my people; it was the 24th of December, 1908. Four days afterward, the terrible earthquake came and destroyed the beautiful cities of Messina and Reggio. It was the 28th of December, 1908."

The charred remains of homes, the smell of smoke in the air, and people's cries for help. It was almost too much to bear. I watched as my family gathered what little they had left, struggling to make a new life for themselves. I heard the conversations they had, the desperation in their voices. The way they clung to each other, never wanting to let go. As I flipped through the pages of my diary, I was filled with an overwhelming sense of sorrow and despair. I knew this tragedy would stay with me for the rest of my life.

I sit at the edge of my bunk, journal in hand, my heart racing as I recall the day my parents brought the news to me. I'm going to America! In my native Calabria, I'm now seventeen, and my parents have decided I can join my brother and sister in the United States. I take my pencil and begin to write, my thoughts tumbling onto the page in excitement and fear. My hand trembles as I describe the moments leading to this momentous decision. I pause, overwhelmed by all the emotions. I take a deep breath and keep writing, determined to capture this moment that will forever change my life. I look to the future, my eyes filled with hope and possibilities. I know this is only the beginning of my journey, and I'm ready for the adventure that awaits me.

"In 1911, I left my family and came to America with their consent. I sailed from Naples on the 18th of May, 1911 with the steamship 'Mendoza' of the North German Lloyd. She reached New York City on the 30th of May.

"As I was underage, my father and mother had a man who was coming to America to look after me until we reached New York City. When we arrived, I went to Fitchburg, Massachusetts, where my brother John, my sister Maria Angela, and her husband were living.

"I worked in Fitchburg in different jobs for about six months, then I moved to 272 Water Street in Springfield, Mass. My first job in Springfield was with West Box Company, $11.02 per week for 58 hours of hard work. I worked here for over three years."

The cold winds of an impending war blew through Italy as my family prepared to leave their home behind. I wrote in my diary detailing the emotions that filled the air, from the fear of the unknown to the hope of a better future.

"I wrote to my father and mother asking them to come to America with my three sisters and my brother Francesco to join us. They came all, and I was so glad to see them that tears ran down from my eyes."

My padre, walking with a slight limp, and my madre, her eyes red from the tears she had shed. My siblings stood close by, their faces full of courage and determination. I knew that, together, we would find a way to survive.

"I bought some furniture the best I could and I rent a house on Merrick Street in West Springfield. We were all happy. My father was old and unable to do any work. My mother worked hard in the house while Frank, Mary, Lucy, and I worked in the factories. My sister Mary was married there, then my sister Lucy."

A few months after our family had settled into our new life in America, the world was suddenly plunged. On July 28th, 1914, the First World War began - one of the most devastating wars in human history. I remember the news spreading like wildfire; everyone was in a state of shock. The streets were filled with chaos and confusion as people questioned what would happen next.

As I opened our apartment door at 52 Sprague Street, a wave of chaotic energy rushed over me. The Parisi family had taken over the four-family house, and their presence was unmistakable. My parents and I, my sister Lucy and husband Joe Dialessi, brother John, and his wife Rose Parisi, all shared the same roof. I heard the laughter and chatter of my nieces and nephews as they ran up and down the hallways and in and out of the rooms. I could smell the aroma of freshly cooked Italian food emanating from the kitchen. I watched my sister Lucy and her husband Joe embrace each other with love in their eyes and my brother John and his wife Rose hugging on the sofa. I settled into the warmth and comfort of the family and filled my diary with the memory. The atmosphere was alive with joy, and I couldn't help but feel an immense sense of satisfaction.

"From there, we moved to Sprague Street, where my sister Catherine got married. About this time, I'm working with the International Shade Company at Harrison Avenue, Springfield, and here I learned some of the trade of electro-plating.

"While I was working here, my place was near the window, looking to the candy shop, where many girls were working. On the top floor of the candy shop were four girls who made some special candy. They looked at my window and greeted me every morning. So, one day, I met two of the girls outside, and they brought me some candy. This is how I was acquainted with them, and one of them, in later years, became my sister-in-law.

"After a few minutes, a young and beautiful girl arrived. She was bashful and asked her sisters to go home. As soon as I saw her and looked in her eyes, my heart began to throb, and I thought that it would burst my chest. I saw before me, with the pure midday light shining full on her, a young lady in the prime of her beauty, who moved with an innate grace, who looked with inbred fascination. My heart flew to her, and since that moment, I have found no peace until I make her my wife, the queen of my heart, the sweetheart and companion of my life.

"That afternoon, I followed them to find out where they live. My first question to her was her name, which I learned from her sister Michelina

that it was 'Faela,' Raffaela. She said to me why I want to know her name? She attracted me so much that I was like a stupid. Here I said to myself, my mother gave me a heart and this angel taught it to beat. I thought I was sick with heart trouble, but after she disappeared from my eyes, my poor heart became normal. After I saw them safe at home, I went back to my house, where my mother and father were waiting for me.

"The same night, I took a walk in front of their house, and after an hour or so, I saw the beautiful Raffaela on their piazza. There she was, the angel of my dreams, my ideal, my inspiration. I have fallen in love at first sight. I would have gone there on the piazza and take her into my arms, no matter what the consequences would be. But I checked myself; an idea came to my mind, some pride. I said to myself, I am a fool; why should I let that woman inspire such a passion in me? I went away with some friends, and I spent the night with them. After midnight, I returned home and went to bed, but I could not sleep. Her image was before me; her keen, bright blue eyes were sparkling before me. All that night, I dreamt about the beautiful Raffaela.

"Monday morning, when I went to work, I started early, and I waited for the beautiful Raffaela at the corner of Harrison Avenue and Dwight Street. Finally, she arrived. I called her by name, and she turned around and looked at me but did not speak. I walked fast and reached her. I took her hand into mine, and I said to her, 'Why Raffaela you did not speak to me?' I felt as if an electric shock had struck me. She pulled her hand quickly and said, 'Go away because I can't speak to you; my brother and my father might see me.' And then when I go home, I get the word of it, and I said to her, but I want to speak to you. She said, No.' But I insisted, and finally, she said to me, 'Wait for me here tonight, and we can talk for five minutes.' I said, 'Yes, I will,' and went to work.

"That night at 6 o'clock, I was at the corner. She arrived more beautiful than before. I 'saluted' her, and I began to talk. I said, 'Raffaela, I love you. Will you marry me?' She said, 'I am too young, and I don't know anything* *about love. I accompanied her until she dismissed me. We talked about many things. The next day, I met her again, and finally, she said, 'You ought to see my father and mother before I can say anything.'*

"After this, I tried to get acquainted with her people, but I did not succeed. Every morning and every night, and sometimes during the noon hour, I saw her, and I spoke to her of my ardent love for her. Finally, she consented to marry me if her parents would approve of the match.

"Finally, on November 28, Thanksgiving Day, 1918, we got married in the Mount Carmel Church in Springfield. Then the 17th of December, 1919, at 11:30 she gave birth to our boy Antonio. I was so glad when my mother, my mother-in-law, and the midwife called me into my wife's bedroom and showed me the baby boy, my first child that I took into my arms and kissed him many times. Then I kissed my wife, and I thanked her for the present she gave to me. I was a father; I thought I was the happiest man in the world."

Nine years had passed since the last of my family had come to America, and now I have taken on an American name, Joseph. I paused, taking a deep breath, and looked around as I realized my life had changed forever. I saw the hustle and bustle of the new city, the unfamiliar faces and customs, and the dizzying array of languages and dialects that filled the air. I knew I had no choice but to adapt. I began to move forward, my steps a little lighter, and a new determination in my heart. I reminded myself of the opportunities that this new life could bring. I had to be strong, and I had to survive. I smiled, and I was ready to begin my new life.

The Parisi family chose Sprague Street in West Springfield, Massachusetts, as their home, and thus, the saga of a new life for us began.

Like in Italy, the area was home to hardworking, honest Italians and those living in the darkness of the "Black Hand." You could feel the tension in the air as the family unpacked their possessions, the cries of the children echoing off the brightly wallpapered walls. The Parisi family had to learn to adjust to the culture, language, and crime that had taken root here. Conversations were hushed when the "Black Hand" was mentioned, and they knew to avoid certain areas. But no matter the challenges, the Parisi family persevered, determined to make a life for themselves in West Springfield.

When I saw it I opened the door to run away for my safety but the professor called me and said "Do not fear she is the servant and if she does not treat you alright let me know." The professor left for Palermo and the government told me that his mind does not work alright sometimes as he has been insane once.

The next day while the professor was absent I left Messina and I went back to my people, it was the 1st of December 1908. four days afterward the terrible earthquake came and destroyed the beautiful cities of Messina and Reggio it was the 28th of Dec. 1908.

In 1911 I left my family and I came to America with their consent. I sailed from Naples the 18th of May 1911 with the steamship Koenig Luisa of the North German Lloyd. We reached New York City the 30th of May.

As I was under age my father and mother had a man who was coming to America to look after me until we reached New York City. When we reached (N.Y.) I went to Fitchburg Mass. where my brother John, my sister Mariangela and her husband where living.

I worked in Fitchburg on different jobs for about

The Diary of Giuseppe "Joseph" Parisi

Giuseppe and Raffaela on Our Wedding Day

La Famiglia Parisi

Back Row, L-R, Anthony F. Parisi (son of Francesco Parisi and Doris Grimaldi), Carmella "Cam" Marvici-Farella and Pasquale "Patsy" Marvici (daughter and son of Joe Marvici and Agata Parisi), Agata Parisi-Marvici-Garreffa (sister of Joe Parisi), Anthony F. Parisi (son of John Parisi), Giuseppe "Joe" Parisi, Frank A. Parisi (son of John Parisi), Mary Angela Parisi-Viola (sister of Joe Parisi), John B. Parisi Jr. (son of John Parisi), Maria Parisi-Selvatico (sister of Joe Parisi), Vincenzo "Jimmy" Selvatico (son of Michael Selvatico and Mary Parisi), Lucia Parisi-Dialessi-Puibini (sister of Joe Parisi), Onofrio "Joe" Selvatico, Carmella Dialessi-Richardson, Anthony "Sharky" Dialessi and John "Barney" Dialessi (daughter and sons of Joe Dialessi and Lucia Parisi).

Front Row, L-R, Cecelia Parisi-Cirillo and Antoinette Parisi-Mancini (daughters of Francesco Parisi and Doris Grimaldi), Cecelia Selvatico-Harrington, Giacinta "Dea" Selvatico-Winston (daughters of Michael Selvatico and Mary Parisi), Cecelia Parisi-Augustino (Joe Parisi's daughter), Mary "Dolly" Parisi-Roberts, Annunciata "Nancy" Parisi-Bonfitto and Cecelia "CeCe" Parisi-Galarneau (Daughter's of John Parisi)

Giovanni "John" Parisi, the Author's Grandfather

Francesco "Frank" Parisi, the Author's Father

The Trial Begins

"Are you conscious of any bias?" asked the judge in the same monotone manner he used to ask all the jurors. "Yes," snapped the juror, his tone and manner indicating that he was not speaking hastily. "I understand that both of these men, the man on trial and the man killed, were engaged in the liquor business. I think that any man engaged in that illicit business should be considered an outlaw. I have no sympathy with them." The judge said, "I understand the defendant is an Italian and advise the men on the panel that if any of them could not for that reason bring in a just verdict, they might be excused."

-JUDGE WEBSTER THAYER

7

The night air was thick with anticipation as I paced back and forth in my small, claustrophobic jail cell. The trial was about to begin tomorrow. I had already confessed to the police that I had killed Carlo Siniscalchi, but now I had to fight for my own life and avoid the electric chair. As sweat trickled down my forehead, I felt a strange mix of nervousness and relief. The moonlight illuminated the room, and I could feel my heart pounding against my chest as I thought about the words I had spoken to the police. I knew that the jury would decide if I was guilty of first-degree murder or manslaughter in self-defense. I took a deep breath and closed my eyes, trying to quell the anxiety that was slowly taking over my body.

I feared the consequences of my actions and what the jury would decide. My conscience told me I should accept responsibility for my actions and whatever punishment I was given, but my desire for freedom was too strong. I was torn between doing what was right and doing what was necessary to save myself. Tomorrow, the jury would determine my fate. I had to remain strong and fight for my freedom, no matter the cost.

As I unfold the crinkled pages of the *Springfield Daily News*, the headline on the front page screams, "Parisi Placed On Trial For Murder."

"Trial for Giuseppe Parisi of West Springfield for the murder of Carlo Siniscalchi of Springfield, December 20, 1921, will begin tomorrow in Superior Court, Judge Webster Thayer presiding. The sitting is a special one called for trial for Parisi's case and that of Eugene Scibelli, charged with the murder of Antonio Bonavita in 1921."

Trial, Day One, Monday, March 19, 1923

I woke up to the familiar chill of my jail cell, but today was different. I peeled back the covers and sat up, feeling a wave of anticipation ripple through me. I was finally going to trial and wanted to be ready for it. I walked over to the small basin and poured the freshly brought water over my head, feeling its warmth seep into my skin. I shaved with a steady hand, and when I was done, I looked into the mirror and saw a man I hadn't seen in a long time. I was ready. I put on the three-piece suit my wife had left for me on my first day of trial, feeling the fabric wrap around me like a second skin. I stood tall despite the weight of the situation pressing down on me. I was ready. I heard a guard's voice echoing down the hall, and I knew my time had come. I was ready.

I was immediately led to the prisoner's cage as I entered the courtroom. My wife and three children, Anthony, aged three, Cecelia, two, and Michelina, nine months, all greeted me with the warmth of their eyes. My father, Antonio Parisi, and my mother-in-law, Mrs. Frances Mazzarino, were also present, accompanied by my two brothers, John and Frank Parisi. The atmosphere was heavy with emotion as I felt my family's loving embrace, their warm embraces radiating through the cold bars of the cage. I heard the quiet sobs of my mother-in-law as she hugged my children, her tears mixing with those of my own. I looked into the eyes of each of my family members, silently thanking them for their support and love.

I greet my team of attorneys - Joseph B. Ely, William C. Giles, and Robert W. King. Attorney Ely, the former Springfield District Attorney and candidate for Governor of Massachusetts, gave me a firm handshake. Across the room, District Attorney Charles H. Wright and Assistant District Attorney Charles R. Clason were already prepping for the case for the Commonwealth. The atmosphere in the room was edgy, as we all knew that Judge Webster L. Thayer would be presiding over the murder trial.

The Chief Justice, Walter Perley Hall, summoned 150 potential jurors to the courthouse. Judge Thayer, presiding, informed them they should be ready for a 10-day trial and that he would do his best to speed up the counsel if the case dragged on. His stern voice echoed through the vast courtroom, the unease clear. "We will begin by selecting twelve jurors this morning," Judge Thayer declared, "And from them, a foreman will be chosen."

The assessment of the jurymen quickly proved that a large majority could not "conscientiously" return a death verdict. It also developed that many had read of the case in the newspapers and formed an opinion that might be prejudicial.

"I don't want anyone to feel that I believe everything I'm told," said Judge Webster Thayer in excusing potential jurors on the ground that his "conscience" wouldn't allow him to give a verdict of the death penalty. "It's getting infectious," he remarked to another and went ahead to put him through an examination.

At precisely 6:06 pm, the jury to try me for the murder of Carlo Siniscalchi of Springfield had been assembled. Exhaustion was already beginning after Judge Webster Thayer spent the entire day questioning 110 of the 150 potential jurors. Alphonse Lapore, a Holyoke automobile dealer, was chosen as foreman.

All eyes were on the judge as he rose, the sound of his gavel echoing off the walls like a clap of thunder. Silence descended like a veil over the room, thickening the air as the judge's gaze swept over the crowd. "Order!" he demanded, his tone heavy with authority. Judge Thayer's booming voice echoed off the walls of the courtroom, announcing that Main and Union Streets--the scene of Siniscalchi's tragic demise--would be put under close scrutiny the following day when court resumed at 9:30.

The Springfield Republican newspaper prompted a flurry of activity as news of the account spread, with citizens eagerly grabbing their latest edition to get the scoop. "Parisi, in the prisoner's cage, while showing the effects of his long confinement in jail, appeared in the best of health. Beyond slight, nervous motions of his hands, he seemed at ease. During the morning, his father, wife, and three children were in the courtroom but were not present at the later session."

Trial Day Two, Tuesday, March 20, 1923

The criminal court was just moments away from convening for the day when Sergeant John Maloney and Patrolman Patrick Keane were alerted to a suspicious bulge under Herbert Horton's shirt while entering the courthouse. Drawing their weapons, the two officers approached the man and demanded he raise his hands, revealing a revolver tucked away in his belt. In an instant, Herbert was apprehended, and the courtroom was thrown into chaos. The two officers stood firm, their guns still pointed at the accused. No one dared to move, all eyes glued to the drama unfolding before them. With a swift motion, Sergeant Maloney confiscated the revolver and cuffed Horton.

"You have to come with me," an additional officer who answered the plea announced, his voice steady and unyielding.

Horton looked away, knowing that nothing would change the inevitable. The police officers grabbed his arms and hauled him away. The crowd let out a collective breath as the two officers holstered their weapons and resumed their post at the courthouse door.

I stared at him, my heart pounding as I wondered his intentions. Was he planning to take a shot at me in court? He didn't say, and I never found out. His face was stony and unreadable; all I could do was wonder if I was about to face an unexpected challenge.

Soon after the court convened, the jury, accompanied by Judge Thayer and counsel, was taken to view the scene of the shooting. The trip took about an hour, and the neighborhood of the alleged crime was thoroughly examined. Looking after my interests in "this connection," my attorney recommended that I waive my right to accompany the jury to the viewing.

District Attorney Wright addressed the jury before viewing the shooting scene to " explain on the map the locations of importance in the case," his finger tracing a route on the detailed plans before them. He methodically pointed out the location of Siniscalchi's car to my car near the corner of Main and Williams Streets, to the route he took following the shooting. Judge Thayer went with the jury on the trip, their shoes tapping in unison against the pavement as they walked to the scene of the shooting. On the way, Wright pointed towards the drugstore near the scene, pointing out the exact spot where the doctor had been standing. The jury took in the sights- the buildings, the alleyways, and the shops- taking mental notes of each detail as they followed Wright's directions, his voice steady and unwavering. When they finally arrived, they were met with the reality of the crime, the air heavy with the knowledge of what had happened. Wright's explanations had come to life, and the jury stood, silent and sad, as they took in the scene.

After returning to the courtroom, Judge Thayer rose from his chair, his stern eyes scanning the jury. He cleared his throat and spoke in a booming voice that echoed off the courtroom walls. "Before the District Attorney can make his opening remarks," he said, "I must remind you that opening statements are not evidence. They are not a part of the record. You must consider only what comes from the lips of the witnesses." The jury nodded in agreement, solemnly understanding the importance of the Judge's words. He paused momentarily before adding, "Do not be swayed by any statements - no matter how convincing - until you have heard all the evidence."

Attorney Wright stood up, his tailored suit emphasizing the authority of his position. He cleared his throat and launched into his opening remarks. "The grand jury has indicted Joseph Parisi for the murder of Carlo Siniscalchi," he began, his voice ringing out in the hushed courtroom. "It was a shocking crime: a shooting in broad daylight on Main Street at 4 p.m., December 20th, 1921. There can't be any dispute about that." He paused momentarily, letting the situation's gravity sink in. "It's a heinous crime that cannot be overlooked."

"It is claimed by the Commonwealth that Parisi is guilty of murder in the first degree, that he killed Siniscalchi with deliberately premeditated malice aforethought, but the degree is to be decided by the jury.

"Siniscalchi had lived here for a long time and was spoken of as an Italian leader. Whether he was is of no consequence. He went into a music store, where he had some conversation with the proprietor. He had hardly left the store when the owner heard shots. Siniscalchi left the store, went to the car, sat down behind the wheel, and started the automobile when Parisi walked up, drew a revolver, and fired six shots, three or four of which took effect, the second fatally. No Matter what their previous relations were, the attack was unprovoked. It was a premeditated attack. Parisi walked up and shot him dead. Siniscalchi put his hand on his chest, sank back, gave a gasp, and died. Siniscalchi's last words were wishing the music store proprietor a 'Merry Christmas' unless he said something to Parisi.

"Parisi claimed to the police that Siniscalchi drew a gun, and he shot him. He said Siniscalchi and he had quarreled about alcohol. The Commonwealth expects to show you that Parisi's story was false, that he shot Siniscalchi while the latter was trying to start his car and before he had a chance to do anything in his own defense."

Judge Thayer sternly addressed the jury, his stern gaze lingering on each of them. "Do not dare even think of discussing the evidence you have heard here today," he warned. He reminded them of the evidence yet to be presented, "The defense has not had their say, the closing arguments have not been made, nor have I, the presiding justice, even had the chance to make my judgment." He paused, letting the seriousness of the situation sink in. "Keep your minds open," he concluded.

The courtroom was packed, every chair occupied. I hung on every word, my expression stoic and my demeanor composed. No trembles of fear or unease betrayed my mounting apprehension. The air was tense, each syllable pronounced in a solemn hush. I felt the piercing gazes of the jury as if they could read my innermost thoughts. My stomach knotted with dread, but my face remained expressionless.

The large map of the site of the alleged crime hung prominently beside the witness stand, illuminated by the courtroom light. The tension in the air seemed to thicken as the prosecution called its first witness, and the trial was on.

Dr. Charles Furcolo, the first witness called by the Commonwealth, testified, "I was Siniscalchi's physician, and in the Springfield Drug Company's store, near the scene of the fatality, when I heard the shots and James Pepe came rushing in and told of a shooting. We rushed immediately into the street to find Siniscalchi lying between two seats, his head on his chest." At Mr. Wright's request, two chairs were brought into the courtroom. Dr. Furcolo stepped forward and recreated the scene, positioning the chairs to show how Siniscalchi had been found. His solemn expression seemed to convey the gravity of the situation. "James Pepe could not get in by the door on the other side of the car and climbed over the body of Siniscalchi."

Dr. Furcolo said, "As Pepe and I were pulling him into the hospital, his coat and jacket came off. The nurse and I found a wallet with $40 in bills and silver in his pants pockets, and a handkerchief. The automobile door was open when I got there, and it was open all the way to the hospital. I had to hold the door partly open and hold him with my other hand. I noticed the broken glass on the other side of the car."

Cross-examined by Attorney Ely;

Attorney Joseph B. Ely paced around the witness stand, his sharp eyes fixated on Dr. Furcolo. "So," he began, his voice trailing off into a menacing whisper, "you claim James Pepe was a chauffeur and had on occasion driven Siniscalchi's car?"

Dr. Furcolo fidgeted in his chair, the courtroom eerily quiet. He glanced around nervously before nodding his head in agreement.

Ely stepped closer. "You're sure of this?"

Dr. Furcolo gave a definitive nod. "Yes," he said, his voice barely a whisper, "I'm sure."

"You know Siniscalchi possessed a revolver?"

"I did not see one; the only place a revolver could have been was in Siniscalchi's overcoat, and had it could have fallen out of there."

"You knew he owned one?"

"I object." Mr. Wright's objection was granted.

"I knew he owned a revolver," Furcolo admitted.

"You know he owned more than one?" The courtroom hung on the question. Furcolo shifted in his seat and nodded. "I know he had quite the collection."

Ely's eyebrows lifted, his gaze intent. "Quite the collection of firearms?"

Furcolo paused, tension rising in the air. He met the attorney's gaze and nodded. "Yes." Murmurs rippled through the courtroom as the realization of Siniscalchi's arsenal settled in.

Ely's next question was piercing, "Is there a special compartment in this auto for the purpose of housing a concealed revolver?"

"Yes." He replied, but the answer was so damning that it was excluded from the record.

Redirect by District Attorney Wright;

Mr. Wright clenched his jaw, eyes blazing with fury, as he gritted out his question to Dr. Furcolo. Had he really said that the only place a revolver could have been was in Siniscalchi's overcoat, and had it fallen out of there? He didn't remember making such a statement. The room was dead silent, the only sound coming from the ticking of the clock on the wall. "Did you say that?" Wright demanded, his voice low and menacing.

Dr. Furcolo nervously cleared his throat and shifted in his chair before replying. "I...I may have, but I'm not sure." Wright's nostrils flared as his fists curled at his sides. He was determined to get the truth.

Mr. Wright glared across the courtroom at Dr. Furcolo as the two quarreled. It began with Wright unexpectedly grilling the doctor during cross-examination, accusing him of not recalling statements he was alleged to have made. Dr. Furcolo, taken aback, tried to defend himself, but his words only seemed to enrage the lawyer further. Wright's voice rose with each successive comment as if he were trying to assert his dominance. As the argument intensified, the room seemed to grow colder, the air heavy with tension.

Dr. Furcolo's answers became increasingly frantic, his brow furrowed in frustration, while Mr. Wright's expression remained one of cold contempt. It was clear that he didn't appreciate the tone of the doctor's words.

Mr. Ely's voice was smooth like silk as he spoke to the district attorney, "Don't get mad." His words hung in the air, almost taunting the district attorney.

Mr. Wright clenched his jaw and fixed his gaze on Ely. " I'm not going to get mad at you, Ely," he said, his voice controlled but tight.

The next witness, James Pepe, took the stand with an air of confidence. His hands trembled slightly as he adjusted the collar of his suit, his day job as a chauffeur having provided him with the means to buy the more formal attire. He testified that he had been in the Springfield Drug Company's store when the shooting occurred. Just as Dr. Furcolo entered, he had stepped out, heading towards Clark's Clothing to buy a pair of socks. As he approached the store door, only twenty-five feet from Siniscalchi's automobile, he heard the sudden crack of gunfire. Instinctively, he froze on the sidewalk and then, as if drawn by a string, stepped into the doorway of the store. When the shooting stopped, he cautiously appeared and went to Siniscalchi's car.

He testified, "Siniscalchi was sprawled out in the car. One leg was almost out the door. His body was leaning over to one side. I saw a cigarette holder on the floor but no revolver in the car. I... I... I shook Siniscalchi, my fingers trembling as I reached into the car. I quickly backed away and ran to the nearest drug store for a doctor." His voice quivered as he spoke. He vehemently denied having a gun at the time, though he admitted to having carried one in the past. He shifted in his seat, his eyes darting around the room. He was desperate to leave the courtroom, but he knew his duty.

The door of the car hung open. Pepe scrambled in a hurry to fetch Dr. Furcolo from across the street. As the doctor made his way into the vehicle, Pepe revved the engine, and they sped off to Wesson Memorial Hospital, where doctors and staff were waiting. Dr. Furcolo quickly sprang into action, leading the way as he and Pepe carried the body into the hospital corridor. The doctor's face was etched with worry, and his breath came in short gasps as he laid Siniscalchi down with care.

Pepe testified that he had "met Mrs. Pasqualina Siniscalchi on High Street while on the way to the hospital. He took the Siniscalchi car to her home and, afterward, returned to his hotel room."

The next witness, State Representative Julius Carman of Springfield, who owned a grocery store just a few blocks from the alleged crime scene, had a chilling account to tell. As he watched from a distance, he spotted a man, whom he could not identify as Parisi, running towards him, a gun firmly clutched in his hand. He was asked what was the first thing he had done when he saw the man approaching with a gun after the shooting.

"My first instinct was to get out of there as quickly as I could," he replied, his voice quivering as he recalled the incident. He glanced around the courtroom, his gaze settling on the gun in the evidence box. No words were needed to convey his dread from that day. He said, "I was rather relieved when he saw the fugitive start running in the opposite direction."

Then, he made his way to the scene of the shooting. When he arrived, he noticed Siniscalchi sitting motionless, his head slumped against his chest in the front of the car seat. The stillness of the air was punctured only by the distant sirens of approaching police. He could feel the dread of the moment hovering in the air as he stared down at the lifeless figure.

Cross-examined by Attorney Ely;

Attorney Ely furrowed his brows in frustration as he stared across the courtroom at the defiant Carman, pressing him for answers to his questions. "Please just answer my questions," he said through gritted teeth.

Carman shifted uncomfortably in his seat, his words getting caught in his throat as he tried to respond. He glanced nervously at the clock, its hands ticking and echoing in the silent courtroom, as he realized he'd miss his train back to Boston if he didn't hurry. The judge intervened, clearing his throat to break the tension.

"We'll continue this examination in the morning," Ely said, his voice echoing off the walls.

Carman quickly stood, gathering his belongings before turning to Ely with a tight smile. "Until tomorrow," he said before quickly walking out.

The next witness was Robert Accorsi, a watchmaker at the corner of Hubbard Avenue and Main Street. He was standing at the rear of his store, diligently minding his business, when he suddenly heard a series of sharp bangs echoing outside. He could tell there were three or four gunshots in total. Stepping out of his store, he saw the street filled with chaos, people running around in all directions. Two men then got into the car and drove away, but the witness couldn't determine who was in the crowd around the vehicle.

Cross-examined by Attorney Ely;

Attorney Ely asked Accorsi sternly, " What was Mr. Siniscalchi's business?"

Accorsi smirked slyly, saying, "I'm afraid I don't know."

Felix Delizia, the last man to testify, owned a jewelry and music store from which Siniscalchi had appeared moments before the deadly shots were fired. Delizia stated, "Siniscalchi came into his store to talk business. I saw him to the door, walked to the back of the store, and a few minutes later heard shots fired in the street. I rushed into the street and saw Siniscalchi sitting in a relaxed position in his car."

Cross-examined by Attorney Ely;

Mr. Ely looked around the courtroom and asked, "Carlo has quite a number of guns, did he not?"

The witness shifted in his seat, eyes darting around the room. "I don't know about that," he replied.

Mr. Ely pressed further, inquiring if Carlo did a lot of shooting at target practice.

The witness shook his head and said, "I knew Carlo only as a customer in my store." The courtroom was silent, all eyes on the witness as he nervously fiddled with his hands. The only sound in the room was the creaking of the old wooden benches as people shifted in anticipation.

Mr. Ely narrowed his gaze. "Was there ever any indication that Carlo was a shooter?"

The witness shook his head again. "No, sir," he said. "I never saw him with any guns in my store."

Trial Day Three, Wednesday, March 21, 1923

District Attorney Wright produced a typed report of the testimony made at the inquest held after Siniscalchi's death, which he referred to in examining one or two of his witnesses. Mr. Ely whispered, his outstretched hand quivering with anticipation, if he might see the volume. The district attorney was about to comply but swiftly snatched it away with a sharp intake of breath.

"Won't you trust me?" Mr. Ely smiled, his lips stretching into a thin line.

"I should say not-- with this," the district attorney retorted, a flicker of anger igniting his eyes.

Mr. Ely bowed his head apologetically, a quiet chuckle escaping his lips. "My dear friend, if I am not entitled to that much trust, I don't want to see your old book anyway."

The laughter was quickly subdued into an eerie silence, only broken by a sharp rap of the gavel.

The Springfield Daily News has unveiled its latest edition, providing a complete overview of the latest news. "An interested observer of all the proceedings is Mrs. Parisi, wife of the prisoner, seated in the front row every day, accompanied by some of Parisi's relatives. At recess, she goes to the prisoner's cage and talks earnestly with her husband. On occasion, she has one of her little children, a boy, with her, but today none of the children were present. Mrs. Siniscalchi had not appeared in the courtroom until today but was in an adjoining room, within the district attorney's call at any time."

District Attorney Wright continued to call witnesses today, and Howard Shear was the first of them. He testified that he had been driving along Main Street near Park when he noticed a crowd of people following a man near the electric trolley garage. Shear said,

"The prisoner in the dock, Parisi, was the man who was running and who was caught."

Shear also testified that he saw a gun in Parisi's left pocket. One of the police officers took it away, and Parisi was taken away in a patrol car. A revolver that was shown to the witness was declared by the witness to "resemble the one that was taken from Parisi." However, he could not positively identify it.

Patrolman Thomas Dowling, who had arrested Parisi, stepped forward as the next witness. He was a reserve officer at the time of the shooting, but four days later, he was promoted to a regular officer.

Dowling recounted that he had been on a trolley car at Main and Howard Streets when the shooting occurred. He then rushed to the Siniscalchi car and saw a growing crowd. "I saw Siniscalchi behind the steering wheel, his hands hanging limp at his sides. I couldn't see any revolver in the car," he declared. Dowling continued, "I followed Parisi as he ran up Main Street and Park Street. When I reached 25 Park Street, I found him standing in the doorway." He added, "Many children were in the street, so I couldn't shoot at Parisi while he was running."

Officer Dowling approached Parisi, who had both hands tucked in his coat pockets. Dowling ordered him to "throw up his hands," and Parisi obeyed. Dowling then identified the weapon as a Smith & Wesson revolver that he had taken away from Parisi. He secured the gun in evidence and handed it over to Detective Lieutenant Fenton at police headquarters.

Cross-examined by Attorney Ely;

Ely's eyes darted to the gun resting on the evidence table. "Did you take the shells out of the gun?" He cautiously stepped closer, his stomach sinking.

Dowling shook his head, his gaze never leaving the gun. "No."

Ely's hand slowly reached out, his fingers trembling as he grabbed the gun. He opened it, his heart beating faster as he saw the empty chambers. He exhaled, relieved, as he gently placed it back on the table.

As Dowling drove the prisoner to Wesson Hospital, he said Lieutenant Fenton interviewed Parisi about the shooting. Parisi had described how he saw Siniscalchi reach his hand to his right hip pocket, his voice quivering as he said, "Siniscalchi has 'done' him for about $400." The officers exchanged glances, a silent understanding that this was a serious crime. Dowling gripped the wheel, his foot pressing down on the accelerator, the situation's urgency palpable in the air.

Officer Dowling testified, "When we reached the hospital and found out Siniscalchi was dead, we took Parisi into police headquarters," he said. He remembered Parisi telling Fenton that he thought Siniscalchi had a gun and was reaching for it. But all the other details, the officer admitted, were a blur. Adrenaline was still coursing through his veins from chasing after Parisi, and the officer could hardly remember what he said.

Dowling fidgeted in the witness box, beads of sweat forming on his forehead. His gaze shifted towards the jury, who sat blankly, unable to recall a single detail of Parisi's words regarding Siniscalchi calling him to his car. "Captain Frank Quilty interviewed Parisi at police headquarters in the presence of the witness and other officers," Dowling testified, his voice trembling.

Attorney Ely's voice boomed through the courtroom as he scrutinized Dowling, demanding to know of his knowledge of Carlo Siniscalchi's reputation. Dowling stood on the witness stand, his brow furrowed in concentration, as he tried to recall the details of his earlier acquaintance. He remembered the day Sergeant James Moriarty introduced him to Siniscalchi as he was being broken in as a reserve. "Did you know the general reputation of Carlo Siniscalchi relative to him being aggressive?" asked Attorney Ely.

"I couldn't say what his reputation was," Dowling finally said, his voice barely audible above the buzz of the courtroom. Dowling opened his mouth to speak, his voice quivering as he began to say, "On one occasion, I heard..." but before he could finish, District Attorney Wright's objection cut him off.

"What did you hear on that occasion?" Ely pressed, his voice a low growl. Again, District Attorney Wright objected. The Judge slammed his gavel down on the bench, and a lengthy discussion followed at the bench. The tension in the courtroom was intense, and all eyes were on the judge as he finally declared a suspension of the matter for a time.

Mrs. Helen Clark shakily testified next that she was at the store of her husband's cousin, Abraham Clark, when the shooting occurred. She recalled the events with a trembling voice, "I heard the shooting. I was in the store and ran to the door and out, colliding with a man running. Siniscalchi was sitting and leaning toward the rear with his hands down. I remained until Pepe and Dr. Furcolo entered the car and drove away. Some man in the crowd, before this, had partly stepped into the car, placed his hand on Siniscalchi's chest, over his heart, and then got out."

Cross-examined by Attorney Ely;

Clark said, "The man leaning into the automobile had one foot on the running board and one on the curbstone."

"How close was he to the car?" questioned Ely.

The witness replied, stretching out her foot, "he was about a foot away."

"That's a very small foot," said Ely, to which she replied with a giggle, "Well, it's the only one I have to measure by." At this, the crowd erupted into laughter.

Guy Moran, of West Springfield, a salesman of Lincoln cars, took the stand and declared, "I sold Siniscalchi his Lincoln Limousine. After the shooting, I had to do some repairs. The car was adorned with festive wreaths, but the upholstery was smeared with blood, mostly on the left side. A bullet was even lodged in the upholstery." Moran stated, "Mr. Siniscalchi asked for two pockets, one on each side, when the car was bought. One pocket was in the upholstery, the other in the slipcover," Moran testified.

James McPhee, the police reporter for the Springfield Union News, testified, "I examined the Siniscalchi car parked in the Wesson Hospital driveway. I spotted a flattened bullet, its sides mangled and distorted, near the left door of the car. I carefully pocketed the evidence and made my way to police headquarters." The witness then pointed to a hole in the car's woodwork, its edges charred and blackened. "I found it here," the witness said, his voice echoing in the silent courtroom. McPhee nodded, his brow furrowed with concentration as he took in the scene.

Harry Cook, the proprietor of a cigar store on Cross Street, testified next of being invited to ride with Siniscalchi the day of the shooting. "Carlo picked me up on Water Street and drove me to the Third National Bank building at 3:30 that afternoon."

Cross-examined by Attorney Ely;

Attorney Ely eyed Harry suspiciously. "Are you associated with Mrs. Pasqualina Siniscalchi in business?"

Harry shook his head. "No. Never have been."

The attorney continued. "Were you at Mrs. Siniscalchi's house on Monday?"

Harry hesitated, his brown eyes shifting away. "I cannot tell you," he said, his voice soft but firm. He said, "I visited Pasqualina Siniscalchi from time to time, and I think I was last there four or five nights or perhaps a week ago, at which time her brother-in-law, his wife, a woman neighbor, and her children were present."

George Gale, a streetcar conductor of Chicopee, testified, "My car had stopped so that the rear door was nearly opposite the hood of the Siniscalchi machine. I heard one shot and the breaking of glass. At a second shot, I looked out the rear door of the car and saw the Siniscalchi car about three feet away, Siniscalchi's arm drawing up to his chest. Still, I'm sure that I saw his arm after it had rested on the slain man's chest." After the second shot, Gale said he heard three more. Gale said, "The man doing the shooting was standing at the right of the automobile and about three feet from it. After the shooting, the man ran south. I cannot positively identify him."

When Gale had finished his testimony, District Attorney Charles Wright called Mrs. Robitaille as one of the Commonwealth's witnesses. He said, "The woman does not speak English, but an officer had volunteered to interpret her testimony."

Judge Thayer refused to allow someone involved in the case to act as interpreter despite Attorney Joseph Ely's willingness to step in.

An adjournment was taken a few minutes before 4 pm.

The Boston Herald reported, "Mrs. Pasqualina Siniscalchi, widow of Carlos Siniscalchi, for whose murder Joseph Parisi is on trial before Judge Webster Thayer and a jury, is expected to take the stand tomorrow."

Rafaella Parisi, my devoted wife, sat in the courtroom's front row, her gaze darting between me and the witnesses as if searching for an answer. Her eyes were glued to every word of the testimony, and when recess was called, she hurried to my side, her voice a hushed whisper. Attorney Ely joined in, too, offering words of comfort and reassurance that I acknowledged with a grateful, heartwarming smile. While the courtroom remained silent, our hushed exchange of comfort and solidarity profoundly affected the onlookers, who watched with wide-eyed awe.

The Weather
CLOUDY TONIGHT; COLD WAVE; TUESDAY FAIR; COLD

Springfield Daily News

5 o'Clock Edition
LATE NEWS

43d YEAR, No 283   SPRINGFIELD, MASS., MONDAY EVENING, MARCH 19, 1923   ONE CENT

PARISI PLACED ON TRIAL FOR MURDER

*Facing Trial for Murder
Before Judge Thayer and Jury*

JOSEPH PARISI
(Photo by The Republican Staff Photographer)

*Parisi and His Wife
Confer During Recess*

JOSEPH B. ELY

CHARLES H. WRIGHT

JUDGE WEBSTER THAYER

The Confession

"Parisi asked me where I was taking him, and I told him he was going to the hospital to be identified. When he heard the word 'hospital,' his eyes widened, and he begged me not to take him there, saying that they would kill him too. He fidgeted and muttered something about trouble with money before quickly adding that he would talk later."

- LIEUTENANT FENTON, SPRINGFIELD POLICE DEPARTMENT

8

District Attorney Wright stood before the press; his brow furrowed in thought as reporters shouted questions. He shifted his weight from one foot to the other, the microphone crackling as he spoke. "I can confirm that the investigation is continuing into the killing of the Italian leader, shot while seated in his car at Main and Union Streets."

He raised his eyebrows and glanced around the room, his voice hushed as he leaned in close. "I have a feeling this was plotted by persons 'higher up' in Springfield's bootlegging ring," he said, looking away, his expression unreadable. The room buzzed with whispers. Wright responded, his voice firm, "Siniscalchi was murdered on the eve of a scheduled appearance before this district attorney. Draw your own conclusions."

He also revealed that he had called in the State Police to aid in getting to the truth in the case. When asked if he believed the confession, Wright declared, "That confession is a 'PHONY' - except the part dealing with the actual killing of Carlo Siniscalchi." Wright gestured to the reporters with a peculiar expression on his face. "Take a look at this," he said. "You'll notice a peculiar feature - the wording of the threat Carlo is supposed to have made against Parisi. They are almost the exact words Carlo used when he threatened police officers during the liquor raid on Water Street. Peculiar, isn't it?"

The reporter's eyes widened in surprise. The District Attorney paused momentarily, letting the words' impact sink in. He surveyed the room before continuing, his voice low and intense. "I'm saying that Parisi's confession does not appear true to me. I'm not going into detail right now, but I urge you to consider this."

The reporters raised their hands to ask more questions, but Wright held up his hands and shook his head. "That's all I have to say about this matter for now. We will keep you updated as the investigation progresses." With that, he stepped away from the podium, leaving the reporters in a flurry of confusion and speculation.

Trial Day Four, Thursday, March 22, 1923

Raffaela entered the courtroom, cradling our tiny bundle of joy, Michelina. Every inch of the room was filled with people, and officers were stationed at the bottom of the stairs to ensure no one got any closer. Despite their best efforts, the crowd was too much, and the majority eventually gave up, leaving for the next court hearing. The atmosphere was emotional as Raffaela passed by, Michelina's gentle cooing the only sound in the room. The officers watched her go, impressed by her courage in facing such a daunting situation.

District Attorney Wright called Mrs. Florence Robitaille of Holyoke as the first witness that morning, her testimony in French through an interpreter, Paul Emmons. She recounted her experience, "*J'étais passager*... I was a passenger on the Forest Park trolley car, which stopped at Main and Union Streets just as the shooting took place. I saw nothing of the shooting. I heard glass breaking and was hit in the arm by one of the bullets. I fainted and did not know what occurred afterward. I heard no noise before that caused the breaking glass."

The next witness, Miss Dorothy Sloane of Hartford, who worked as an assistant supervisor at Wesson Hospital at the time of the alleged murder, sucked in a sharp breath the moment she laid her eyes on the blood-soaked clothing presented as evidence. "That's Siniscalchi's," she confirmed, her voice trembling. Her gaze followed the officers as they carried the body away to the operating room. Soon after, the clothes were removed and taken away by the police. Dorothy was overwhelmed by the sight before her. It was a moment frozen in time, the reality of the situation a heavy weight on her shoulders. She paused momentarily, her mind spinning, before steeling her resolve.

District Attorney Wright stood before the jury, his voice echoing in the hushed courtroom. "The witness testified that Siniscalchi was robbed of 'about $45 in cash, a diamond ring, and a diamond stick pin was taken from his clothing," he said, his gaze quickly turning to Lieutenant Fenton.

Joseph Maronne, an orderly at the hospital, stepped forward to testify. With his own eyes, he saw Lieutenant Fenton searching through Siniscalchi's clothes: a coat, vest, slip-on sweater, silk shirt with collar, and tie. Maronne, however, "did not recall" what items the detective took from them.

Detective Lieutenant Patrick Fenton, in charge of the investigation by the Springfield police, testified that he arrived at the hospital at 4:15. He was met with Siniscalchi's lifeless body. At 5:15, he returned to the hospital to collect Siniscalchi's clothes.

Cross-examined by Attorney Ely;

Ely interrogated Fenton, pressing him for answers. "Did he tell you that Siniscalchi reached for his hip pocket?"

Fenton shook his head. "Not on the way to the hospital."

Ely's eyes narrowed. "He told you Siniscalchi reached for a gun?"

Again, Fenton denied it. "Not on the way to the hospital." The room was thick with tension as Ely bore down on Fenton. He finally spoke, his voice calm. "I made no record of conversations with the prisoner on the trip to the hospital." Lieutenant Fenton said, "Parisi asked me where I was taking him, and I told him he was going to the hospital to be identified. When he heard the word 'hospital,' his eyes widened, and he begged me not to take him there, saying that they would kill him too. He fidgeted and muttered something about trouble with money before quickly adding that he would talk later." Fenton continued, "Parisi remembered shooting once or twice, and he got very agitated and refused to talk anymore. I had no other conversation with him during the trip. I was present later when they interrogated him at police headquarters. Captain Frank Quilty directed the questioning while a stenographer noted what was said. It was about a half hour after our return from the hospital."

Lieutenant Fenton stood in the witness box, recounting his presence at the trial of Carlo Siniscalchi, convicted of slashing Patrolman Learned across the cheek and sentenced to a short term in jail.

"Do you know of Carlo Siniscalchi's reputation as a confrontational and vindictive individual?" asked Mr. Ely.

Lieutenant Fenton's eyes narrowed as he recalled the man and replied gravely, "It was evil." He could still see the jagged gash on the patrolman's neck and the anger in Siniscalchi's eyes.

District Attorney Wright's objection was so vehement that the jury was sent out of the room. There was a heated debate between the two attorneys about whether or not to allow testimony concerning Siniscalchi's character, mentioning his "aggressiveness and maliciousness."

Judge Thayer firmly declared, "The jury has the right to know what kind of man the deceased was at the time of the shooting. He stated that this could be more compelling evidence than just the general reputation of the deceased." His voice reverberated off the courtroom walls, echoing his stern decision throughout the room.

Attorney Wright's brow furrowed as he spoke, his voice tinged with dread. "I have confidence in Mr. Ely but not in his client, Parisi," he said. "I don't want to give him the chance to present anything that might make Siniscalchi look dangerous or like he was in serious conflict." The tension in the room thickened as if the walls themselves had absorbed it.

Attorney Ely's response was soft but firm. "I think we have plenty about that now," he said.

Mr. Wright hesitated, his gaze darting around the courtroom before settling back on Mr. Ely, "Well, we'll know more about that later," he said. Wright's expression was serious as he nodded in agreement with the truth of Mr. Ely's words. "I'm well aware of Siniscalchi's record," he said, "but I believe Parisi should be the one to tell it, not the others."

Cross-examined by Attorney Ely;

Attorney Ely asked Lieutenant Fenton about Siniscalchi's infamous ability with a revolver.

Fenton nodded, his eyes wide, his voice low with reverence. "From what people have told me, it was excellent."

"He was a crack shot?"

"Yes."

Ely pressed on, "Did you ever see a revolver that he owned or carried?"

"No," Fenton said, "but it was always known that he did carry one."

Attorney Ely recalled Reporter James McPhee back to the stand for testimony about Siniscalchi's reputation. His eyes narrowed, and his lips thinned as he spoke. "Did you know of him as a man who carried a gun?" Ely asked.

McPhee nodded. "Yes."

"Did you know of him as the leader of a gang?"

McPhee sighed. "Yes."

"And his reputation?"

The silence in the courtroom seemed to stretch on forever as the jury took in the answer. "Siniscalchi's reputation was rotten."

"Parisi's comment regarding Siniscalchi's reach for a gun echoed throughout the interview in Captain Quilty's office. We must introduce this evidence," Ely declared, his voice pounding into the conversation like a hammer.

Wright shook his head, his lips thinning into a bitter line. "Objection," he muttered.

"It has been touched upon in the testimony by Patrolman Dowling," Ely continued, undeterred.

The court considered the situation momentarily before finally giving the order to admit the evidence. A collective sigh of relief filled the room, yet the tension lingered like the smoke of a freshly extinguished flame.

District Attorney Wright rose to his feet, his voice booming through the courtroom as he declared his intention to introduce my confession into evidence. Attorney Ely nodded formally, allowing it to be read out in the absence of the stenographer who had taken the notes. The room seemed to hold its breath as Wright began, the anxiety clear as each word echoed around us.

CONFESSION

<u>Giuseppe Parisi's Confession</u>

Taken by
Detective Captain Frank W. Quilty
Witnessed by
Lieutenants Fenton, Raiche, and Bicknell
and
Patrolman Dowling
at
Springfield Police Department
December 20, 1921

Q. What is your name? (Quilty)

A. Joseph Parisi. (Parisi)

Q. Where do you live, Joe?

A. 52 Sprague Street, West Springfield.

Q. What is your business?

A. Storekeeper.

Q. How long have you been running a store over there?

A. About seven or eight months.

Q. You came over to Springfield this afternoon, and what did you do?

A. Yes, I go in Lyman Street to buy some stuff for my store.

Q. From there where did you go?

A. I go to Peter Wolk on Lyman Street and then I go to Italian store.

Q. Then where did you go?
A. I go down Bridge Street to Crockett's jewelry company and I buy a chain and locket, for chain I pay $28 and I buy a set looking glass and brush for $11.

Q. And then where did you go?
A. I go to Ware Pratt, front of post office, and buy silk shirt, $6.95, 40 cents war tax, make it $7.35, then I go down Water Street to see my mother-in-law.

Q. Where does your mother-in-law live?
A. 345 Water Street.

Q. What is her name?
A. Frances Mazzarino. My mother-in-law was not there. Nobody was there, so I turned my car at Freemont Street and go on Main Street.

Q. You went up Freemont to Main and up Main?
A. Up Main across, then I turn my car down William Street and I stop there. My car is over there now, this side of the church. Then I walk up right-hand side of the sidewalk and I see Siniscalchi in his car, his limousine car.

Q. And where was his car?

CONFESSION

A. On the right-hand side on Main Street.

Q. On Main Street?

A. In front of Delizia's store. I don't see him and I was walking right side of street when I hear a noise somebody knock on glass. I turn around and I see him and he call me to come there. He opened the door and told me some bad words.

Q. What were the bad words?

A. You ----------, you keep away from Water Street or I'll kill you and don't try to sell any alcohol to anybody on Water Street at all. When he said that to me I said I do as I please, nobody boss me.

Q. When he said that you said what?

A. I said I do as I please. Nobody boss me. When he said that he turned around, put his hands in his pocket, so I—

Q. Put his hand in what pocket?

A. The right hand in the right side. When I see he make that motion I pull my gun and I shoot him.

Q. How many shots did you fire?

A. I can't remember.

Q. About how many?

A. I fire I so nervous and I don't know how many I fire.

Q. Would you say that you fired two shots?
A. I don't know what to say. I fire two shots.

Q. Would you say you fired more than two shots?
A. I won't say because I don't remember.

Q. When Siniscalchi reached in his back pocket--- was it in the back pocket?
A. Yes.

Q. When Siniscalchi reached in his back pocket as though to draw a gun, you didn't see any gun?
A. I see him put his hand in his pocket like that. I saw something shiny, I thought was gun see. He puts hands like that, I see something shiny. I thought was magazine. Colts, what do you call it?

Q. An automatic gun?
A. Yes, an automatic gun.

Q. Well an automatic gun isn't shiny?
A. Well I saw him put his hands in pockets and pull a gun anyway.
Q. We want to get the truth. Just what did you do when he put his hand in his back pocket?
A. I see him put the gun like that (demonstrating).

Q. You didn't say that before?

A. I didn't see him fire any shots. When I gave answer "I do what I please" he put his hand in his pocket and pull his gun. When he pull his gun I fire first.

Q. What did you do then?

A. I took my gun and fire at him.

Q. You said that.

A. I ran away to Hubbard Street and then turn to Willow Street and then to Park Street.

Q. Where were you arrested?

A. On Park Street. A fellow came in plain clothes and said he was a special officer. He said you under arrest and I said all right. He take me in garage and I stay there.

Q. Is there anything else you want to say about it, Joe?

A. That's all I want to say. When I turn to go Park Street I want to give myself up, I don't try to run away. I afraid somebody come after me from Siniscalchi's gang.

Q. What did you do with your revolver after shooting?

A. I put it in my pocket.

Q. Was it in your pocket when you were arrested?
A. Yes.

Q. Why would Siniscalchi tell you to keep away from Water Street?
A. I don't know, I imagine because he wants to do everything himself.

Q. How long have you known Siniscalchi?
A. Since he came to Springfield.

Q. About how long is that, do you know?
A. May be eight or nine years.

Q. Did you ever have trouble with him before?
A. No. The first time when I have trouble about the alcohol. This time I had trouble.

Q. What trouble is that?
A. He sold me fifty gallon alcohol, $15 a gallon in October, I can't remember, in October sometime. He tell me to come down and get it in night when it was dark. When I go down there my car outside, I go in his house.

Q. Outside where?
A. In Wilcox Street, I go in his house, ring the bell and the young girl come out in house. I ask for Carlo and he come outside and tell me to come right in garage. I go right in with him over there and I give him $750.

Q. Was this in the garage you gave him the $750?
A. In the garage, yes.

Q. Where in the garage?
A. In Wilcox Street, he close the door when we got in. He put the money in his right pocket and then I asked him where I got to get the stuff. He raised his hands and gave me a slap in the face and he tell me to keep away from Water Street and if I say anything he is going to kill me.

Q. If you say what?
A. If I say he going to kill me and he take my money.

Q. Have you talked with him since about the money?
A. No.

Q. Well, Joe, you say this afternoon you parked your car on William Street by the Italian church?
A. Near the corner where the church is, the ice cream store, you know.

Q. On William Street?
A. Yes.

Q. Then why did you go up Main Street?

A. I want to go over to corner Wilcox Street to see a shoemaker. He was a friend of mine over there.

Q. Well, why were you on the other side of Main Street from where the shoemaker shop is?

A. I go over to Italian bank first. When I leave my car I go over to Italian bank and I was walk on that side.

Q. Did you go in the Italian bank?

A. I go over to read bulletin on the outside.

Q. What was the bulletin you were so interested in?

A. The bank sent money in Italy. You see we send some money to Italy. From $1 we get $3 of Italian money.

Q. Did you read the bulletin?

A. Yes.

Q. What is the rate on Italian money, do you know?

A. I don't remember now. I think is 26 and little more on a dollar.

Q. And then although your friend whom you were going to see in the shoemaker shop lived on the left hand side of Main Street you walked up Main

Street on the right hand side where Siniscalchi was?

A. I don't see Siniscalchi when I walk up. I don't see Siniscalchi there.

Q. But it developed later that he was on that side?

A. I don't know he was there. I don't see anybody.

Q. But you saw when you got there that he was there?

A. I don't see anybody when I got there.

Q. The first you saw of Siniscalchi was when he rapped on the window of his car?

A. Yes and I look around and I see him in his car.

Q. Was he alone?

A. Yes, alone.

Q. What is the name of your friend that works in the shoe repair shop?

A. Joe Luvern.

Q. What were you going to see him for?

A. I just go there all the time. He is friend of mine.

Q. Well if that is the case, Joe, why didn't you drive your car up to the shoe repair shop?

A. Because a lot of cars in Main Street, so I leave my car in William Street. I stop my car there because my sister-in-law live there. After I going over the bank I want to go down and see my sister-in-law in house, see.

Q. Where does your sister live in William Street?

A. On William Street on front of church.

Q. What is her name?

A. Mary Mazzarino.

Q. You say she is your sister?

A. My sister-in-law. My wife's sister.

Q. Is this the gun you used in shooting Siniscalchi?

A. Yes, that's mine.

Q. Did you load it up again after you fired?

A. No, sir.

Q. You notice, Joe, that six shots have been fired out of here?

A. Yes. (Parisi is here shown a Smith & Wesson, .32 caliber revolver containing six empty shells, No. 551234.)

CONFESSION

Q. How long have you had this gun, Joe?
A. About a month and a half ago or two months. I bought that gun over here on Worthington Street. I don't know the name.

Q. About a month and a half?
A. I bought the gun after the shooting on Water Street, see.

Q. Where did you buy it?
A. On Worthington Street.

Q. Do you know the name of the store?
A. I don't know name. That store in front of Worthington Street in Victoria Hotel.

Q. You mean O.C. Alderman's?
A. I don't read the name.

Q. On what side of Worthington Street from Main is it?
A. On the right hand side. They didn't have any in there they sent to get it for me.

Q. You have been carrying it every day?
A. No.

Q. Why did you carry it today?
A. I carry it to protect myself.

Q. Well why did you carry it particularly today?

A. I carry it every day since the shooting on Water Street after I bought that gun. I carry gun in pocket of my car and when I go out I put it in my pocket.

Q. This has been your custom ever since you bought the gun?

A. Yes, since I bought the gun.

Q. Well, this is all you have to say, Joe?

A. That all I say for tonight, maybe tomorrow I will talk some more, see.

Q. Well what do you mean later you will talk some more?

A. Well you know I can't remember everything.

Q. But as you tell it to me you tell it of your own free will without threats or fear on your part?

A. This is all true, yes.

Signed: *Giuseppe A. Parisi*

The medical examiner, Dr. Frederick Jones, who performed an autopsy on the body of Siniscalchi on the night of the shooting, testified that there were three bullet wounds in the body. He demonstrated on Lieutenant Fenton where the bullets entered. Dr. Jones' skilled hands gingerly traced the path of the bullets, one in the right arm, one in the left hand, and a third across the chest.

The medical examiner took out a little paper package holding the bullets, each one individually marked and kept. He spread out the bullets, marking each one's entry point into the body with a piece of chalk on Siniscalchi's overcoat. "This is the bullet that killed him," the examiner declared as the courtroom fell silent.

He rolled up the bullets and carefully placed them back in the package, emphasizing that they had remained in his possession since the autopsy. The direct examination was over, and Attorney Ely could only imagine the impact of these visuals on the jury.

Cross-examined by Attorney Ely;

Attorney Ely analyzed Dr. Jones with his piercing gaze, his mouth forming a thin line as he asked, "Is it possible for one bullet to make two holes in a coat if it were folded?"

Dr. Jones simply replied, "Possibly."

Ely pressed on, "Not only possibly, but probably, right?"

The doctor nodded. "Yes."

"And if Siniscalchi were reclining, reaching for a gun, his coat would be folded back, wouldn't it?"

"Yes."

The room fell silent as Ely paused, his mind processing the answer. After a moment, he took a deep breath before uttering, "Well, so much for that."

Attorney Ely then made an effort to show that the bullet that had lodged in the top of the driver's seat was the same one that had passed through Siniscalchi's sleeve. And that Siniscalchi had his elbow raised at the time in the position of a man reaching for a weapon. Dr. Jones was asked to use Ely as a model to illustrate the wounds' locations. Ely stepped back and protested, "But I don't want to be marked as an exhibit in this case!" His voice echoed around the courtroom, attracting the disdain of District Attorney Wright.

Dr. Jones gazed at Ely skeptically as he asked, "Does that mean a man with his arm bent at the elbow might not have had his arm at the wheel but might have had a gun in his hand?"

"Yes," Dr. Jones answered.

Ely furrowed his brow and continued, "And that would be a position for quick firing?"

Dr. Jones shrugged and replied, "I don't know."

Attorney Ely's expression hardened as he probed, "Perhaps you are not an expert?" Ely shook his head, his eyes wide with uncertainty.

Assistant District Attorney Charles Clason declared that Mrs. Pasqualina Siniscalchi, the widow of the slain man, would be the Commonwealth's final witness, if called at all before it rests its case.

Attorney Ely then strongly suggested that I would also take the stand, testifying that I had reason to fear Siniscalchi and that I had shot him in self-defense. The room stilled as my attorney's words echoed through the chamber. Every gaze in the courtroom was fixated on me, and I felt my palms sweat. Clason's face was a mask of determination, while Siniscalchi's widow glared at me with a menacing expression. The atmosphere in the courtroom was thick, and I knew that my fate lay in the balance. I had to take the stand and face the truth of what I had done - that I had killed a man in fear for my life.

Trial Day Five, Friday, March 23, 1923

Colonel Roy Jones of the Smith & Wesson Company, the renowned expert on revolvers, was recalled to the stand. He

176

stepped up to the window behind the witness stand, three bullets carefully balanced in his hands. He handed a magnifying glass to Judge Thayer, then to the counsel and jurors, pointing out the "crimps" and flattened surfaces. His voice was soft but serious as he explained what these markings signified - that the fatal bullet had been fired first. As he handed the magnifying glass to each person, they could see the scratches inside the gun barrel. Colonel Jones' conclusions were clear - these scratches indicated that it was the first bullet fired.

Attorney Wright raised his index finger and pointed towards the vest, a questioning expression on his face. "What is that hole in the vest?"

"A moth hole," the witness replied.

Attorney Ely turned his gaze to the witness, his eyebrows raised. "Are you qualified as a moth expert?"

Judge Thayer leaned forward in his chair, his eyes scanning the witness. "I believe that almost everyone who has clothes knows what a moth hole is," he said. "The witness is qualified to state whether or not a bullet made the hole."

Jones nervously returned to the stand during cross-examination, his eyes shifting uncomfortably between the lawyers.

Cross-examined by Attorney Ely;

"Where were you the day of the shooting?" asked Attorney Ely.

Jones cleared his throat. "At the Springfield Revolver Club." "And when did you begin your investigation?"

"Last Monday," Jones replied. He wiped his forehead, beads of sweat gathering on his skin.

Ely raised an eyebrow. "How much time have you spent on it since then?"

"Practically the entire day Monday and some time since," Jones said.

Ely leaned in, his voice low and menacing. "Do you think you can tell the sequence of bullets, their course, and the position of the deceased, despite not being present at the shooting and only having a partial description of the defendant?"

Jones shifted in his seat. "Yes, sir."

Mr. Ely's lips curved into a smirk. "Suppose you put these things all in and then explain them,"

Jones's heart raced. "That's an acrobatic feat. How can I locate them all at once and explain them all at once?"

Mr. Ely's gaze bore into Jones's. "That should not be difficult for an expert."

Jones then placed the garments and pointers in position to illustrate the bullets' location and course. Colonel Jones then used five pointers, passing through the clothing on the form to show the course of all the bullets that passed through the body or clothing.

"All your conclusions," Ely asked, emphasizing each word, "are based on testimony that the deceased was at the back of the steering wheel?"

Jones nodded. "Primarily."

The lawyer glanced down at his notes. "You heard Dr. Furcolo's testimony that Siniscalchi was seated in the middle of the seat?"

Jones gave a single nod. "Yes, but Dr. Furcolo was not present at the shooting."

Ely furrowed his brows, his gaze piercing the detective. "If there are indications on the bullet that hit the window that it struck some round hard substance, causing it to ricochet, and there are no marks on the steering wheel to show where it struck, is it not possible that it struck a revolver?"

Jones shifted in his seat, his eyes narrowing. "I have no evidence that there was a revolver."

The witness was shown a photograph of the Siniscalchi car and asked to point out the location of the bullet marks on the car. "If Siniscalchi had his arm raised and was reaching for his hip pocket to get a gun," Ely began, his eyes narrowing, "would it not cause his elbow to rise?"

The witness nodded. "Yes, it would."

"In that case, would the elbow holes be higher than the other holes?"

"Yes, they would."

Ely paused, his voice becoming quieter. "And would they be pretty near the level of the holes in the back seat?"

The witness hesitated before answering, "It could be brought near the same level."

Ely looked intently at the witness. "Are you sure there was an arm inside the sleeve?"

The witness nodded, his voice confident. "I am sure there was an arm inside the sleeve of the overcoat."

Ely was silent for a moment, then asked, "Have you heard evidence that the coat was buttoned?"

The witness shook his head. "I am not certain that I have." "Even with the bullet holes as shown, is there anything to prevent the coat from being worn open?"

"No, sir. I don't know of any."

Colonel Jones said in answer to Attorney Ely's question that the folding back of the coat might account for two bullet holes in the Siniscalchi garment, with one bullet. Some portion of the body would have to come forward while a man was reaching to his hip pocket for a gun.

Attorney Ely indicated by sitting in a chair the manner of a man reaching for a gun, and Colonel Jones said Ely's elbow was five or six inches above the chair.

Attorney Ely's question hung in the air - "It is about on the level with the top of the chair?"

Jones shook his head and replied, "No, it's above it."

The "expert's" bandaged hand was a topic of conversation. He had a sheepish grin on his face as he explained how he'd gotten the wound, "I didn't know the gun was loaded," from a revolver he was asked to examine at police headquarters.

The room was suddenly filled with laughter, my attorneys and I included, as we pictured the scene in our minds. Jones blushed, embarrassed of his mishap.

More expert testimony on revolvers and shooting and gunshot wounds was then given by Dr. Irving Calkins when he took the stand. Dr. Irving Calkins stepped forward, an imposing figure with his champion revolver shot of the world record. He narrated his accomplishments with a brief yet powerful speech, and the room was filled with awe.

Attorney Ely gave District Attorney Wright a knowing look and said, "You needn't go any further to qualify Dr. Calkins as an expert revolver shot."

Dr. Calkins had known Siniscalchi "fairly well" and belonged with him to the Springfield Gun Club. His expertise on revolvers, shooting, and gunshot wounds was unparalleled. His hands moved gracefully as he spoke, emphasizing each point with a punctuated gesture. He was a masterful storyteller, and his words painted a vivid picture for the jury. The room was filled with admiration as Dr. Calkins concluded his testimony, and the jurors were left with a deepened understanding of the case.

Dr. Calkins had an air of conviction as he assumed the posture in District Attorney Wright's chair in front of the jury. He gestured as if Siniscalchi was sitting in his car, his right arm bent forward, grasping the wheel. In this position, he claimed that Siniscalchi was struck by the first bullet, paralyzing him, after it had penetrated his arm and entered his lungs. Unable to move, he remained in the same position while the following bombardment from the pistol rained upon him.

The courtroom was silent as all eyes were glued to the gruesome dummy standing at the center, clothed in Siniscalchi's garments, with sticks protruding from the bullet holes. It was a morbid sight that seemed almost unreal. Dr. Calkins stepped forward, pointing to the series of bullets that had been lodged in the dummy. He began to explain the story behind each one, and the audience hung onto his every word. The room's atmosphere changed as he spoke, with a sense of dread and fascination consuming everyone present. The details and the tragic display made the scene even more powerful. It was a moment that none of them would forget.

The Commonwealth rested its case at 12:45. The noon recess was declared following the announcement by District Attorney Wright that his case was all in.

Wife of Man on Trial For the
Murder of Carlo Siniscalchi

MRS. JOSEPH PARISI

Siniscalchi's Clothing Worn When He Was Killed
Being Exhibited in Courtroom at the Parisi Trial

Left to right—Col Roy D. Jones, revolver expert; Attorney Joseph B. Ely and District
Attorney Charles H. Wright, with jury in background. Wooden pointers in overcoat show
course taken by bullets.

Defending a Murderer

"We will show you that Parisi acted as any reasonable man would have acted when he found himself facing this vindictive and quarrelsome man, the king of a gang, the man who had hired another man to make an attempt on the life of Parisi only a few weeks before."

- DEFENSE ATTORNEY JOSEPH B. ELY

9

The cold air of the brick walls of my cell pressed against my skin as I paced back and forth. My mind raced with worry and dread. Four days of the prosecution's case had passed, and now it was my turn. Would I be able to avoid the electric chair? My palms were sweaty as I ran my hands along the rough surface of the wall. The ghostly sound of my steps resonated through the silence of the jail. With each step, the anxiety in my chest grew tighter and tighter. Would I be able to make it out of this alive? "You can do it," I whispered to myself. "You can make it." But I knew it was easier said than done. I would have to summon all my strength and courage if I had any chance of success. I took one last deep breath and collapsed onto my bed. I closed my eyes and tried to imagine a different outcome. A future where I wasn't condemned to death. A future of freedom and possibility. I had to believe that this future was still possible. I had to think that I would make it out alive.

Trial Day Five, Friday, March 23, 1923

Just before 2 pm, the courtroom erupted with anticipation as Joseph Ely, my attorney, stood to deliver his opening remarks. His words filled the room, and Judge Webster Thayer nodded in approval. As the jury leaned in, a United States Federal Court Judge, Elisha Brewster, appeared in the room. Judge Thayer noticed him and beckoned him to sit on the bench alongside him. Judge Brewster accepted the invitation without hesitation and joined the judge.

Opening Remarks by Attorney Ely;

Attorney Joseph Ely strode powerfully to the center of the courtroom, hands clasped firmly in front of him. He cleared his throat, and his thunderous voice reverberated through the hushed room. "Gentlemen of the jury," he began, his eyes piercing each juror." This man whom the Commonwealth claims to have murder in his heart went in this store and bought a chain and locket for a gift," he said. "Parisi then went to the Ware-Pratt store and bought a silk shirt, another gift, for some person to give on that beautiful holiday, Christmas. Then Parisi went to see his mother-in-law on Water Street. She was not home. He then went to visit his sister-in-law on William Street. She was not at home. He left his car in front of his sister-in-law's house. He then went to see a friend at the Italian bank. Parisi had the habit of sending money to Italy and had business at the bank.

"We will show you how Siniscalchi came to Springfield from New York. We will show you his record in Brooklyn and New York. We will show you his reputation as a quarrelsome and vindictive character. We will show you that Siniscalchi, in broad daylight, assaulted and slashed an officer of the law on his post of duty on Water Street.

"We propose to show you that when Siniscalchi left the dock where Parisi now sits, he told another officer of the law, Lieutenant James Daly, who had testified against him, 'You --------, I'll get you yet.'

"We will show you his record for carrying a gun. We will show you that Siniscalchi persuaded Parisi to buy fifty gallons of alcohol and that when Siniscalchi got the money from him, he said, "Get out; if you tell, I will kill you.

"On another occasion, when Parisi was on Water Street, Siniscalchi and another man shot at Parisi's car. The defendant was informed that the other man fired the shot at Parisi at the demand of Carlo Siniscalchi. More evidence will show you that he was the leader of a gang.

"Such a man the defense claims Carlo Siniscalchi to have been. Such a man the defendant knew him to be. Piemontese said in Concord Reformatory, 'When I come out, Parisi won't be alive.' The defendant was against a gang of such character that the protection of the police could not shield him. Consequently, he purchased a revolver.

"As Parisi was making his way north on Main Street, having no thought of murder in his heart, the chain and locket in his pocket, he heard the rap on the window of the car. Siniscalchi beckoned to him to come over. Siniscalchi threatened him. When Parisi said, 'I do as I please,' he said it to the man known as the 'King of Little Italy.' When Parisi said that, Siniscalchi reached for his hip pocket, and this man did not wait for the shot but drew his gun and shot in self-defense. He ran away because he thought some member of the gang would get him, and he wanted to give himself up.

"On December 20, 1921, he was taken to York Street Jail and has been there since then. We will show you that Parisi acted as any reasonable man would have when he faced this vindictive and quarrelsome man, the king of a gang. This man had hired another man to make an attempt on the life of Parisi only a few weeks before."

Attorney Ely's powerful words echoed throughout the courtroom, bringing a sudden close to his opening address. The judge, nodding in approval, waved a hand for recess. I stepped out of the dock, my legs unsteady with anticipation, and went to the restroom. As I lit up a cigar, I couldn't help but feel a wave of relief, knowing that I had been granted a moment of respite in this overwhelming situation.

During the recess, Attorney Robert King rushed through the overcrowded hallways of the courtroom, rounding up witnesses in a flurry of activity for my defense. The courtroom was packed, and the hallways even more congested as the testimonies began.

Attorney King ushered in Phillip Brologo of West Springfield, a friend of mine. We had ridden together that fateful day when I visited my mother-in-law on Water Street. Brologo made an amusing entrance when he was placed on the witness stand, plunging instantly into a narrative of the events that took place the day of the shooting. The interpreter began to translate, but Attorney Ely laughingly interrupted, asking to be given a chance to question him. My friend was so nervous that he stumbled over his words as if he had been practicing what to say. Unfortunately, his story didn't provide any help.

Miss Mary Keehan, the nice lady behind the counter at Adams & Crockett's jewelry store, took the stand and testified that she had sold me a diamond pendant that afternoon of the shooting. The pendant was placed in evidence. It was a cherished present for Raffaela, but one she would never receive. My heart sank into my stomach as I remembered Mary's warm look as the pendant passed over the glass countertop. She wished me luck, and I could barely manage a thank you before my feet had me hurrying out the door. I could feel the heavy weight of sadness as I realized that Raffaela's gift was now part of a criminal trial rather than a tender moment between us.

Patrolman Charles Learned testified that he had been a police officer for eleven years and had known Siniscalchi since 1913. He pointed to the scar on his cheek, a result of Siniscalchi's attack on him on Water Street in 1915. District Attorney Wright tried to object, but Judge Thayer said evidence like this was allowed to demonstrate Siniscalchi's habits, temperament, and character.

"What was Siniscalchi's reputation for being hostile and vindictive?" Ely asked.

"Bad," Learned replied.

"Did he carry a gun?"

"I heard he did," the Patrolman answered, his finger still lingering on the scar Siniscalchi had inflicted.

Detective Lieutenant James Daly then took the stand, his gaze fixed on the jury. Daly testified that he was present at the trial of Siniscalchi for slashing Patrolman Learned and that Siniscalchi threatened to "get" him as they passed each other in the courtroom. Daly shuddered, his throat tightening as he remembered the brutality of Siniscalchi's attack on Patrolman Learned. As Daly spoke, he could feel the late Siniscalchi's eyes burning into his back.

Judge Thayer interrupted Lieutenant Daly's testimony with a stern question to District Attorney Charles Wright, demanding to know if he proposed to present any positive evidence to dispute the police officers' "bad" character assessment of Siniscalchi. Staring into the hall, Wright observed the swarm of officers summoned and waiting in anticipation to be called. The district attorney said that he did not, and Judge Thayer suggested that Attorney Ely need not "have the whole police force testify," prompting a nod of agreement from Ely. He was well aware that he was disliked by most of the police department, except for the ones on his payroll.

Trial Day 6, Saturday, March 24, 1923

The Springfield Daily News reported, "Testifying as to his fear of the man he is alleged to have murdered, Joseph Parisi drew tears to the eyes of the spectators in Superior Court this morning when he was called to the witness stand to give his version of the events when Carlo Siniscalchi was shot and killed as he sat in his automobile at Main and Union Streets."

At 9 am, I was called to the stand by Attorney Ely;

I raised my hand, proudly declaring my age: twenty-nine.

My journey to this country began in Italy back in 1909. From there, I made my way to Fitchburg. Though I stayed there for only a few months, I eventually moved to West Springfield, where I've lived for the last 14 years.

On November 23rd, 1918, I was wed with joyous celebration. Our family has grown since then, with a spirited three-and-a-half-year-old boy, a vibrant two-and-a-half-year-old daughter, and a precious nine-month-old girl born while I was in jail. As I look at them, I can't help but smile at how much has changed since that day.

One day, I drove down Water Street and spotted Mike Piemontese and Carlo Siniscalchi. Before I knew it, four or five gunshots echoed through the street. When I got home, I frantically searched for bullet marks on the auto, but nothing was there.

"Will this alleged shooting be connected with Siniscalchi?" Mr. Wright inquired.

"We will connect it with him," Attorney Ely responded, his eyes narrowing and his mouth set in determination.

Attorney Ely leaned forward, his brow furrowed in intense concentration. "Who do you think was the man responsible for putting Piemontese up to kill you?" he asked, his voice low and urgent.

The room suddenly seemed to press in on me, the air heavy with the weight of my answer. I took a deep breath before finally speaking. "Carlo Siniscalchi," I said, my voice barely above a whisper.

I hesitantly testified my events of that day of the shooting to the court.

"Did you have any intentions to murder Siniscalchi?" Attorney Ely's voice broke through the room, sharp and inquisitive.

"No sir, never," I replied, my voice trembling.

Cross-examined by District Attorney Wright;

After recess, Wright began with a barrage of questions about my bootlegging activities.

"Parisi said he was born in Calabria, Italy, and Siniscalchi was from Naples. Is that true?" he asked, his voice cutting through the tense silence of the courtroom.

"Yes, sir," I replied, feeling my heart thump against my chest.

The prosecutor's gaze sharpened. "Did you ever hear that Piemontese shot at you because he heard you were going to kill him?" asked the prosecutor.

I glanced around the room, my eyes settling on the jury, before responding. "No, sir."

"You knew it was against the law, didn't you?" asked Mr. Wright, savagely pressing the line of inquiry about my liquor activities.

"Yes, sir."

"You say you yelled when Carlo slapped your face," he said, his voice cold and accusatory. "Is that all you generally do when a man slaps you in the face?"

My eyes were blazing as I spat out my reply. "It was all I did on that occasion."

District Attorney Wright asked, "Were you afraid of him on the day on Main Street?" His voice was low yet piercing.

I nodded, my heart fluttering in my chest. "Yes."

The district attorney raised his eyebrows. "And yet you went right to his car?"

"Yes," I said, my voice barely above a whisper. "I thought he was going to pay me back my money."

"Did you have an idea that other people would be hit if you shot Siniscalchi on that crowded street?" he asked, his voice taut. "Did you think two or three others might be killed?"

"I was too nervous to think about the people," I replied, my hands shaking.

"And you didn't care, did you?"

"I was nervous and did not know."

"When did you first meet Siniscalchi?"

"About ten years ago."

"And you had been buying alcohol from him before the shooting?"

I nodded. "Yes."

I said that I had been at Siniscalchi's house several times with friends of his. Carlo and I drank wine together. I said I did not go to Siniscalchi's home after the slashing of the police officer until Carlo sent him a card after he got out of jail. Carlo had a party in Agawam, sent me a ticket, and asked for $20. I said I would not take the ticket but sent Carlo the $20.

192

Wright insisted, his frustrated voice laced, "Why did you refuse the ticket?"

I swallowed hard, my fear evident in the stagnant air. "Because he was a bad man, and I feared him."

"You were not afraid of him when you bought alcohol off him and when you killed him," Wright accused.

I shook my head, my eyes wide with terror as he replied, "I was afraid of him all the time."

Wright studied him, searching for a hint of truth. "Were there not other men from whom you could have bought alcohol?"

I nodded. "Yes, but I knew he had it, and I wanted to get it to do business with him."

"Who was the man to whom you gave the $20 for the party?"

I shrugged helplessly. "I don't know who he was. It was soon after Siniscalchi got out of jail." I felt a chill run down my spine when I heard Siniscalchi's name.

Wright persisted, "But you remembered that you were afraid?".

I nodded, my throat tight. "Yes."

"When did you first begin to get afraid of Siniscalchi?"

"Right after I came to Springfield," I said, my voice small.

"Why did you go to his home and drink wine with him if you were afraid of him?"

I looked away, feeling a heavy weight on my chest. "I had been in no trouble with him. Somebody else took me down. I knew he was a bad man, but I thought he wouldn't hurt me."

"So, you weren't afraid of him then?"

I shook my head, refusing to meet his gaze. "Yes, I knew he was a bad man all the time."

Wright continued, "Why did you go into the liquor business?"

I ran my hands through my hair and sighed, "To make money."

Wright raised an eyebrow, "So, you didn't go into the business because Siniscalchi wanted you to?"

I shook my head, "He wanted me to go into the business, and I wanted to make money."

"You never paid Siniscalchi by check at any time?"

"No," I said firmly.

"You had an account at the Chapin National Bank?"

I nodded, "Yes." I continued, "I withdrew about $200 from the bank just before I bought the alcohol. I had about $600 at my house at the time."

Wright asked, his brows furrowed in concentration, "On the night when you had the trouble with Siniscalchi at the garage, you went down there alone?"

I nodded, my lips pursed. "Yes."

"You drove there in your brother's Hudson car just before 7:30?"

I nodded again, my eyes flitting to the side. "Yes. It was my brother's car."

"The one you used in the liquor business?"

I shook my head, my voice firm. "No, it was my brother's car."

"How long did Piemontese live in West Springfield?"

"Two months," I replied, my thoughts wandering back to those days.

"Where did he live?"

"At 28 Sprague Street, in my mother's house. He later went into the army."

"You are a Calabrian?"

The question hung in the air as if daring me to answer. I could feel my heart thumping in my chest and my palms sweating, but I forced my voice to remain steady as I replied, "Yes."

He continued, "Siniscalchi came from Naples?"

I nodded. "Yes."

"Is there a Calabrian gang here?"

My throat felt tight as I shook my head. "No."

"You know the Puglianos?"

I could feel my body tense up, and I clenched my fists. "Yes."

"Cardone?"

I paused, wondering if I could trust him. "Yes."

"Scarfo?"

I hesitated, then finally said, "Yes."

He leaned forward, his voice taking on an edge as he asked, "Why were Piemontese and the others trying to get you?"

I shook my head, my mind racing as I tried to find an answer. "I don't know."

"You don't know why these men were always after you?"

I shook my head, my hazel eyes darkening. "I don't know."

"You never went man-hunting yourself?"

I clenched my jaw. "No." The room was silent; the only sound was the clock ticking on the wall.

"You think Piemontese is in Worcester now?"

I shrugged. "I've been told so, but I don't know where he lives."

Mr. Wright's further questioning felt like ice in my veins. I had to tell him what had happened - I had to tell him about the Piemontese shooting. I told him I'd gone to Siniscalchi's house to talk about it. He'd invited me into a room, and we'd talked together.

"Why weren't you afraid to go?" He asked.

I hesitated for a moment, my heart pounding in my chest. "He told me to go, and all my people knew I was going. I was afraid he would think I had something against him about the shooting if I didn't go," I replied.

I was on the stand for what felt like an eternity, my nerves jangling as I tried my hardest to remain composed. As I finished my testimony, Attorney William Giles patted my shoulder reassuringly.

"I think we'll be done by Monday," King said with a meaningful look, "but I'd wager the jury will get their hands on the case by Wednesday."

The courtroom was heavy with anticipation as I stepped off the stand. I could feel the eyes of the jury burning into my back as I made my way to the defense table. Everything seemed to move in slow motion as I waited for the adjournment to be called, eventually taking place until Monday.

Trial Day 7, Monday, March 26, 1923

The courtroom was filled with people ranging from elegantly dressed women to laborers. The unease in the room was unmistakable, and the sound of shuffling feet and hushed conversations resounded off the walls.

I took the witness stand again this morning at 9:30 a.m. for further cross-examination. The District Attorney, Wright, grilled me with questions about the $750 taken from me in the garage across the street from Siniscalchi's house.

"You did not tell anyone about it until after you shot Siniscalchi, did you?" He probed.

I felt my palms begin to sweat as I shook my head. "No," I replied, my voice trembling. "I was afraid everybody would know about it."

He raised an eyebrow skeptically. "You did not even tell your wife?"

I shook my head again, feeling the weight of the courtroom's gaze. "No," I answered, my voice barely a whisper.

Wright furrowed his brow as he asked, "Piemontese went away to the war, and when he got back, you tried to get some money from him?"

"Yes," I replied, my voice barely a whisper.

"You weren't in the army yourself, were you?"

Shaking my head, I answered, "No."

"And you were twenty then, still unmarried?"

I nodded, unable to form words.

He continued, "You thought Siniscalchi was bigger than the police, and you couldn't get protection against him?"

My eyes darted around the room as I whispered, "Yes."

"Wasn't there anyone you could have gone to to tell them of your fear of Siniscalchi?"

"I didn't know you at the time," I whispered, my voice trembling.

District Attorney Charles Wright's words cut through the silence of the courtroom like a sharp knife. "So, you never told any officer of the law or anyone that Siniscalchi had threatened your life until after you had shot him dead?"

My heart thudded in my chest, and I nervously played with the hem of my shirt. I shook my head slowly, my throat too tight to speak. I had never told a soul about Siniscalchi's threats.

"I think that question has been asked at least ten times already, and each time answered in the same way," Attorney Ely said with a pointed look. Judge Thayer's voice rang out from behind the bench. "Let him answer it just once more."

I took a deep breath and looked up at the jury. In a small but sure voice, I said, "No. I never told anyone about the threat of Siniscalchi, adding that I did not know the district attorney then."

"You thought the police were afraid of him?" Wright asked.

I nodded, my thoughts racing. "Yes," I said in a voice that was barely a whisper. "I thought he was a powerful man. Everybody was afraid of him." I could almost feel the tension radiating off of Wright, who seemed as scared as I was of Siniscalchi.

"Siniscalchi was a great man, wasn't he?"

"Yes, he was a bad man."

"You didn't think Police Chief Belmer of West Springfield was afraid of Siniscalchi, did you?"

My eyes glanced at Chief Belmer. "No, I thought he was a friend of Siniscalchi."

"So, you did not ask Belmer for a permit to carry a gun?"

"No."

"You didn't tell the State Police about the threat? "Did you think the governor and the state officials were afraid?"

I stayed silent, not telling the State Police about the threat. The governor, the state officials - were they afraid too? I couldn't answer; I kept my head down and said nothing.

"The only liquor business you ever did was with Siniscalchi and the people you sold it to?"

"Yes."

"Didn't you tell the police after your arrest that you knew all about how to make alcohol?"

"Yes."

Wright's deep voice pierced the silence of the courtroom as he asked me, "You had a gun in one of your pockets and both hands in your pockets?"

I nodded, my fingers shaking as I testified, "Yes, my right hand was in my pocket."

He then inquired, "Why didn't you take it out when you went on Main Street?"

I hesitated, my throat tightening before I replied, "I...I forgot to take it out."

His hard gaze never left me as he repeated, "You knew it was against the law to carry it on the main street?"

I nodded again, barely able to get the word out, "Yes."

He persisted, "You felt it in your pocket?"

I shook my head and replied, "I did not feel it; I knew it was there."

When Siniscalchi called me, I said I was walking with my hands in my pockets and hesitantly walked toward him. My heart was pounding, and I knew that something was off. I could feel the sweat dripping down my forehead as I slowly approached the car.

Wright asked, "Was that when your heart told you not to go?"

I leaned back, my gut clenching as I answered, "Yes."

He probed further, "But you still went over to the car?"

I could feel my heart pounding in my chest as I replied, "Yes."

"He opened the door?"

I nodded, "Yes."

He paused, his voice almost a whisper as he asked, "You thought he wanted to give you the money?"

I swallowed hard before murmuring, "Yes."

He looked at me, his gaze intense, "Your heart told you to go and get your money the second time he called?"

I shifted my weight, my voice barely audible, "I was afraid it would look bad if I didn't go."

He asked, his voice tense with fear, "Were you afraid of him right on Main Street in Springfield?"

I nodded, my heart racing as I remembered that afternoon. "Yes," I whispered. "I thought it was best to do what he told me."

He pressed further, "Why were you afraid of him that afternoon after he had gotten your $750?"

I shrugged, my mind spinning with fear. "I don't know just why," I murmured, "but I thought he might think I would tell the police about what Piemontese said."

He raised an eyebrow. "You walked right up to Carlo's car?"

I nodded, my hands trembling as I remembered the fear I felt. "Yes."

Here, at Wright's request, I demonstrated, at the jury panel, how I stood with my right foot on the running board, with hands in pockets.

Wright's voice was heavy with suspicion as he asked, "Was your head inside the car?"

My eyes darted around, unsure of what to say. I finally muttered, "I don't know."

He inquired further, "What about your arm? Was it in?"

"No," I replied, shaking my head.

"How far away was your gun?"

"I don't know," I answered, my voice almost a whisper, "but it was outside the car."

The memory of that day came back to me suddenly. I remembered how my hands had trembled as I held the gun, my breath coming in short, ragged gasps. I had no idea how I did it. "Carlo said, 'You son of a -----, I told you not to come down Water Street and sell alcohol anymore, or I'll kill you.'"

With the aid of a chair, I showed how Carlo drew his gun. I jumped back and pulled my gun when I saw Carlo reaching into his pocket. His strained position and the pistol in his hand made me shake my finger and point it toward the jury to demonstrate the situation.

"You saw the gun in his hand?" He asked.

"Yes," I replied, my voice trembling.

"You mean to say this gunman Siniscalchi, crack shot, who could fire through the neck of a bottle without breaking it, had his gun out first, and the police were afraid of him, and you are alive today?"

I nodded, my eyes wide with fear. "Yes."

"You could have got away, and he could never have shot you in a thousand years," he said, his voice rising with the implication.

I shook my head, my eyes wide. "I didn't have time to think," I answered, my voice quivering with fear.

"You saw no way of getting away?" he questioned, his eyes searching mine.

"No," I replied, my breath catching in my throat.

"When a man points a gun at you, you duck back, don't you?" he continued, his voice low and insistent.

"He didn't point. I didn't have time to think what to do," I responded, my hands trembling.

"You didn't want the bullets to hit the lady on the car?" he persisted.

"No," I said, my gaze dropping to the ground.

"Didn't want to hit anybody but him?"

"I didn't want to hit anybody, not even him," I said, my voice barely audible.

"Why did you run away?" he asked, his voice ringing with curiosity.

"I was afraid somebody would kill me," I whispered.

Wright asked, his voice laced with curiosity and disbelief, "Why were you running?"

I replied, my voice heavy with defeat, "I was going to give myself up to the police."

"You were trying to get lost in the crowd, weren't you?" Wright questioned.

"No," I answered firmly and determinedly.

Wright continued, "Didn't you see the policeman in uniform, Dowling, running after you with a gun?"

"No," I said, my breath catching in my throat.

"Have you ever said so to Officers Manning, Bligh, and Fleming?"

I paused for a moment, my heart pounding in my chest. I could almost taste the cigar smoke as I recalled my encounter with the three officers. "I saw three men. They gave me a cigar, and one lighted it for me. I told them I have a headache," I finally replied. The officers then asked me if West Springfield people told me to look out or I'd have trouble with Siniscalchi, to which I said, "No." I was not being honest. I could feel a pounding headache caused by the cigar the officers had given me, making my head spin. I begged them to postpone the questioning till the next day, but they refused.

I sat there, being questioned in the interview, with a male stenographer present. I could feel the sweat trickling down my back and my heart pounding. "It must be, I said, if it's there," I muttered, my voice wavering.

District Attorney Wright announced he was done questioning me. The judge nodded towards me, and I slowly stood, my legs shaky beneath me. I carefully made my way down the steps of the witness stand, my heart pounding in my chest. I could feel all eyes in the courtroom on me as I walked, my strides measured and deliberate. I finally reached the floor and exhaled, relieved that my ordeal was over.

Eugene Scrivani, a police detective from New York, stepped up to the witness stand to testify. He identified Carlo Siniscalchi from a photograph and was asked about his reputation by Attorney Ely.

He replied gravely, "Well, it wasn't too good."

He then recounted a story about the time he had to arrest Carlo, who was carrying a gun. The air was tense with the tension of the courtroom as the detective spoke. The judge eyed him intently, noting every detail.

Attorney Robert King called witness Michael Piemontese to the stand. On October 15, 1921, as Parisi drove by in his automobile, Siniscalchi declared, "This is the time to shoot him." Piemontese drew his revolver and fired four shots, but he maintained he hadn't meant to kill Parisi. Siniscalchi offered to supply bail, and Piemontese was sent to Concord Prison. While he was there, a man from New York visited him. With a trembling voice, Piemontese admitted, "Parisi will be dead before I get out of Concord." Fear of Siniscalchi was evident in his voice.

Cross-examination by District Attorney Charles Wright;

"Didn't you tell Judge Heady you shot at Parisi because he slapped your face?"

He shook his head, his eyes filled with regret. "I said that, but it was not true."

"How long did you serve?"

"Fifteen months," he replied with a heavy sigh.

"You're out on parole now?"

"Yes," he muttered, his gaze cast down.

Wright leaned in, his voice low. "Didn't you tell Judge Heady and Prosecutor Madden that Parisi had robbed you and that he wanted you to be a member of his Black Hand in West Springfield, and that you wanted to be sent to Concord to get away from that gang so they couldn't hurt you?"

He swallowed hard, his hands trembling. "I told them that, but it was not true." Piemontese's face was filled with worry as he told Mr. Wright and the representatives of the institution and the parole board in the Concord Prison the same story he'd been telling.

The room was filled with an uncomfortable silence as Wright looked at him and asked, "You cried when you talked with us?"

Piemontese shook his head. "No."

"Why did you tell us a lie?" Wright demanded.

The witness looked down at his feet as he replied, "Because I wanted to get out of jail as easy as I could."

"Parisi never slapped your face, took your money, and sent you around to collect Black Hand money for a man whose wife was sick?"

"No," Piemontese answered quietly.

"You told us after you had refused to do that they took you to Parisi's house to try you before the Black Hand?"

Piemontese shook his head. "I do not recall."

Wright's eyes narrowed as he looked at the man, the corners of his mouth turned up in a smirk. "What are you smiling at?" he asked.

The man's expression shifted, his lips thinning into a tight line. "I never smile," he answered.

Wright's brows raised. "Are you afraid of anyone here while you are talking now?"

The man shook his head. "No."

Wright's gaze fixed on him, his voice low. "Are you the man who goes out and shoots people when you are told to do so?"

The man's face hardened. "No."

Wright leaned in closer, his eyes darkening. "Why did you do it because Siniscalchi paid you?"

The man dropped his gaze, a hint of fear in his voice. "Because I was afraid of Siniscalchi. He was feeding me in his house."

"Do you come here and lie for money?"

Piemontese's face contorted with anger as he slammed his fist down upon the witness stand, his chest heaving with deep breaths.

"I ain't no liar!" he growled, his voice trembling angrily. "I'm a bricklayer now, and I ain't got no need to lie for no money!" The rage in Piemontese's expression had dissipated and was replaced with a look of injured pride. He stood for a moment in the stillness of the courtroom before stalking out.

The courtroom was silent as Attorney Ely stepped forward, his voice barely above a whisper. "The defense rests."

Raffaela, my wife, and our children have been present throughout the entire trial, and Raffaela has accompanied me during every break. We'd all grown accustomed to the sterile white walls of the courthouse, the smell of polish as we walked across the marble floor, and the sharp rap of the judge's gavel.

My three-and-a-half-year-old son, Antonio, let out a soft whimper as the courtroom emptied for recess. With his tiny fingers, he approached the dock and tugged at the heavy bronze padlock that secured the gate. The emotional toll of the trial was evident as tears welled in my eyes.

The sound of my son Antonio's desperate cries echoed through the courtroom, piercing my heart. I had promised my family that I would be home soon, and I had to fight for my life to keep it. The stale courtroom air seemed to close in on me, suffocating me with its intensity. I could feel the stares of the jury and the judge, their judgment weighing on me like bricks. "Please, papa, let's go home," Antonio whispered, wiping away his tears. I looked into his trusting eyes, and my determination was renewed. I had to win this case for them.

Trial Day 8, Tuesday, March 27, 1923

"More than 2,000 people sought entry to the Hampden County courthouse today, March 27, to hear the final arguments in the case of Joe Parisi, who for more than a week has been on trial charged with the murder of Carlo Siniscalchi, Italian leader," reported *The Evening Gazette of Worcester*.

Judge Thayer's booming voice echoed in the courtroom, commanding that extra chairs be brought in to accommodate the crowd of attorneys and others gathered outside. He insisted that every available inch of space should be used. His stern gaze swept the room, lingering on each person as if to ensure his orders would be followed. The bailiff scurried to gather additional chairs, hurrying them into the courtroom until barely an inch of the floor remained exposed. The attorneys crowded in, murmurs of anticipation rippling through the room as everyone wanted to hear the attorney's final arguments.

Closing Argument by Joseph Ely for the Defense;

At 9:35, my senior counsel, Joseph Ely, stepped up to the jury box. He paused, taking in the attentive faces of the jury, and let out a deep breath of appreciation. His brow furrowed as he began to speak, his voice filled with misgivings. "I'm not sure I did justice to this case," he said, his gaze flickering towards me. "I have great misgivings as to my ability to present all the points tending to show the innocence of the defendant, Joseph Parisi." He paused again, his lips pursed as he lost himself in thought. He stood tall and proud, his suit pressed and neat, his hands clasped behind his back. His gaze moved slowly across the room, resting briefly on each jury member. "I will do my best," he said, a steely determination in his voice. He cleared his throat and began to speak, every word carefully chosen to present the case. He spoke with conviction, his deep voice carrying throughout the courtroom. His hands were a blur as he gestured and emphasized his words. He made a powerful argument and laid out every detail of the case precisely and fairly. The jury was mesmerized.

"You have heard the evidence, and now it rests with me to sum up and bring to your minds a proper picture of the relationship between this defendant and Carlo Siniscalchi. I want to briefly sketch his life from when he was born in Calabria, Italy, to when he met Carlo Siniscalchi. Picture yourself a youth of 15 years, set down among people he did not know, not knowing our language, our manners, our laws.

"Parisi spent a few months in Fitchburg and then came to Springfield and worked steadily for the West Box Company for six years. He then worked for the International Shade Company. He then went into business in West Springfield. He bought a general store in West Springfield with his brother about six months before the events, which you are now considering. Is that the history of an evil man? Is the story of this industrious young man that of a criminal and murderer?

"During his 15 years in this country, he met Carlo Siniscalchi. Now, Carlo Siniscalchi came from Naples. An officer in New York tells us he found him with a gun in his hand. The common report says he was driven out of New York, and we know in Springfield, his life has been one long chain of crime and disaster.

"We know he interfered with justice, tried to intimidate the police at the point of a revolver, and that on Water Street grabbing an officer of the law by the arm and with his brother, held him while Michael Fiore slashed the officer across the face.

"We know Carlo Siniscalchi was a vindictive and quarrelsome person. He served two years in jail for assaulting Learned, the officer. He threatened Officer Daly. When Carlo Siniscalchi got out of prison, cards were received by Italians, Parisi among them, calling for contributions to set him up in business.

"What was the business? Even his friend Delizia did not know.

"Carlo Siniscalchi had no legitimate business. You, jurors, cannot realize the fear that played around the hearts of Parisi and others because of Siniscalchi's position on Water Street. He was known as 'the King of Little Italy.' Graduating from his confinement in jail, following the party in Agawam, to whom all were required to contribute, we find Carlo Siniscalchi in 1921, on evenings, attired like a gentleman in evening clothes, and driving up and down Main Street in a beautiful Lincoln Limousine, afforded only by those of great industry or who engage in unlawful business.

"Nothing that I can say can be half as dramatic and forceful as the simple statements of this defendant, picturing Siniscalchi. How did Siniscalchi get this power? Through love and confidence? No. It was because he was known to carry in his pocket a revolver, a vindictive and quarrelsome man.

"The common impression of these simple-minded people was that Siniscalchi could intimidate the very officers of the law themselves. It was their impression of this great man, this 'king of Little Italy,' rising to power through fear, threats, and intrigue, not through lawful American institutions.

"He became a law unto himself, engaged in an unlawful business, and was capable of making a poor fellow like Piemontese attempt to take the life of a fellow man, Parisi.

"That's the kind of man Parisi shot!

"I could almost wish to establish the innocence of this poor young fellow, Parisi, that you had lived for a few months on Water Street. Then you would know things as they really were.

"Parisi seems to be drawn into association with Carlo Siniscalchi and engages in the business of buying and selling alcohol. We all admit it was an unlawful thing for Parisi to do. Would you send Parisi to the electric chair or prison for life for that?

"Let him who is without blame cast the first stone!

"Carlo Siniscalchi has told Parisi he would kill him after taking $750 from Parisi, leaving Parisi only $200 in the bank. Parisi went home, ashamed but also afraid to tell the police about this king of a gang, crack shot, who carried a revolver at all times. Parisi has been frank and has told you things that hurt him and things in his favor.

"Now, one day, Joe came to town and went on Water Street, violating the king's orders. He took some provisions to his mother-in-law's house. They were at dinner, and although he wouldn't wait, he took a little taste to show his goodwill. Later, he saw Siniscalchi and Piemontese in a store.

"Shortly afterward, he was shot at, and he did not know Piemontese was put up to it by Siniscalchi. The Commonwealth admits Piemontese shot at Parisi.

"Now, if the defense wanted to bring here a witness who was a model because he had never told a lie and had always been honest and straightforward, it would probably not be a man who could be hired, as Piemontese was, to take the life of a fellow man. Piemontese is not of Parisi's choosing; he is the man Siniscalchi hired to kill Parisi. The district attorney will say Piemontese admitted he lied in police court when he said Parisi was a Black Hander. But who was Parisi trying to protect? Himself? If he had said he was hired to kill Parisi, would Piemontese have only been sent to Concord Reformatory for 15 months?

"Piemontese was only the muscle, the villain, the bodyguard, the doer of rotten and dirty deeds for Carlo Siniscalchi.

"His testimony yesterday was his only noble act. Do you wonder that under the taunts of the district attorney, 'you came here for the pay,' he got mad and yelled, 'I'm telling the truth today.' Piemontese told the truth yesterday, perhaps during his parole from jail. Do you blame him for getting mad as he did yesterday?

209

"Nothing that Joe Parisi says is denied from the lips of any living soul. When he tells you of the 'phone message of Siniscalchi, not to say anything to the police,' he tells the truth. It was Siniscalchi's guilty conscience that was at work. If he were drawn into the Piemontese shooting affair, he would get into the hands of the police and lose his money and power. So, Carlo, later at a meeting, asked Parisi to forget that Piemontese did not mean to shoot him. Siniscalchi procures a Santaniello to go bail out Piemontese, and when the latter comes into court under such obligation, would you expect he'd say to Judge Heady, 'Carlo Siniscalchi told me to do this,' would he be likely to be paroled?

"Now Parisi heard Piemontese say that he would be killed before Piemontese got out of jail, so Parisi bought a revolver to protect himself. Piemontese's statements in prison that Parisi was the leader of a gang may be quoted by the district attorney, only to impeach Piemontese's credibility. Still, Parisi was a funny gang leader if he never had a gun until he heard that he would be killed before Piemontese got out of jail.

"Coming down to the day of the shooting of Siniscalchi, do you think Parisi had murder in his heart when he came over here shopping, in the center of Springfield, for jewelry and other goods? He had no accomplice. His simple mind is shown by his pride in the little locket, which he thought was a diamond. He was proud to give it to his wife when he returned home as good a husband and father as when he went away.

"The locket and the brush and comb he bought for Christmas, my God! Do you think a man would be thinking of Christmas presents with murder in his heart? He's a friendly man, full of the holiday spirit. He goes out to waste a few minutes of his time after a few calls. The power of the Commonwealth has been at its disposal to check up on this story because his confession tells it all.

"Confession! That's a hard name for an act that is in every way justifiable.

"We plead self-defense."

"But they say no gun was found. He always carried one. Has a collection of weapons. Pepe, a driver for Santaniello, cousin of Siniscalchi, finds himself within almost arm's length of the affair by a peculiar coincidence. He could tell you of any conversation if there was any.

"He tells you he turned his head away and waits until it's over. The young lady who came out of the store and Carman said to you that Pepe was not there. Pepe was the first man to see Siniscalchi alive after the shooting; he tells you so. He rushes to the automobile and then to the store. Rushes back and meets Mrs. Siniscalchi on her way to the hospital. Who needs that car, Mrs. Siniscalchi or the garage? Why doesn't it remain in front of the hospital? The car is rushed right back home, with the gun, of course!

"The evidence leads to the irresistible conclusion that a gun was in the car and a gun was taken away to protect the reputation of Carlo.

"Who says he had his hands on the wheel? Colonel Jones, the expert with significant experience with guns, who in the police station shot himself in the hand and offered the time-worn excuse he didn't know it was loaded, he would swear a man's life away with that evidence.

Judge Thayer's gavel cut short a buzz of laughter in the crowded courtroom.

District Attorney Wright stepped closer to the model that had been rigged up with Siniscalchi's clothes, watching intently as Attorney Ely began his demonstration of his theory of the shooting. With practiced ease, Ely adjusted the coat as he spoke, pushing it back like a man leaning forward to draw a gun. He gestured to the bullet holes he had pointed out, and when he felt Wright pressed too close, Ely gently but firmly pushed him back, never breaking stride in his theory. The room was tense as Ely's words echoed in the air, each detail he spoke of meticulously woven together to paint a vivid picture of what could have happened on that fateful day. With a flourish, Ely concluded his demonstration, standing back from the model with a satisfied grin.

"This is as Parisi says, and again, Parisi is right," cried Attorney Ely. "Siniscalchi probably looked on Parisi as an easy victim, who never carried a gun, who shrieked when he slapped him, with whom he could do as he saw fit. He was not expecting it would not be necessary to do more than draw his revolver; with Pepe there, there was no necessity for the incredible energy and quickness. Carlo was probably surprised; he was not quick enough, and the prey had escaped!

"Now, if I have not brought to your mind the overlord of this Italian community, Siniscalchi, Joseph Parisi, an honest working young man of twenty-nine, honest and diligent father of a family, who, fearful of this overlord's will, commands and trickery if I have not presented him as the kind of man he is, then I have failed in my duty to this defendant.

"Bring them together in your minds, Parisi and this cool, cunning devil, Siniscalchi—one a quiet, industrious boy, one a terror of a community.

"Then are you going to find Parisi guilty of murder in killing Siniscalchi, having shot with malice this demon of whom he was so afraid, into whose meshes he had been drawn? Is he guilty of any crimes beyond a reasonable doubt? He has been in jail since December 20, 1921. His Christmas presents are two years late. Confinement is not a pleasant thing.

"When you leave this courtroom at the end of this case, you will go home with the exuberance of release, to take your loved ones in your arms and plant on them the first kiss since your absence.

"So, act toward this young man that you can go home with the abiding conviction that you have served both the ends of justice and mercy. Do justice to the Commonwealth and this lady who sits beyond, Parisi's wife, this defendant, and the baby who has never sat at its father's knee."

Recess was taken at the end of Attorney Ely's argument. He spoke for one hour and fifty-five minutes.

Closing Argument by Charles Wright for the Prosecution;

District Attorney Wright stood before the jury, his look steady and determined. "This man sits in this dock today guilty of murder unless he can show that Siniscalchi had a gun. He had no right to empty six shots into Siniscalchi's body unless Siniscalchi had a weapon. Parisi has to show you that Siniscalchi drew a pistol, that he threatened violence and assault with it, and that Parisi feared that he was to receive grievous bodily injury.

"Now, think of it, Siniscalchi, a crackshot, desperate gunman, vindictive, quarrelsome man, had his revolver out first, and yet Paris is alive today. Parisi fires six shots into Siniscalchi's body. Yet, Siniscalchi is supposed, according to the defense, to have had out an automatic revolver, which pulls so easily. Try it and see how easily one pulls; the bullets fly in rapid succession. If Siniscalchi had had such a gun out, the bullets would have been in Parisi's body before he could shoot.

"But Parisi sits here today with no sign of injury, and there is not one ounce of evidence that one bullet was fired in his direction. And where is the gun of Siniscalchi? Not a witness tells you they saw one. Every living witness for the Commonwealth tells you they saw none.

"But this man who is afraid of Siniscalchi walks right up to him with his gun. If Siniscalchi had had a gun, would Parisi have run away after the shooting? No, he would have remained, stood right where he was, and told the police, 'Yes, I'm sorry, I shot him, but look at the gun in his hand. There he is dead with his gun.' How impossible to refute such a situation if he had taken that course of action!

"The only question is: Did Siniscalchi have a gun? Did he start to use the weapon before the defendant shot him? If such were not the case, Parisi would be guilty of murder. If Siniscalchi had had a gun, he would be alive here today. Parisi was in no danger, with Siniscalchi in the automobile. He could have leaped behind the car door, opened back, and fled. Does anyone suppose Siniscalchi would have gone chasing Parisi around Main Street to shoot him? No, if Siniscalchi had had a gun, both men would have been alive here today.

"A friend of Piemontese. Piemontese shed a little light on this case when he said Parisi would be killed before Piemontese got out of prison. Yet he remained in jail and never did a thing to prevent the murder. Then he tells us in Concord Reformatory that he was in mortal terror of Parisi. And now, on the witness stand, he says it's all a lie. And you saw the fury he went into when I cross-examined him."

"The motive," continued the district attorney, "who had the motive to do violence? Who was actuated by fear, hate, or other sentiment? We find that this defendant had liquor dealings with Siniscalchi. Parisi says that Siniscalchi took his money, slapped his face, called him names, and threatened him. Later, they met in front of Goldstein's and offered to square it.

"What motive had Siniscalchi? These were his only dealings with Parisi. Who had the motive, the man with $750 in his pocket?

He had wound up the deal as he had wanted. What motive? Fun? Who had a motive? Parisi had every reason in the world—Parisi, whose face had been slapped by Siniscalchi.

"You are not here to try an Italian feud, not to find out the merits of one crowd of gunmen as against another gang. We ought to have them all in jail, these gunmen who kill one another in their excitement. In his excitement, this man did not know how many shots had been fired. He might as well have shot any of you or your wives or children. The bullet that hit that woman on the trolley car might have sent her to eternity. Of course, he did not intend to kill her. He was excited.

"These gangs say it will be easy to escape conviction by saying that the murdered man had a gun. They say nobody will pay attention to the district attorney or the evidence if a story shows self-defense. These Calabrian gunmen were too busy to go to war. They had to figure out how they could escape the consequences of their violations of the law.

"Siniscalchi has gone to his final judgment. His lips are sealed, and he cannot tell you about this crime. You have the duty to do justice to this crime. That is our case. Siniscalchi, an expert shot, with an automatic in his hand, and this defendant was able to escape alive! Put yourself in Parisi's situation in running away from the scene of the shooting and decide if you would try to get away from the police if you wanted to give yourself up."

Springfield Daily News

The Weather
PARTLY CLOUDY TONIGHT
SUNDAY FAIR

5 o'Clock Edition
LATE NEWS

PARISI SAYS SINISCALCHI WAS ARMED

KING CASE MYSTERY MAN SON-IN-LAW OF MORGAN PARTNER

Scene in Court Room While Parisi Was Testifying at His Trial for Murder

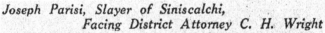

Joseph Parisi, Slayer of Siniscalchi,
Facing District Attorney C. H. Wright

"HIS LIFE OR MINE" IS PARISI'S DRAMATIC SELF DEFENSE PLEA ON STAND

Spectators in Tears as Alleged Murderer Tells of Shooting of Carlo Siniscalchi—District Attorney Wright Questions Parisi About His Alcohol Dealings—Case May Go to Jury Wednesday

Murder Trial Witness Who Told Of Attempt on Life of Defendant

MICHAEL PIEMONTESE

The Verdict

"It is not essential in order to create imminent danger that a gun actually be drawn, provided the conduct of the deceased was of such a nature and character that would have created in the mind of a reasonable man that there was imminent danger of great bodily injury."

- JUDGE WEBSTER THAYER

10

J udge Webster Thayer pulled at the room's attention with eloquent instructions by those who heard it. He broke down the varying degrees of murder, carefully laying out the law that governed them. As he droned on, the jury hung on his every word, notably when he delved into the nuances of self-defense and its relation to the crime of murder. His voice echoed throughout the chamber, bouncing off the tall walls and marble statues as he spoke with authority and clarity. The jurors took notes, transfixed by his masterful delivery of the law. He paused every so often to allow time for understanding and to let the gravity of his words sink in. There was an air of anticipation as the jury eagerly awaited his next words.

Trial Day 9, Tuesday, March 27, 1923

The judge addressed the jury, "I request you not to allow the fact that the defendants are Italians to influence or prejudice you in the least degree. Under the law, they are entitled to the same rights and consideration as though their ancestors came over on the Mayflower. Guilt or innocence of crime does not depend on the place of one's birth, the proportion of his wealth, his station in life,

221

social or political, or his views on public questions prevent an honest, just, and impartial administration and enforcement of the law."

The jury was presented with a staggering amount of evidence, including Siniscalchi's blood-soaked clothing and the six bullets that had been found in his body and the surrounding area of the shooting. The officers carried the exhibits to the jury room, their faces grave with the gravity of the situation, so the jurors could refer to them in reaching their decision. The stenographic record of the entire week of court proceedings was also placed in their hands, allowing them to review everything that witnesses, counsel, and the judge had said.

Judge Thayer's voice boomed through the courtroom as he instructed the jury to retire and deliberate the case that afternoon. His words reverberated off the marble walls as the jurors filed out, their heads turning to glance at each other in confusion and anticipation. They were enveloped in a heavy silence as they gathered in the jury room. The air was thick with the tension of uncertainty, punctuated only by the clock's steady tick on the wall. After a few moments of awkward silence, the foreman spoke up, his voice shaking slightly. "Alright," he said, his voice gaining strength and conviction with each word. "Let's get started."

My pulse raced as I sat in the courtroom, my future in the hands of the jury. I nervously hoped that they would decide on an acquittal, but the possibility of a guilty verdict for first-degree murder loomed before me. If that were the case, my fate would be life behind bars or the dreaded electric chair. I shuddered at the thought, my hands trembling as I waited for the jury to bring in their verdict.

The jury deliberated on my case for what felt like an eternity. As I sat there, my mind drifting, I watched my cellmate Eugenio

Scibelli stand silently in the courtroom, his eyes shifting between District Attorney Charles Wright and his lawyer as they spoke. Scibelli saw his only option was to take the deal, and he reluctantly pleaded guilty to manslaughter.

The judge sentenced Eugene Scibelli to serve three to five years in state prison for shooting and killing Antonio Bonavita on December 4, 1920. I could feel the tension as the judge's gavel echoed through the halls. I heard muffled sobs from the back of the courtroom, a reminder of the gravity of this situation. Eugene's face was expressionless, but his hands shook as the judge read out his sentence. He would never be the same.

Scibelli, with the aid of a court interpreter, bowed his head in gratitude to Judge Thayer for his leniency. Mrs. Scibelli, the widow of Bonavita, who had married Eugene after the shooting, sat close to him in the prisoner's dock. She gently placed a hand on his arm and whispered words of comfort in the Italian language they both shared. The courtroom was tense and silent, with the only sound being the rustle of clothes as the judge leaned back in his chair. Eugene looked at his wife, his eyes filled with appreciation as if he were trying to thank her for standing by him during this difficult time.

The Judge shifted in his chair, the sound of his robes rustling through the silent courtroom. He cleared his throat and began delivering a long speech, emphasizing the consequences of taking the law into one's own hands. He acknowledged from the evidence presented that Scibelli had indeed shot in self-defense. Still, he did deserve some punishment for taking Bonavita's wife, angering him so much that he tried to kill Scibelli. Murmurs echoed throughout the courtroom as the Judge's verdict was announced. He hammered the gavel against his desk, and the sound of justice was heard.

Suddenly, the foreman from my case entered the courtroom. The jury's question to Judge Thayer echoed through the courtroom, their voices filled with deep anticipation, "After a threat is made, is it necessary that a man actually draw a gun or simply make an attempt or motion to draw a gun to constitute a self-defense?" As the judge carefully considered the question, the tension in the room rose, and I could feel the oppressive weight of the electric chair slowly fading away as the possibility of acquittal began to take its place. The judge's response was thoughtful and measured, giving me a glimmer of hope that I could walk free.

The attorneys, witnesses, and other spectators filled the courtroom to capacity, all aware that the jury's decision hinged mainly on that one question. Without any solid evidence of an actual gun by Siniscalchi, it was clear that the defense theory was significantly weakened. When the judge finally spoke, his voice was unmistakably favorable to my defense, and a wave of optimism swept through the room. Everyone was encouraged that the chances of an acquittal were strong.

Judge Thayer's response was, "It is not essential in order to create imminent danger that a gun actually be drawn, provided the conduct of the deceased was of such a nature and character that would have created in the mind of a reasonable man that there was imminent danger of great bodily injury, he possessing the same knowledge and information that the defendant possesses concerning the deceased. It is a question of the imminence of the defendant losing his life or suffering great bodily injury."

The courtroom was filled with more than fifty of my friends and family who came to support me, anxiously awaiting the jury's decision. Every face of the jury was carefully studied, searching for any indication that I would be acquitted and come home. In some way, a small group was fascinated that two of the jury seemed particularly interested in Judge Thayer's instructions, sparking a hope-filled rumor that spread through the hall like wildfire. My family and I could only hope that it was true - that the jury was ten to two for acquittal. Every moment seemed like an eternity as we waited for the verdict.

Onlookers shuffled impatiently around the room, their faces a mask of anxious anticipation. Some sat in silence, others muttered among themselves, eagerly awaiting the door on the right side of the room to swing open any minute and the jury to appear with their verdict. There was an air of tension in the room, thick with the collective anticipation of those present.

"What do you think they'll decide?" one man whispered to his companion, a woman with her hands nervously clasped in her lap.

"We'll have to wait and see," she replied, her voice almost a whisper in the serene atmosphere.

The minutes felt like hours as the room waited, the silence punctuated only by the occasional sound of a shuffling foot or a cough. Raffaela perched on the hard wooden bench near the prisoner's dock, her gaze flickering from me to the ground and back. I sat in the dock or paced restlessly up and down the narrow confines of the cage, my feet thudding heavily against the floor, a reminder of the harsh reality of the situation. I offered her reassuring smiles, trying to keep my face calm and gaze steady. The anxiety in the air was intense, but even in the dim courtroom light, I could still see the love in her eyes. "Take care," she said, her voice thick with emotion. She reached through the bars and touched my arm, her fingers calm and gentle.

"I will," I replied, my throat tight. I wanted to reach out and wrap her in my arms, to keep her safe in this cold and unforgiving place, but I could only stand there and hope she could feel my love radiating from within.

Surrounded by a symphony of sympathetic spectators, Raffaela leaned in close and carried on an energetic chat with me from a seat beside the dock. My mother, Maria, joined in every now and then, her voice low and subdued. As the night wore on, the strain began to tell, and Raffaela's head nodded, and she dozed off, her breathing soft and steady. I, however, kept my composure and chatted calmly with court officers and friends until nudged by my mom, Raffaela's eyes fluttered open, and she resumed her close talk with me.

At about 1:30 am, when there was no sign of a verdict on the horizon, I was released from the tight confines of the dock and escorted to one of the restrooms in the corridor. The air was musty, and the walls were lined with wooden benches, each creaking in protest as I passed. I could hear the muffled voices of the jury in the background, deliberating on the verdict, and my heart pounded in anticipation. I took a moment to catch my breath, and the room's silence seemed to echo my inner turmoil.

I sat there, puffing on my cigar, yet still keeping a tranquil air that had been present throughout the trial. My confidence in my expectations of a not-guilty verdict was apparent in my posture - not arrogant, just self-assured. All who looked in my direction remarked on the honesty and intelligence that my face portrayed and the cheer that my demeanor exuded, as Attorney Ely would later describe as something more genuine than shallow or contrived.

Interested friends and many attorneys milled constantly around the courtroom door, their voices buzzing in the corridor like a swarm of bees. The room itself was thick with the chatter of the Italian language, the deep character of their native tongue vibrating through the air. The jury suddenly appeared and took their seats. Judge Thayer sat in the center of the room, his presence commanding an eerie stillness that seemed to swallow all sound. Not a word was spoken as he sat to receive the judgment.

As the clock ticked away the minutes, my heart raced faster with every second. I sat in the courtroom with nerves of steel, trying to stay composed. My wife and I sat side by side, our facial expressions unchanging. We were both prepared for what would soon come. The clerk finally asked for the verdict. Time seemed to stand still for a moment until the foreman uttered one word:

"Guilty."

No one moved a muscle. My wife's composure remained intact, her gaze fixed forward. I sat stoically, my heart pounding harder, never revealing my inner turmoil.

The jury's verdict of manslaughter came with an unexpected request for "extreme leniency," a plea that the presiding Judge took into deep consideration. My friends crossed their fingers in the hope of a short prison term for the killing of Siniscalchi. The tension in the courtroom was deep as the jury's suggestion for clemency echoed through the harsh walls. Every eye was on the Judge, his stern face betraying no emotion as he weighed the implications. He knew that the sentence he imposed would have far-reaching consequences, and his decision would shape the future of many. The silence was broken only by the faint rustling of papers and the occasional cough from the gallery. All eyes were on the Judge, their silent prayers for clemency hanging heavy in the air. The Judge finally leaned forward and, with a voice full of authority, declared, "A sentence will be pronounced after Attorney Ely produces witnesses to testify as to the defendant's character." My friends were delighted. The Judge had finally heard their plea, and a weight had been lifted off their shoulders. The jury's recommendation of compassion had been heard, and the future looked bright.

The jury members admitted they were in a deadlock for hours, unable to agree on a verdict. Whenever they thought they had reached a consensus, one man would shoot it down. Clearly, he was holding out for acquittal, and his stubbornness prevented them from coming to a conclusion. The room was tense and heavy, and the air was thick with anxiety. The jurors shifted in their seats, exchanging glares as they tried to come to a decision. Not until nearly 2:30 am did the lone juror finally relent and consent to a verdict of manslaughter. It was whispered that the recommendation for extreme leniency had been added at his insistence.

<u>Trial Day 9, Wednesday, March 28, 1923</u>

Attorney Joseph Ely stood passionately before the court, his voice booming passionately as he begged for mercy for his client, the most sincerely spoken of anything of the kind in the courtroom in years. Every plea seemed to resonate throughout the courtroom, and the jury, who had already found his client guilty of manslaughter in the killing of Carlo Siniscalchi, watched in awe.

"Your Honor, I urge you to consider the jury's recommendation of extreme leniency," Ely implored. His voice was solid and steady as he spoke, and the courtroom was silent, hanging on his every word.

Attorney Ely stood before the judge, looking pale, tired, and worn, as if the burden of the case had taken a toll on his physical being. His voice was strained as he spoke, "I feel so strongly in this case. I can't help but feel that any sentence for this boy in the dock would be like a sentence for me if it were only for six months." He paused, letting the gravity of his words sink in, before continuing, "I would feel that I had to serve it myself."

Attorney Ely slammed his fist on the desk as he declared, "I stand as strongly for law and order as anyone, but that it was a peculiar trick of fate that the man responsible for much of a certain kind of crime – gunplay, robberies, assaults - Siniscalchi, has been killed by a man about when the law had woven a net. It's unfortunate he had been caught in this web, for the dead man was a real 'scourge,' responsible for all of this."

"It seems to me that if the defendant had come in without a trial and pleaded guilty to manslaughter, your honor would be in a position to say that he shot in the heat of passion, not with that malice recognized in the crime of murder, giving way to the feelings of his nature in this passionate outburst and taking the life of a man.

"But Joseph Parisi is not before you on a plea whereby you may be judge of facts. He is here on a verdict of a jury of twelve men who gave 11 hours of consideration of the facts in the case. These twelve men believe that no wrong should be done to this prisoner; it seems that the jury's deliberations in this respect should be considered.

"I yield to no man in respect to belief in law and order and in not wanting this fair city to become known as the home of gunmen and murderers. We have altogether too much gunplay, and I want to emphasize that for one reason. Innumerable murders, shootings, stabbings, and gun-toting had been committed, and the man who, more than any other individual, was responsible for the conditions existing was the man who persuaded Piemontese to lay in wait and shoot the defendant.

"I am not saying this upon the theory that the defendant should be rewarded for ridding the community of this scourge, but because he felt himself denied the protection of our laws and courts."

"This case is somewhat beyond mere professionalism with me," said Mr. Ely. "With Parisi's ability, disposition, and unusual genius in expression, I can see great opportunities in the future for better conditions among the Italian people. When he is free, I pledge myself, not as a lawyer, not as Joseph Parisi's counsel, but as an individual, to try to see that his efforts are directed in that way with an ambition in my heart to guide him with that end in view.

"I beg your honor not to spoil that opportunity by too severe a sentence. Let us, at the earliest possible moment, avail ourselves of this remarkable personnel for the benefit of the community. That's my plea.

"For an error of judgment, he is before you for sentence. He knew Siniscalchi as a vindictive man and that he had already attempted his life. Perhaps Siniscalchi had no gun and was merely threatening him and making a pretense of reaching for a revolver. In either event, Parisi had reason to conclude that another attempt was being made to shoot him." "This man has a family. They are entitled to consideration. I know how difficult your honor's task is. The defendant has already served 14 months in jail, awaiting trial. That should be taken into consideration. I feel so keenly that I have failed in presenting this case that any penalty, even as low as a sentence of six months, would be almost like making it a penalty upon myself."

District Attorney Wright now stood before the court, his hands clasped firmly in front of him, and declared, "Springfield is the finest city in the world, yet the sad fact remains it has been given over as the battleground of gunmen. During my past three years in office, I have investigated twenty-four murderers, the majority of them from Springfield. This does not include the four or five underwood alcohol indictments which have not been brought before the court." His words seemed to strongly point an accusing finger at the police, who remained silent. The atmosphere was tense, and the air thick with implied accusations. Judge Thayer's face contorted with disgust as he heard the district attorney's figures, shaking his head in disbelief at the "appalling" conditions in Springfield.

"Neapolitans or Calabrian mean nothing to me. Every man with a gun will go to jail if I can send him there. Every man who shoots down another is going to be tried for murder if I can get a grand jury to let me try him. I am not going to let Springfield be a battleground for gunmen.

"I believe that if the victim had been a man of good standing with no record for crime, that the verdict would have been murder. Piemontese told one story in jail, and another on the witness stand under oath. God Almighty only knows what the truth is. The gun of Siniscalchi has been eliminated from the case by the verdict. No one else except Joseph Parisi testified to having seen it. It was not due to any restraint of this "outburst of passion" that the woman and her little children at the rear of that trolley car are now alive; it is time that these people who think they must carry guns learn that they cannot shoot where the innocent will be shot down."

Preliminary to passing sentence, Judge Thayer said, "When the clerk read the indictment to the jury," he said, "his instructions were in case they should find the defendant guilty to the state of what he was guilty and say no more. The jury has added its recommendation, which I consider a bad policy. I fear it might be a dangerous precedent in our courts."

Judge Thayer spoke sternly, bringing the case to a close with the resounding declaration, "Crimes of that character must be stopped." His gavel slammed down with a final, resounding thud, imposing a stiff sentence-

"Seven to ten years."

My heart sank as my gaze shifted to my wife, Raffaela, who was fighting back tears. As the handcuffs were placed on my wrists, I had a few last words with Raffaela and my lawyers before being taken away.

Judge Webster Thayer's face took on a severe expression as he addressed my counsel, Joseph Ely. "If you can produce evidence of facts in the case which the court believed had not yet been brought to light," he said, authoritative and clear, "I am willing to reopen the case." He paused, running his gaze over the court before continuing. "The jury has gone outside its jurisdiction in recommending clemency. All the law requires is a verdict of guilty or not guilty of a charge which the jurors shall determine, and nothing more," he said, his words carrying the weight of the law.

Since the trial began on March 19th, my wife, Raffaela, remained stoic, our anxiety quiet during the harrowing ten days. The only visible emotion of the people who had begun to hope for a light sentence was a shade of disappointment, a heavy air of sadness that weighed heavily on us all. No hysterics, no one shed a tear. Yet, with every passing second, the disappointment grew, sinking into our hearts like a stone. The faces of those who had held out hope for a light sentence were now drawn, the spark of hope extinguished. In the face of such a dreary outcome, we stood in solidarity, expressing our disappointment silently.

PARISI FOUND GUILTY OF MANSLAUGHTER

Joseph Parisi, Convicted of Manslaughter This Morning

SEVEN TO 10 YEARS
FOR JOSEPH PARISI

Final Chapter Added to Killing of Carlo Siniscalchi Year Ago — Defendant's Lawyer Urges Clemency

My Time Away From Family

"On both sides of the river, the city was bustling with the roar of cars and the clinking of glass bottles. Despite the strict laws of Prohibition, business was booming. The smell of whiskey hung in the air as people ventured out into other rackets, the scent of money and success driving them to take risks."

-AUTHOR NICHOLAS PARISI

Undici Parte

11

T he iron bars of York Street jail in Springfield clanged shut
behind me for the last time as I stepped inside, the sound
echoing off the stone walls. I'd been sentenced to 7 to 10
years in state prison by Judge Thayer just the day before, and now
I was waiting for the transfer that would take me away. The air was
stale and heavy, and I could feel the weight of my sentence pressing
down on me like a physical force.

I've been granted the right to speak to reporters and make a
statement to the public. I'm trying to confront the future with
courage and hope. The walls of my cell seem to be closing in on me
with every passing minute, and the sounds of distant footsteps and
muffled voices echo in my head. I'm drowning in a sea of my own
thoughts, feeling both scared and resigned to my fate. I made a
passionate plea for a representative from both The Republican and
The Daily News to come and accept my appreciation of the fairness
of the trial's reporting in those papers. I had something special in
mind as a gift for the libraries of both papers. With proud
sentiment, I retrieved an item from my cell—"Naples and Southern

Italy"—which I asked to be accepted as a little gift from me. I asked that the writings and pictures from the book be featured in The Sunday Republican in the future as a token of my gratitude.

My voice quivering, I stand before the reporters and take a deep breath, trying to remain composed. "I'm doing my best to stay strong and remain optimistic," I say, "but I can't help but feel like I'm the victim of an unpleasant situation."

I gazed in admiration at the page, my heart swelling with pride as I read Edward Hutton's vivid description of Calabria. The words painted a picture of rolling hillsides dotted with ancient olive groves and vibrant wildflowers, and I could almost feel the sun on my face.

"Calabria, what a beautiful country," I murmured, my voice filled with awe. I could practically feel the history and culture of the place seeping into my bones. I lingered over the pages of my beloved book, unable to bring myself to part with it and its promise of the glories of my native land. With a fond caress, I read, "Calabria is a paradise." The thought that its wonders could be brought to the attention of newspaper readers filled me with a sense of duty and purpose. I knew I had to share it with the world.

I gestured to the scenes of breathtaking beauty adorning the colored engravings, and a wave of nostalgia washed over me. "I left it at fifteen years," I sighed, "but how well I remember these places like it was yesterday."

Despite being deeply disappointed by the trial's outcome, which I had confidently expected would be an acquittal, I maintained goodwill toward everyone involved.

I spoke in a soft, gentle accent. "I'd very much like," I said, "if you would tell the people how grateful I feel to my lawyers, Joseph Ely, William Giles, and Robert King, who worked so hard for me. Mr. Ely worked for me not like a lawyer for a client but as a good friend. I can never repay him. I can't find the words to express the gratitude I have for him. I also thank my good friends who came to court and stood by me so nobly during my trial and the strangers who also came to the court and showed so plainly by their manner that they had sympathy for me. One and all, I thank them for their kindness.

"I feel that I am the victim of a cruel circumstance in this case, but I hope to show that I am a good citizen, and when I am released, I am going to devote myself to being a good American citizen and making other young Italians the same.

"Sheriff Clark has been so good to me that I cannot thank him enough, and all the guards in the jail have been the same."

I uttered my words without a trace of hostility, my voice firm but not angry. My body language revealed no animosity; my stance was relaxed and open. I wanted to make sure my point was heard, loud and clear, without any subtlety of hostility.

I said, "The local Italian paper, L'Eco, had not treated me fairly in the month leading up to the trial. The paper printed an article on the 'emotional case,' referring to the matter that was about to come before the courts for consideration. The paper speaks of itself as 'with the people' and 'for the people,' but such a paper should be impartial; that paper is partial." I explained, "It had printed no article about the recent Frank Magoni case, in which a prisoner on bail had left the court before the jury's verdict, and I do not see why it had singled out my case for special attention."

"To both Ben Hapgood, secretary of the Chamber of Commerce, and John Hendron of the West Box company, who had testified strongly in my favor before the imposing of the sentence, I wish to express my thanks and appreciation to you for what you have done for me. It was very kind of you to come to court, and I want you to know that I greatly appreciate it. I hope to get out someday and prove to you and the rest of my friends that my reputation is as good as you testified at my trial.

" I am the victim of a cruel circumstance."

I was overwhelmed with gratitude for all the friends who had taken the time to visit me and bestow upon me a generous money present "so as to have something to carry away with me." The jail officials went above and beyond in their courtesy, warmly inviting me to the office each time a reporter came to call, allowing us to speak in a corner for over an hour without interruption.

As I was speaking to reporters, thanking everyone who supported me during the trial, Federal Prohibition Agents joined forces with West Springfield police to raid the house of my brother-in-law, Joseph Dialessi, on Sprague Street. The officers reported discovering ten quarts of liquor and three gallons of grain alcohol. I could feel the tension in the air, the heavy weight of the law descending upon him. I could hear the officers' voices echo through the house as they shouted orders and pounded their fists on the door. My brother-in-law, Joseph, was dragged out in handcuffs, his face a mask of disbelief.

A few days later, I was transferred to my new home for the next seven to ten years: Charlestown State Prison.

As the prison bus drives over the sole bridge into the Charlestown area of Boston, essentially sealing it off, the sight of the Massachusetts state prison stands before them. The soot-covered stone fortress, constructed during the Civil War, has a look of decay on the outside, mirroring the abject lives of those within. Inside those dingy walls was the electric chair that had snuffed out sixty-five souls since 1901. Before that, executions were carried out through hanging.

The heavy metal cell door clanged shut behind me with a finality reverberating through the prison walls. I stood there, the stark reality of the next seven to ten years of my life settling in.

I was joining a few prisoners who had achieved international notoriety, including Charles Ponzi and anarchists Nicola Sacco and Bartolomeo Vanzetti, all Italian immigrants. I could feel the tension in the air, a sense of dread that seemed to hang over the entire prison. Everywhere I looked, there were reminders of the power of the unforgiving justice system and the helplessness of those who had been caught in its grip.

Charles Ponzi's ambitious investment plan was simple yet dangerous; he lured investors in with the promise of a high return while he used the new investors' money to pay off the old. His infamous Ponzi scheme had no actual investment going on. When authorities caught wind of his scheme, Ponzi was arrested and pleaded guilty, spending two years in federal prison. But the darkness didn't end there. After his release, Ponzi was immediately convicted of larceny at the state level and spent the next seven years at Charlestown State Prison. Upon his release, Ponzi is set to be deported.

Nicola Sacco and Bartolomeo Vanzetti, two Italian anarchists, were accused of a heinous crime - the murder of Alessandro Berardelli and Frederick Parmenter during the April 15th, 1920, armed robbery of the Slater and Morrill Shoe Company in Braintree, Massachusetts. With a flimsy case against them and no money recovered from the theft, the two men were tried by prejudiced Judge Webster Thayer, the same judge who presided over my case. He had a deep-seated anti-radical sentiment in America and declared them guilty, sentencing them both to death.

Back in West Springfield, life went on like nothing had changed. Bootleggers and police engaged in a never-ending war of cat and mouse, their sirens and gunshots echoing through the night. I closed my eyes, the last vestiges of freedom slipping away like the echoes of the distant sirens.

The police raided "The Pavilion" on Bridge Street, West Springfield. Luigi Pugliano, the owner, had been supplying liquor to the patrons. But what the police discovered was no ordinary hooch: it was moonshine. Joseph Dialessi, Pugliano's nephew, was caught standing guard during the chaos. He was married to Lucia Parisi, my sister. As the police searched him, they found a loaded revolver tucked inside his pocket. Joseph was arrested on the spot.

The police had also raided Pugliano's home. In a bureau drawer, they found evidence of forged stamps and seals for use on illegal liquor bottles. Undercover agents had previously made a deal to buy a large quantity of the liquor, and when the police raided the home, they found those pallets of alcohol in the garage. The officers had to duck under the battered-in garage door as they entered, the smell of alcohol heavy in the air. They fanned out, searching the drawers and cabinets, until one of them finally found it: evidence of Pugliano's forgeries. The officers stood in a circle, staring in shock at the evidence until one of them finally spoke. "We got him," he said.

One year later, my brother John Parisi and his wife Rose were cuffed and shoved into the back of a police car for obstructing a federal agent in the performance of his duties. Federal Officer Charles Ray stated that, accompanied by West Springfield Police Officer John Sullivan, he had entered the Parisi residence under a federal search warrant. When John and Rose Parisi appeared in the kitchen, a dispute ensued about the legality of the search. According to Officer Ray, while trying to open the ice chest, John shoved him aside and, with Rose, tried to take the contents of the box. Mrs. Parisi held him in a tight headlock as John threw a bottle of what seemed to be red wine onto the floor and rushed to the other door to discard another bottle contained in the chest. During this entire altercation, Officer Sullivan stood by and did not interfere.

The sun shone brightly, but the mood was anything but cheerful, and the atmosphere was heavy with dread. The couple remained silent, their faces pale and their eyes fearful as their fate was sealed. The agent slammed the door shut, and the car pulled away, taking the couple to face the consequences of their actions.

In court, Officer Sullivan's testimony backed Ray's claim on the search warrant, yet John had already reached the two bottles - shattering them all over the ground. West Springfield Sergeant Joseph Demers, who responded to the Agent's call for help, reported seeing a broken bottle in front of the Parisi's doorstep, with a small amount of liquor dripping from it. Rose ran to the door, but unfortunately, neither Officer saw her. The case was dismissed with the conflicting reports from the two officers present in the raid.

Meanwhile, Pasqualina Albano Siniscalchi's world shifted when she found herself widowed, inheriting her late husband's business and immediately needing protection from her rivals - the Parisi and Pugliano families of West Springfield. In 1924, she found the perfect person to provide her with the security she sought - Antonino Miranda. Born in San Giuseppe Vesuviano, near Naples, he had previously lived in Manhattan's Little Italy. His family was known for their criminal prowess; his brothers, Michele and Donato Miranda were no exception.

Michele Miranda stayed in the busy streets of New York City, ready to make his mark. He soon became a close associate of Vito Genovese, the notorious head of the Genovese Family, and Frank Costello, earning the title of Consiglieri. This began the loyalty and links of Springfield to the feared Genovese family, the most powerful of New York's five crime families. Vito Genovese went into bootlegging with his childhood friend, Salvatore "Lucky" Luciano, alongside Frank Costello, Gaetano "Tommy" Lucchese, Meyer Lansky, and Benjamin "Bugsy" Siegel. This business venture would soon become a symbol for the Genovese family.

Donato Miranda became a part of the Boston crew, bridging the gap between the Springfield group and both the New York City and local New England Cosa Nostra Families. He kept the peace in Springfield throughout the 1920's, a period of intense violence, an impressive feat in and of itself. His presence brought an air of calm and stability to the area, his words and actions guiding the community into a period of harmony.

Just months later, in the early hours on Bank Street in Waterbury, Connecticut, my cousin John Musolino, alleged to be the head of the local liquor gang, met his demise. John was driving with my brother-in-law, Joseph Marvici, when he was killed. Two years have passed since that fateful night, yet the chilling memories remain forever etched in John's mind.

John stepped out of the Italian social club and was instantly met with a barrage of bullets. Two men had emerged from a nearby doorway, guns blazing. Musolino was struck, and in the blink of an eye, he lay lifeless on the ground in a puddle of blood. The police arrived shortly after, detaining several people in connection with the shooting. After hours of interrogation, all were released, each declaring their innocence. The street was filled with the pungent smell of gunpowder, and the air was thick with shock and disbelief. The police had cordoned off the area with yellow tape, and the people of the neighborhood huddled in small groups, tearfully sharing their accounts of the tragedy.

Musolino had experienced four life-threatening attempts before this one. As he cruised in a car, two men pulled up and opened fire, but none of the bullets hit their mark. Standing on the street, someone shot at him, this time wounding an innocent bystander. His third ordeal happened while he was traveling between Meriden and Waterbury when shots rang out, grazing his ear and killing Joseph Marvici. The fourth try on Musolino's life came in New Haven on July 14th, 1922, when his cousin Alfonzo Cozzo was shot and killed, mistakenly believed by the police to have been intended for Musolino himself.

After the shooting, police gave chase to two men they had seen fleeing the scene. When apprehended, the men told the officers that they had given two men a ride in their car shortly after the shooting. They drove a few blocks, and the two men suddenly jumped out and vanished. The police believe that these men were Ralph Averga and a companion. They scanned the area with flashlights, searching for clues that would lead to the suspects, but their efforts were fruitless. They had to be somewhere, but where? With a sense of urgency, they resumed their pursuit. A revolver with four expended cartridges was found in an alleyway across the street from the scene of the shooting, and a short distance down the street, a second revolver was found.

Musolino expressed several times before he was shot that his life was in danger and four gunmen always accompanied him as bodyguards.

A year and a half after John Musolino's death, Ralph Averga was apprehended in San Francisco in connection with the murder. As the San Francisco police agreed to detain Averga, extradition papers were requested from Springfield. The bustling city streets grew still in the wake of the news, the gravity of the situation settling heavily on the hearts of our family. As the morning chatter dimmed, the only sounds were the heavy footsteps of the police escorting Averga to his cell. As he spoke, Averga's face drained of color, and his solemn pronouncement rang through the air: "I didn't do it." His eyes were wide and pleading, his hands clenched into tight fists at his side as if begging for someone to believe him. The room was still silent except for his words, and it seemed like the entire world was holding its breath. The only thing that could be heard was the sound of Averga's heart pounding against his chest, his fear and anxiety evident. He stood there, waiting for someone to answer, his gaze fixed on the floor, his expression a mix of desperation and despair.

Six months later, my brother's night quickly turned for the worse. The sound of handcuffs clicking shut echoed through the night as they were arrested for their alleged involvement in a brutal assault on West Springfield Police Officer William Hartley. Frank and John Parisi's fists flew like thunder, crashing into Hartley with enough power to send him crashing to the ground. West Side town officials arrived to find him in an unconscious state, Hartley's uniform ripped and his body covered in cuts and bruises, a grim testament to the Parisi's brutality. No one spoke as the men stood over the unconscious form of the officer, a guilty silence hanging in the air.

Hartley's probing questions had riled the group, and each man's fists clenched as John Parisi growled menacingly: "The next man I'm gonna get is the chief of police - and I'm gonna shoot him." The officer's face blanched as he was wheeled away, vowing to report this to his superiors.

John's feet had barely hit the floor of his West Springfield home after bailing out for the officer's assault. The sergeant's authoritative voice cut through the air and shattered the silence. John was soon back in custody, this time for the crime of "threatening to shoot West Side Chief of Police Marshall Belmer." The air around him was tense as he stood on the street corner, surrounded by a group of cops, illuminated by the harsh streetlight. His voice was eerily calm as he retorted, "You don't have the guts to take me in!"

The following month, when the Parisi brothers entered their pleas of "guilty," the town of West Side knew justice would be served.

But as soon as the hearing began, with the first witness on the stand, a figure strode through the courtroom door. All eyes followed Chief Belmer of the West Side police as he made his way to defense counsel. A whispered agreement was struck between the two, and the proceedings abruptly ended with a plea of guilty and just a small fine. The court was filled with a mixture of shock and disbelief as the verdict was declared, the atmosphere a thick, tangible presence. Conversations rose and fell like the waves of the ocean, each one carrying its own unique reaction to the abrupt conclusion of the trial.

District Attorney McKechnie's face was a boiling cauldron of rage when the agreement was finalized. His voice echoed off the room's walls as he clarified that he was not a party to the deal. The Parisi's were each fined only $200 for beating a police officer, and it was too much for Attorney McKechnie to bear. He could not stay silent and immediately called County Commissioner John Hall to share his feelings. His voice was sharp, and his words were strong, making it abundantly clear that he expressed his discontentment with the preferential treatment given to the Parisi's.

Attorney McKechnie, stern yet authoritative, demanded that Commissioner Hall remove Chief Belmer for his part in stopping the trial. He argued that the interruption had likely cost the town the chance to lock away the troublesome Parisi brothers behind bars. The sun shone brightly through the dusty windows of Hall's office, illuminating the tension that had descended upon the room. Hall sat silently, eyebrows furrowed as McKechnie pressed his point. Finally, after what seemed like an eternity, Hall slowly exhaled and nodded in agreement.

The West Springfield county commissioner sent a sharp letter to the board, demanding that Belmer be held accountable for his actions. He charged that the chief set "too cheap a price on crime" and demanded that he be punished for interrupting the trial of John and Frank Parisi last week when the pair were being prosecuted for assault on Officer Hartley. The boardroom was tense as the commissioner read the letter, his voice echoing off the walls. He spoke of Belmer's carelessness, how he had jeopardized the trial, and the need for justice to be served. His words were met with a solemn silence as the members of the board weighed the gravity of Belmer's actions.

The next day, Chairman Walker of the West Springfield Board of Selectmen vehemently defended the chief's "good faith" action regarding the Parisi case. After severe scrutiny, the board found nothing to validate Mr. Hall's claims and thus dismissed his request to remove the chief from office. "We've made sure to inspect the chief's conduct thoroughly," Walker said, emphatically pounding his fist on the desk, "and I'm proud to say that he has passed with flying colors. There is no basis for Mr. Hall's allegations, and I will not stand for such unfounded accusations."

Later that year, eleven jurors, their faces sincere yet determined, had just finished signing a petition to Massachusetts Governor Fuller, requesting my full pardon from the Charleston State Prison. I was convicted of manslaughter, and now, after years of waiting, I would be given a hearing by the Board of Parole. As the last signature was added, the clink of the pen seemed to echo throughout the silent courtroom. I could feel the weight of their conviction, the hope that I would be free soon. Although I had been in prison for many years, I was still filled with optimism, knowing that soon I could be reunited with my family.

Joseph Ely declared his commitment to represent the petitioners, who believed I had done my time in prison. The warden of Charleston prison praised my exemplary behavior while I was there, expressing his desire for me to become a responsible citizen once again. Every day, I strived to make the most of my opportunities and, as a result, earned the respect of the prison staff. My hard work was not going unnoticed.

I nervously sat in front of the parole board, my hopes of an early release resting with them. But as soon as I saw the stern expression on the administrator's face, I knew my request was denied. I felt a heavy weight settle on my shoulders, and my stomach sank. I knew this was the end of the road.

Later on, the Massachusetts State Police and Connecticut Troopers received a tip from an informant: a convoy of vehicles was heading from New York to Springfield with a large load of illegal alcohol. The police set up a roadblock outside Southwick, Massachusetts, but the lead car smashed through. The officers gave chase, but the car was too fast, eventually losing them in Feeding Hills. The other three cars weren't so lucky; as the troopers rushed towards them, the occupants scattered, trying to flee the scene.

"Big Nose" Sam Cufari's truck roared down the street, the 150 gallons of alcohol rattling and sloshing in the back. A blast from a shotgun rang out from the nearby police, causing Cufari to screech to a halt. Gunfire erupted from the officers, bullets whizzing in the air as the men scrambled for cover. Cufari, his arms bleeding from the shots, was given first aid and rushed to Wesson Memorial Hospital, where he was placed under guard. Those arrested with

Cufari were Abe Steele, Nick Camerotta, Joseph Mineo, Angelo Pasquale, and Arthur Sarno, all of Springfield.

The river was alive with the illicit business of bootlegging. On both sides of the river, the city was bustling with the roar of cars and the clinking of glass bottles. Despite the strict laws of Prohibition, business was booming. Conversations were hushed, but the thrill of the illegal activity was intense. The smell of whiskey hung in the air as people ventured out into other rackets, the scent of money and success driving them to take risks. The streets were lined with shady characters, bargaining and trading for their next big score. "You looking to make some money?" a voice asked from the shadows. The city was alive with the promise of opportunity, and no one was about to let Prohibition get in the way.

As I stepped out of the prison gates on March 29, 1927, the feeling of freedom washed over me. The sun seemed brighter, the air seemed fresher, and I could finally breathe in the day's freshness. After being locked away from the world for five and a half years, I was finally free. I felt like I had been reborn. Walking along the path, I couldn't help but take in my surroundings. The sound of birds chirping, the smell of flowers, the sight of trees, and the feeling of the warm sun on my skin. I was ready to start my new life, even if I'd still be on parole for the next six years. I smiled to myself as I thought about the future. I was ready to make a new start. This was a new beginning, and I was determined to make the most of it.

As I made my way out of the prison, I could see my family waiting for me on the other side. My wife, Rafaela, had tears streaming down her face while my children jumped up and down in excitement. I opened my arms wide, and they all rushed into my embrace. The reunion was filled with laughter, joy, and a renewed sense of hope. I was finally reunited with my family and couldn't have been more thankful.

Three years later, in 1930, a year after the stock market crash and the beginning of the Great Depression, my defense Attorney, Joseph B. Ely, was elected the Commonwealth's first Democratic governor in 14 years and only the fourth in 40 years. He was the "wet" candidate, promising to fight for the lifting of Prohibition laws and to accelerate public works projects. Ely won two terms as Massachusetts's governor but declined the chance to run for a third, saying people should see new faces in public office.

On March 29, 1933, I felt a sense of liberation and accomplishment as the Executive Council of Boston granted me a full pardon with a unanimous vote at the request of Governor Joseph Ely. I watched in awe as the votes were tallied - each more affirmative than the last - until finally, the vote was unanimous. I was overwhelmed with jubilation as the Governor presented me with my pardon papers. I had to pinch myself as I stared at the document representing my freedom.

I was grateful as I thanked Governor Ely, my close friend, and the Council members for their unanimous decision. I knew this moment would open up a new chapter in my life. As I walked out of the chamber, I couldn't help but feel the weight of the world lifted off my shoulders.

I could finally take a deep breath as my six years of parole conditions ended. To celebrate the momentous occasion, I filled out my second citizenship papers.

Parisi Says He Is "Victim Of a Cruel Circumstance"

Man Convicted of Manslaughter in Connection With Death of "King of Little Italy" Declares He Will Emerge From Prison a "Better American"—Thanks The Daily News and The Republican for Fairness in Reporting Trial

Flowers Cover Grave of Antonio Miranda Whose Elaborate Funeral Drew Throngs

Photo shows the flower-covered grave in which the body of Antonio Miranda was laid yesterday, in the same lot with that of the murdered Carlos Siniscalchi, reputed "king of bootleggers." Miranda married Siniscalchi's widow and is said to have succeeded to much of his prestige in the local colony. The flowers alone are said to have cost $20,000.

Governor of Massachusetts, Joseph B. Ely

SLAYER THAT ELY DEFENDED IS GIVEN PARDON BY STATE

Joseph Parisi Wants to Get Second Citizenship Papers —Ely's Plea to Jury in Siniscalchi Case Recalled

Pasqualina "Taken for a Ride"

For some peculiar reason, Fiore lingered at the house's front door, talking to Mrs. Giannini. He was about to slip into their car when he noticed a sleek, expensive sedan sitting in complete darkness at the top of the Worthington Street hill. As the vehicle slowly emerged from the shadows, Fiore could see the glint of its windows in the moonlight. He hesitated, taking his hand off the door handle, and took a few steps back.

12

P asqualina Albano was born in Bracigliano, Italy, in 1889, arriving in Springfield, Massachusetts, with her parents, Luigi Albano and Francesca Izzo, and her older brother, Antonio Albano, in 1890. They settled in their new home on Union Street in Springfield, subsequently having three more daughters, Annina, Josephine, and Rose.

Pasqualina, barely 21, married Carluccio "Carlo" Siniscalchi on September 26, 1912. The newlywed couple made a home for themselves on Water Street in the South End section of Springfield. Over the years, their family grew to include five children: Carlo, Angela, Rose, Theodore, and Gloria.

In 1917, Pasqualina and her husband Carlo Siniscalchi inherited the family's liquor business from her late uncle John Albano and his son Felix. But when the prohibition of 1920 struck, they decided to take a risk and continue selling illicit alcohol. Before long, Carlo had earned the notorious title of "King of Bootleggers." Carlo's rise to power was swift and merciless as he led his gang of bootleggers through the city streets, delivering alcohol to the speakeasies with a knowing smirk.

Pasqualina's world was turned upside down in 1921 when Joseph Parisi's cruel and merciless violence snuffed out the life of

Carlo Siniscalchi. The icy grip of terror left her to bear the weight of the family business alone.

In 1924, Pasqualina quietly married Antonio Miranda in a small ceremony conducted by a justice of the peace in the Thompsonville section of Enfield, Connecticut. Soon enough, in 1928, Pasqualina and Antonio welcomed their only child, Vincent, into the world.

Antonio and Pasqualina continue to run Carlo's bootlegging operation in Springfield until a minor procedure to remove a callus from his foot left Antonio with a deadly case of blood poisoning. His skin began to discolor, turning a sickly shade of green, and the smell of death hung heavy in the air. Vincent and Pasqualina stayed by his side until the very end, Vincent's eyes wet with tears. The gangrene slowly took his life on February 6th, 1930, and he was laid to rest in St. Michaels Cemetery. They said their final goodbyes, Vincent's voice shaking with emotion, and watched as his father's casket was taken away. They watched until the cemetery gates closed behind them, and the weight of his death settled heavily on their shoulders.

Hundreds of mourners somberly filled Our Lady of Mount Carmel church, their presence a testament to Antonio's life. An abundance of floral tributes, sent from as far away as San Francisco and Miami, were valued between $15-20k. The sheer amount of flowers was so overwhelming that the scent of gardenias, roses, and lilies perfumed the air. Antonio is known as an affluent but not flashy real estate agent. Still, the newspapers completely overlooked his significance in organized crime, a detail that seemed to be common knowledge amongst his associates. As the attendees filed out of the church, they nodded and whispered to one another, exchanging stories of Antonio's life.

Pasqualina, now a two-time widow, then chose Michael Fiore, a 34-year-old Italian immigrant, to step into a leadership role to help run her flourishing enterprise.

Michael Fiore is the brother of Vincenzo Fiore, who is married to Pasqualina's sister, Anna Albano. Michael's resume included an attempted murder of Dominick Perrotti in Connecticut and the knifing of a police officer in Springfield.

Pasqualina Siniscalchi-Miranda had taken a stranglehold of the bootleg industry in Springfield, her iron fist of tyranny crushing all who dared to stand up to her. With her first and second husband's untimely deaths, she had become the undisputed "Queen of Bootlegging," her reign was absolute. Her unyielding rule refused to falter as whispers of rebellion began to echo throughout the underworld.

"She's the one in charge, no matter what anyone says," one bootlegger said to another, shaking his head.

The oppressive atmosphere was thick, the air heavy with the scent of fear. Pasqualina had set herself up as a dictator, enduring the dissatisfaction of many, her word the only one that mattered. Nobody dared speak out against her. None of them wanted to be the one to risk angering Pasqualina. They knew what happened to those who crossed her.

Pasqualina and her crew had been accused of a series of holdups and hijacking capers in the city. Over the past several months, fourteen speakeasies had been robbed, with one resulting in the murder of the owner. The police had come knocking on her door several days ago, and she had been questioned in connection with the robberies. She could feel the weight of their gaze upon her, cold and accusing. "Mrs. Miranda," one of the officers said, his voice heavy with suspicion, "we believe you may have had something to do with these robberies."

Mrs. Miranda held her head high though her heart hammered in her chest. "I don't know what you're talking about," she said, her voice wavering ever so slightly.

The officers exchanged glances and then looked back at her. "We'll be keeping an eye on you," one said. They turned and left, leaving Mrs. Miranda standing there, the room's silence uncomfortable.

Michael Fiore, Pasqualina's alleged sweetheart and trusted lieutenant, had aspirations of becoming the "king" of the local bootlegging gang. This evidently did not sit well with some, including her late husband's brother, Michael Miranda, of the Genovese Crime Family in New York. His bold moves threatened the status quo, bringing on a wave of fear and uncertainty.

That autumn night on November 12, 1932, was illuminated by the stars above as Pasqualina and her business partner, Michael Fiore, drove up to Giannini's home on Worthington Street, Springfield. Mr. and Mrs. Domenico Giannini had invited Pasqualina to help plan something special for their upcoming 12th wedding anniversary. Fiore had been "keeping company" with Mrs. Miranda for some time. The car pulled across the street from the house, parking in the alley alongside the post office garage. It was 10:20 pm when they stepped out of the vehicle and headed to the warmly lit home. They were welcomed eagerly by the Giannini's, who were delighted to have them there, and together, they discussed the plans for the anniversary celebration.

Pasqualina walked out of the house first at the stroke of midnight, her footsteps echoing in the dead stillness of the street. She shivered in the cold night air, her breath misting before her face as she crossed to her car. Gripping the key tightly, she unlocked the sedan, slipping inside and starting the motor. The sudden roar startled her, the exhaust fumes billowing in the air as she pulled out of the alley, swung the car westward, and turned to the curb as if to park. She rolled to a stop under a streetlight, motionless except for the rhythmic tapping of her fingers on the steering wheel. It seemed like an eternity as she waited for Michael Fiore to appear.

For some peculiar reason, Fiore lingered at the house's front door, talking to Mrs. Giannini. After saying goodbye, he took one last step off the porch, and his foot met the cold concrete of the driveway. He was about to slip into their car when he noticed a sleek, expensive sedan sitting in complete darkness at the top of the Worthington Street hill. As the vehicle slowly emerged from the shadows, Fiore could see the glint of its windows in the moonlight. He hesitated, taking his hand off the door handle, and took a few steps back.

The sedan crept alongside the Miranda car as it sat idling, its headlights still out. It drew so close that its fenders scraped against it. The driver of the sedan was taking no chances to let Pasqualina escape. In an instant, two shotguns and an automatic pistol appeared from the drawn curtains. The menacing weapons glowed in the moonlight; their barrels pointed towards the Miranda car. The air was tense as the sedan driver pinned Pasqualina to the curb.

Suddenly, the men let loose a hail of lead, the thundering echoes of the guns reverberating through the air. Bullets pounded the driver's side window, shattering it into a million pieces and leaving gaping holes in the windshield.

The relentless barrage of shots tore apart Pasqualina's body. Bloodied and mangled, her left ear was nearly blown off, her eye ripped out, and several slugs embedded in her neck. Her left cheek was mutilated by the force of the bullets, leaving a gaping wound that stretched from her ear to her chin. The air was heavy with the smell of gunpowder, and Pasqualina's agonizing screams pierced through the darkness. She begged for mercy, her voice trembling, as she pleaded for her life. But it was too late; the bullets had already done their job.

Michael Fiore had been just mere steps from the car when the attack occurred. He felt the searing pain of a stray bullet in his left elbow as he frantically scrambled further away from the vehicle. Shards of glass rained down on him, slicing his face as the windshield shattered. Miraculously, he had escaped with only minor wounds despite the killers having ample time to riddle him with bullets just as they had done to Pasqualina. How Fiore had managed to survive remains a mystery.

The bullets flew by with a ferocity that sent a chill down the spine of a neighbor who happened to be up at the time, though their home had no view of the scene. The sound of the shots, too fast to be counted, echoed through the night air.

Harold Lord, a postal employee from Irving Street in West Springfield, had just started walking towards the post office garage when he heard a loud bang. He assumed it was the backfire of an automobile until he saw a blaze of shots erupting from the direction of the sound. He stopped in his tracks, and a feeling of dread washed over him as he realized what was happening. He could feel the shockwaves from the gunshots, and the smell of gunpowder hung heavy in the air. He heard the cries of terror from Fiore as he scrambled to get away from the scene. Harold stood in disbelief, unable to understand what he had just seen.

John Bradley stumbled upon the gruesome scene, a black sedan illuminated by the streetlight, now riddled with bullet holes. He heard the shots and felt the repercussions in the air - a spray of leaden hail that tore through Mrs. Miranda's car. Five men rode in the sizable sedan, the moonlight reflecting off the barrels of their two shotguns. The tires screeched as the murder car sped away toward West Springfield, the headlights off, leaving the two witnesses in the dark and unable to catch the registration number.

The police arrived on the scene to a gruesome sight - the unmistakable intent of the gunmen was abundantly clear. Mrs. Siniscalchi's bullet-riddled body lay sprawled across the front seat, her one remaining eye staring blankly into eternity. Blood was pooled around her, and the car was peppered with bullet holes. The "boyfriend," Fiore, standing on the corner, was unharmed. It was clear that the gunmen had only one target.

More officers arrived, their eyes immediately drawn to the car - penetrated with bullet holes, the windshield a web of shattered glass. They exchanged uneasy glances, the tension in the air almost spiking. "Must have been a machine gun," one of them muttered.

"No, it was an automatic," another countered. A cluster of holes in the windshield bore some evidence of the number of bullets fired.

The neighbors paced around the vehicle, chattering in their melodic native Italian, their hands flailing through the air as they spoke. When asked if they had any knowledge of the shooting, they clammed up, barely meeting each other's eyes. The oppressive silence that seemed to linger in the air was only broken by the distant sound of sirens.

John Bradley felt an icy shiver of fear run through his veins as he stepped forward to talk to the cops. He was one of the only two who had witnessed the gruesome shooting, and he had to tell them what he saw. John's voice shook as he recounted the details to the police. "It happened so fast. I just wanted to get out of there."

He watched in horror as the guns were raised and fired with a deafening roar that echoed through the street. He could still feel the shockwaves reverberating through the air and almost taste the acrid smell of gunpowder. "It was terrible," he said, his voice trembling. "I saw the blood splatter all over the windshield, and I heard the screams of terror from the woman inside. I thought I was going to die." John swallowed hard and then continued. "I saw the shooters. They had cold, emotionless faces, and their hands were steady as they pulled the triggers. I'll never forget it."

The cops looked at John intently, their faces grim. They thanked him for his bravery and for coming forward. John was relieved that he'd been able to share what he saw, but he knew the image of the shooting would stay with him forever. He was still trembling when he finished his statement.

There is no record of the Giannini's being questioned by the police, although they were on the porch during the ambush.

The police hustled around the crime scene, their flashlights scanning the ground for any clues that might help their cause. A few stray bullets marred the garage wall, and even the roof was checked in case some slugs ricocheted upward. "I need to search for more clues," one officer said, shining his flashlight against the walls.

The other nodded, his flashlight darting around the area. "I'll search up top," he declared, taking to the roof. The first officer continued his search, methodically checking every corner and crevice, looking for anything that might help them solve the case.

The car, pock-marked with the evidence of the gunfire, now sits in the post office garage. None of them could agree on a motive, but the damage was done - a stark reminder of the violence that had occurred.

The following day, my eyes slowly opened, and the sound of pounding on my front door jolted me out of my slumber. "Open up," a voice bellowed from outside, "Police!"

I cautiously opened the door and was met with a pair of stern faces. "Where were you last night around midnight?" they asked.

I glanced next to their feet at the newspaper lying on my front stoop. The headline read, "Queen of Bootlegging, Pasqualina Siniscalchi-Miranda, Murdered Last Night." I tried to keep my voice steady as I told them I was in bed with my wife, Raffaela.

Doubt flickered in their eyes as they stood there, and I could sense the questions they weren't asking out loud. "Can you prove it?" they finally said.

I felt my stomach tighten as I tried to think of something to say that would convince them, but before I could find anything, they stepped back off the stoop and left.

Headlines blared across the country, her violent murder making front page news. It was an unprecedented event in the state of Massachusetts, with organized crime rarely putting a hit on a woman. Shockwaves rippled through the community, and people crowded in subdued conversations, whispering about the tragedy.

A bundle of newspapers from *The Boston Herald* hit the ground with a loud thud, its pages rustling in the wind. The headlines screamed of the latest news, informing and captivating the city's inhabitants. "Woman Killed By Machine Gun Fire!" the vendor shouted, trying to garner the attention of the passersby's. He waved the paper in the air as if painting the news in vivid colors. His words echoed off the buildings, reaching far and wide. People stopped to listen, eager to hear what the *Herald* had to say.

"A woman was killed and her companion critically wounded by machine gun fire from a passing automobile in what police describe as a gang outbreak on upper Worthington Street early today. No reason for the crime had been discovered at 2 am. Jealousy or a quarrel over racket dealings were advanced as possible theories. Witnesses said a heavy sedan with drawn curtains was driven close to the Fiore car. Machine gun bullets raked the back seat of the parked automobile."

The Rockford Register-Republic of Illinois reported with a jolt, the news rippling through the small town like a clap of thunder. "Massachusetts Woman 'Put On Spot,' Slain." Eyes wide, the citizens hurried to the paper, eager to read the latest developments. Conversations crackled and hummed as neighbors shared their opinions, their reactions ranging from shock to outrage.

"Lead from a gangster's machine gun today killed Mrs. Pasqualina Miranda and wounded her companion, Michael Fiore, as they were sitting in a parked automobile. She was the first woman ever 'put on the spot' in Massachusetts. Ten years ago, Mrs. Miranda's first husband, Carlo Siniscalchi, an alleged bootlegger, was 'bumped off' by Joseph Parisi. The killers of Mrs. Miranda sped away in the sedan."

"Did you hear the news?" asked one commuter to their neighbor.

"No, what is it?"

"*The Albany Times Union's* got an amazing story out today. Let's have a look!" The two of them stopped and quickly skimmed the headlines. "Liquor Queen 'Put On Spot;' Partner Shot." Their eyes widened in surprise as they read about the latest events to have taken place.

"Springfield's "Queen of Bootleggers" was "put on the spot" as a reprisal for a series of speakeasy holdups and liquor hijackings. This was the theory police worked on as they sought a motive for the slaying of Mrs. Pasqualina Miranda, the wealthy widow of two men who were both bumped off and who herself was a victim of gangland's wrath when her body was riddled with shotgun slugs fired from a passing automobile."

The Springfield Republican reported with a booming voice that shook the city streets, reverberating an impact that could not be ignored. "Mrs. Miranda Shot in Auto on Worthington St."

"Mrs. Pasqualina Siniscalchi Miranda was shot and instantly killed this morning at about 12:10 am while she sat in her automobile by the side of the road across from the post office garage at 781 Worthington Street. Michael Fiore, who was near the automobile at the time, is at Wesson Memorial Hospital with a gunshot wound in his left arm and his face cut in several places by glass. Mrs. Miranda was the widow of Antonio Miranda. Her first husband, Carlo Siniscalchi, was murdered by Giuseppe Parisi of 52 Sprague Street, West Springfield, as the former sat in his automobile on Main Street, near Union Street, on the afternoon of December 20, 1921. Parisi was defended by Attorney Joseph B. Ely, now Governor of the Commonwealth of Massachusetts." The last line read, "The whereabouts of Parisi is unknown."

The body of Pasqualina was brought from the undertakers to her home the previous evening. The door creaked open, and two men cautiously carried in the body of the woman, shrouded in a white sheet. The stillness of the night was interrupted by the sound of their footsteps as they trod carefully up the stairs. The men laid her down in the center of the room, and a solemn silence descended. The only thing that could be heard was the clock ticking, marking the passing of time until the funeral. The air was thick with grief, and the moonlight shone through the window, casting a pale light on the body that lay in repose in the late woman's home.

Old friends and relatives trickled in, forming a solemn line outside the Chestnut Street home. Through the door, a plain bronze casket was visible, Mrs. Miranda's final resting place. A modest floral wreath hung on the entrance, the only adornment in an otherwise somber space. Soft sobs could be heard, followed by a chorus of comforting words. As the hours passed, the line of visitors grew shorter until, finally, the home was empty again. The aura of Mrs. Miranda was still detectable, a reminder of the dangerous existence she had endured and the casualties she had abandoned in her wake.

There was no sign that her funeral would be as lavish as the funerals of her two late husbands, one of whom was killed ten years ago and the other who died in 1930. At Antonio Miranda's funeral in 1930, twenty-three cars were bearing floral tributes, while thirty others carried guests from several cities and towns in the East.

State prison officials in Connecticut were convinced that Michael Fiore, her ex-convict companion at the time of the killing, was somehow involved and in Springfield "for a purpose."

Warden Charles Reed told reporters, "According to the 'prison grapevine,' the same men, leaders of a rival Parisi gang active in control of liquor running in West Springfield, had put the first husband of the Miranda woman, Carlo Siniscalchi, 'on the spot.' These same men had dealt likewise with Fiore's brother several years ago." His voice boomed as he recounted the rumors of Fiore's mission. He leaned forward in his chair, his eyes intense as he finished his sentence. The room was filled with a heavy silence as everyone present was left to ponder the implications of the warden's words.

"On October 7, 1920, Michael Fiore was convicted of a heinous crime - assault with intent to murder a man from New Haven, Connecticut. The man had been shot and was left seriously wounded. As a result, Fiore was sentenced to twelve years in the Wethersfield prison. Fiore was finally released on May 21, 1932, but not without a fight. He was supposed to be paroled before the end of his sentence," prison officials commented grimly, "but he had trouble with the warden, as a result of which he was required to remain in custody for two years longer."

The oppressive stillness of gangland shrouded the search for the killers of Mrs. Pasqualina Siniscalchi-Miranda, the air thick with unspoken secrets. Even the investigators' footsteps echoed through the darkness as if the criminals were determined to remain hidden. The detectives exchanged uneasy glances, feeling the weight of the silence that seemed to be daring them to uncover the truth. They heard only the distant rumble of the city and the occasional eerie caw of a crow as if the criminal underworld were a living being determined to guard its secrets. The detectives grew frustrated; their questions met with a deafening silence. Even their informants could not provide any useful information, as if the gangsters had imposed a code of silence that could not be broken.

Meanwhile, Michael Fiore lays in a bed at Wesson Memorial Hospital, his arm bandaged and covered in a cast that was a telltale sign of the gunshot wound in his elbow. Technically, he was under arrest, although no charge had been placed against him, and a police guard had been stationed at his bedside since his admittance to the infirmary to ensure he had no contact with the outside world. The detectives had questioned him at length, but his unwillingness to cooperate had put their investigation of the cold-blooded murder of Mrs. Pasqualina Siniscalchi-Miranda, reputed "queen" of the local bootleggers and associated groups, on hold. He had refused to offer any information that might put them on the track of the slayers, who had made their getaway in a large sedan.

Because of the type of business Mrs. Miranda was involved in, no motive for the killing has been found by the police, who say that one guess is as good as another. Despite her recent financial difficulties, she was once reputed to be wealthy. Unfortunately, the car in which she met her death had been repossessed by Commissioner Lynch's automobile agency due to her failure to make payments. For two months, the sedan was in their possession before it was returned to her, and it is believed that she was still behind on her payments at the time of her death.

The police carefully examined the bullet-ridden automobile before conducting an autopsy to conclude that the killers had not used a machine gun but instead sawed-off shotguns and an automatic pistol. The officers, in a somber tone, reported that the shooting occurred at an extremely close range. The scene was one of utter devastation, with metal shards strewn across the pavement and blood splattered across the car's interior. People in the area, still in shock, could only describe the sound of the gunshots as deafening, leaving an eerie silence afterward. One witness spoke of the intensity of the moments, "It felt like the world had stopped."

Mrs. Miranda's autopsy was a grisly sight. The coroner concluded that the fatal injury was a compound fracture of the skull caused by gunshots. Four double-O buckshots were extracted from her neck. Evidence of sawed-off shotguns and an automatic pistol at the crime scene showed that multiple assailants had used these weapons. The room was thick with the smell of cordite and the grim reminder of violence. Mrs. Miranda's body lay motionless on the cold steel table, a stark testament to the brutality of this act. In the silence of the room, the coroner spoke solemnly. "It looks like we have a mob hit on our hands."

Police pounded the pavement, dead-set on tracking down the culprits responsible for the attempted hit on Mrs. Miranda. Probably imported from the gritty streets of New York City, the gunmen had arrived with a direct order to put Mrs. Miranda "on the spot." But no matter how hard the detectives worked, they were up against a stonewall. Not a single lead could be found to help them get any closer to finding the culprits. Fiore was with Pasqualina every step of the way, but it was clear he wasn't the target of the gunmen's mission. The same chance to shoot him as they had her was there, but it seemed they had a different plan.

Still, detectives continued their search, determined to bring the gunmen to justice.

Fiore's response to the detectives' questioning was confused and forgetful. His answers were short and almost monotone - "I don't know. I don't remember." His eyes darted around the small hospital room, searching for a way to escape the relentless interrogation. He shook his head in disbelief, unable to recognize the men or recall how many were in the car. He was at a loss for words when asked for a motive for the killing, his shoulders slumping in defeat. The detectives stared him down, their sharp eyes never leaving Fiore's face as he struggled to answer their questions.

The entire detective bureau was out in full force, scouring the scene for clues to the possible hijacking angle in the killing. Rumors were swirling of a "split" in certain circles months ago, a possible motive for the crime. Everywhere they looked, the detectives were met with a silence that seemed to hang in the air, the only sound the rustling of the wind through the trees and the tapping of their shoes as they combed the area. Every minute detail was examined and logged, every bit of evidence recorded; a single piece of information could be the key to unlocking the mystery of the killing.

Finally, after hours of searching, one of the detectives stepped forward and said, "We need to find out who was involved in this 'split.' That may be our best hope of finding out why this happened." Everyone nodded in agreement, and the detectives chased down that angle.

Deputy Chief Fleming and Captain of Detectives Daniel McCarthy met after one of the "dog watch" officers reported that five Italians had come into Springfield during the night and registered at the Hayne's Hotel. To investigate more, the two decided to send a squad of detectives to the hotel. When the detectives arrived, the sun had just been tucked away, leaving behind a sky of deep navy. The hotel was illuminated by its bright red neon sign, which only brought any light to the otherwise dark street. They could hear the Italians' faint chatter coming from the hotel's open windows.

"What do you think we'll find in there?" McCarthy asked Fleming, gazing up at the hotel.

"Let's go find out," Fleming replied, leading the way inside.

The detectives knocked and inserted their passkeys into the locks simultaneously, the doors creaking open just in time for the occupants to realize what was happening. As the detectives stepped into the rooms, the scene that unfolded before them was one of surprise. "This is the police!" one of the detectives yelled as he stepped into the room, making sure all the occupants knew why they were there.

Lieutenant William Lonergan and Sergeant Victor Tetreault entered another room occupied by Salvatore Celembrino and his companion. Their eyes were met with a fully loaded revolver resting ominously on a chair near the bed on Celembrino's side.

No resistance was offered by the New Yorkers, who willingly went with the officers to headquarters. Four of the men taken into custody by police as suspicious characters were released when word was received from the New York City police department saying they were not wanted. The fifth man, Salvatore Celembrino, was in the consultation room of the detective bureau when questioned in detail. Celembrino reluctantly admitted that the gun was his. But he was duly booked for the violation without a permit to carry the weapon. He was released on bail to later answer to a charge of carrying a loaded revolver.

Fiore was now the only one actually in custody, a grim reminder of the slaying that had taken place. Police diligently followed every lead, expecting to take them across state lines to New York.

Mrs. Pasqualina Siniscalchi-Miranda, the recognized "queen" of a bootlegging gang, was honored with a far humbler funeral than that of her late husband, who had met a similar fate. The mourners gathered in the chilly autumn air, all standing in respectful silence as the priest intoned the final rites. The two hundred or more mourners gathered solemnly and respectfully on November 15, 1932, displaying the utmost decorum. The atmosphere was still and quiet; the only sound was the shuffling of feet and the occasional muted sob. The Springfield detective bureau was on hand, their police vehicle parked discreetly on the periphery in case of any emotional outbursts. Fortunately, no violence was seen, and the funeral went ahead in an orderly and dignified manner.

The mourners crowded into Mount Carmel Church, a wall of sound enveloping the room as the majority of the attendees – women and children – sobbed and wailed. Nothing compared to the funeral of her first husband, Carlo Siniscalchi, who was shot to death in his car in the South End eleven years ago. Nor was it as grand as the funeral of her second spouse, Antonio Miranda, who had passed away two years ago from what was described as gangrene poisoning. But the size of the funeral was enough to fill the room.

The soft rumbling of the forty funeral cars filled the air as they slowly drove along the winding road. Sunlight glinted off the countless floral tributes packed tightly into five open vehicles. Mourners from far and wide had gathered, some coming from as far away as New York City, Boston, and Philadelphia.

Eight sturdy pallbearers struggled to carry the heavy bronze coffin with Mrs. Miranda's body inside. Frank Capaccio, Thomas

Santaniello, Antonio Daniele, Alphonso Albano, John Albano, Carmino Albano, Louis Cooper, and John McCarthy shuffled forward one step at a time; their faces strained with effort as they grunted and heaved. The coffin seemed to press down more heavily with each step, the metal creaking as it swayed side to side. The air seemed filled with grief as the mourners silently followed, a sad procession in the frigid fall chill.

The church was filled to the brim, with people standing in the aisles and the lines stretching into the corridor. When the coffin was finally carried out, a large crowd had formed outside, lining both sides of William Street. As the mourners got into their vehicles, their silent tears betrayed the gravity of the situation, and the crowd watched in respectful silence. The atmosphere was thick with emotion, and the sound of sniffles and sobs echoed through the air.

The silence of the cemetery was broken by the solemn chanting of the high mass as Reverend Richard Zambiasi led the service with respectful reverence. Reverend Joseph Costi stood by his side as deacon, while Reverend Valentinelli served as subdeacon. The sun shone brightly through the church's stained glass windows, casting a beautiful prism of light onto the congregation. As Father Zambiasi read the committal service, the strong scent of incense filled the air, and the mourners bowed their heads in reverence. The service concluded with a moment of silence before the mourners left the cemetery, each leaving with a heavy heart. Father Zambiasi stood alone over the grave, offering a final prayer before leaving.

While the long entourage was slowly making its way down the street to St. Michael's Cemetery, surgeons at the Wesson Memorial Hospital worked tirelessly to extract a .38 caliber bullet from Michael Fiore's shattered elbow. With a sickening crunch, the bullet was finally removed, and Michael's arm was left limp and crippled for the rest of his life. The bullet was handed off to the state ballistic expert, and the consequences of the tragedy hung in the air. "I can't believe this is happening," Michael whispered, his voice raw with emotion. The scene was a grim reminder of how quickly life can change, and the bullet was a silent testament to the power of violence.

Michael Fiore was being held under heavy guard at Wesson Memorial Hospital, with no visitors allowed in his room, which a police officer constantly watched over. Deputy Chief of Police John Fleming was overseeing the search for the assassins, and anyone wishing to visit the wounded man had to go through him first. The atmosphere outside his room was tense, the air thick with anticipation as the police guard vigilantly scanned the hallway. There was a heavy sense of security in the air, and it was clear that no one could get anywhere near Michael Fiore without first being cleared by the Deputy Chief of Police. John Fleming stood at the entrance to the room, arms crossed, his stern voice ringing in the hallways as he spoke to each visitor. "No one is allowed in here without my approval. This is a matter of utmost importance, and I will not allow any visitors in until we have captured the assassins."

The underworld was abuzz, rife with speculation of who would take the dubious mantle of Mrs. Miranda, the leader of the local bootlegging and racketeering enterprises. Many believed that Fiore, with his close ties to the woman and her illicit activities, was the likely candidate for her successor. Others were sure he would opt for a more relaxed lifestyle in retirement. Fiore, now in the hospital, was fearful that the woman's assassins would murder him the moment he walked out the doors. He could feel the air of anticipation, a sense of dread, hovering around him. Even his attempts at conversation were met with silence, as though the mere mention of Mrs. Miranda's name was enough to bring the wrath of her killers down upon them.

To ensure justice is served, he has been detained until the mysterious gang war shooting is resolved. The police garage is home to the bullet-ridden car, a grim reminder of the tragedy, covered with a canvas and warning signs telling people to keep away from it. Meanwhile, photographs of the slain woman, taken at the scene of the shooting and the morgue, are kept for evidence. The pungent smell of gunpowder still lingers in the air, a reminder of the violence that had just taken place. As the officers discuss the grim details, their voices echo in the silence, a reminder of the gravity of the situation.

Pasqualina had placed her trust in Michael Fiore, never suspecting his hidden agenda to take over as the leader of her bootlegging empire.

MRS ANTONIO MIRANDO

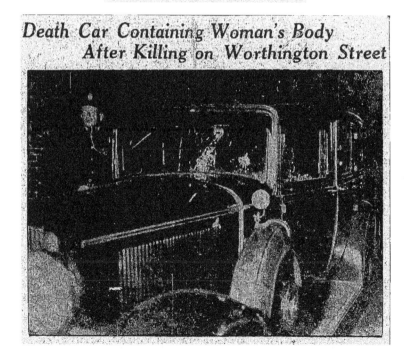

Death Car Containing Woman's Body
After Killing on Worthington Street

Scenes at the Funeral of Mrs Pasqualina (Siniscalchi) Miranda, Victim of Gangsters

Top view shows body being removed from the attractive Miranda home on Chestnut street. Lower view, crowd of curious people watching the body of murdered woman being taken into Mount Carmel church.

Barbershop Slaying

"*Pasqualina was dead and out of their way. She had been warned to keep out of the liquor racket, but following Fiore's advice, she became too active and knew too much. What Miranda didn't expect was Michael Fiore slipping his way in and trying to take control.*"

-GIUSEPPE "JOSEPH" PARISI

13

M ichael Fiore walked out of his house, as he always did, precisely at noon. He made a beeline for the shop, a three-chair establishment, and took his usual seat. Antonio Basile, the barber, immediately started snipping away at his hair. Just as the clippers had started buzzing, Dominic Resigno entered. He wandered to the left side of the front door and settled in the waiting chair. Alphonse Iennaco, the shop owner, sat beside Resigno and eagerly awaited the translation of the newspaper Dominic had brought. The conversation between the two old friends was lively and full of laughter. Dominic's Italian accent was thick, and his hands gesticulated expressively as he spoke. Meanwhile, the clippers kept their steady rhythm, adding to the shop's atmosphere.

Fiore had opted to remain in Springfield, at his brother's home on Union Street, rather than steal away quietly to hide from his enemies. He felt he would be safer here than elsewhere. Little did he know his mistake would come in the form of habit. Every week, he'd make a point to visit the South End barbershop on Columbus Avenue three times a week, at the same time of day. His enemies quickly caught wind of this routine, and during one of his visits, they came to seek vengeance.

As two men barely over thirty years old approached him, he could feel the tension radiating from them. The taller one spoke, his voice low and strained.

"Hello, Mike," he said, his gaze shifting around the room as they shook hands.

Fiore watched in the mirror as the other man slid around the chair, trapping him between the two of them. Basile, the barber, continued to trim the back of Fiore's head, seemingly unaware of the danger. Suddenly, Basile spotted something in the corner of the mirror - the smaller man had drawn a large black gun from under his coat. His stomach dropped as his eyes widened in horror. Fiore tried to move, but the men had cornered him in the chair. He was at their mercy.

Fiore lurched, his eyes widening in terror as the first gunshot exploded from the gun. The slug hissed as it flew through the air, leaving a trail of smoke behind it, slicing his throat open in a sickening six-inch gash. His body slid out of the chair on his back and hit the floor with a thud as Basile and Iennaco sprinted out the door. Desperately, Fiore clawed his way on his hands and knees towards the back of the shop, trying to escape his killers. But the assassins tracked his movements, their steps measured and unhurried, following him to the room at the back.

Resigno lunged forward, attempting to intervene, when a loud bang echoed through the air. His body staggered, and he felt a searing pain shoot through his abdomen. He collapsed to the ground, the smell of gunpowder pungent in the air. He heard the screams of terrified bystanders, and he shut his eyes tight, wishing it were all just a bad dream.

Michael Fiore lay on the floor, his trembling arms weakly reaching up in a plea for mercy. But his pleas were silenced with a single, tragic shot. It tore into his chest, piercing his heart and lodging in the base of his spine. His murderers, their faces twisted in cold indifference, calmly left the building, drove away in a waiting car, and disappeared.

When the mob decides it's time for you to go, they put you "on the spot."

Resigno, tears streaming down his face, stumbled to the corner of Union Street. There, Officer Michael Curley, shouting orders to the traffic, was stunned to see the man collapse into his arms. The sirens of the police ambulance wailed as it raced to the scene, and Resigno was rushed to the Wesson Memorial Hospital.

Thomas Denardo, a special police officer, was one of the first to arrive at Iennaco's Barber Shop. He had been drinking coffee at a café at the corner of Columbus Avenue and Union Street when he heard the loud and unmistakable sound of gunshots. Racing to the scene, he was soon followed by Patrolmen Hallahan and Curley. The street was abuzz with the news that somebody had been shot, and as Denardo stepped closer to the barbershop, he could feel the tension in the air. He was met with the faint smell of gunpowder and a thick silence he could feel in his bones. He slowly opened the door and stepped inside, only to be confronted with the gruesome scene. He could see the lifeless body of Fiore sprawled on the floor, encircled by a pool of blood. He felt his stomach churn with nausea, and he could hear Patrolmen Hallahan and Curley taking in a collective breath of shock.

The detectives surveyed the scene, observing the telltale signs of a struggle that had taken place before and during the shooting. The half curtains, normally extending across both display windows, were in disarray, pulled to the floor like a blanket of evidence. An overturned chair lay in the corner, some newspapers scattered beneath it. The detectives exchanged glances, their minds piecing together the clues left behind.

Detectives removed one bullet from the wall, and another was found in a battered condition on the floor. All of the bullets were copper nickel-plated .38 caliber. Deputy Chief Flemming recalled meeting Fiore just a week ago on the street, warning him that enemies surrounded him and he was in a tough spot, urging him to return to Italy.

The shocking news spread like wildfire, and a large crowd quickly swarmed in front of the shop. An extra squad of policemen was called in to control the increasingly chaotic situation. James Fiore, brother of the murdered man, was one of the first to arrive. He was allowed to enter the backroom, where his brother's lifeless body lay motionless on the floor. The atmosphere was heavy and oppressive, and the somber silence was only broken by the occasional sob of grief. James stood there, helpless and grief-stricken, as the police officers went about their work.

Deputy Chief Flemming's commanding voice echoed through the barbershop as he issued orders. "Put in a call for Sergent John Sullivan, official photographer of the detective bureau. No one is to enter until after he has taken his photographs."

The only sound to be heard in the barbershop was the humming of the bright lights overhead. The tang of talcum powder and the scent of aftershave hung in the air, mingling with the faint traces of tobacco smoke from the night before. A tall barber's chair sat in the corner, its leather seat still warm from Fiore's body. The Deputy Chief stood in the doorway, his stern gaze sweeping around the room. "Nobody touch a thing," he said, "until Sergent Sullivan arrives."

District Attorney Thomas Granfield sprang into action, arriving at the scene of the shooting to launch his investigation. Deputy Chief John Flemming joined him, and the two men combed the area, searching for clues. They headed to police headquarters to interview witnesses and dig deeper into the case. Granfield and Flemming worked tirelessly, their eyes scanning every detail, their ears listening intently to every word uttered by the witnesses.

The deafening silence engulfed the gangland of Columbus Avenue following the killing of Fiore. Despite the police's tireless efforts to uncover clues, they were left with nothing. Not even the residents in the three-block radius of the barber shop could supply any information about the assassins' whereabouts. Alphonse Iennaco, the shop's owner, and Antonio Basile, the barber, were taken to the police headquarters for questioning. But the officers soon released them, as their interrogations supplied nothing of value. The streets remained still and quiet as if the air itself was withholding the truth. Witnesses were tight-lipped, and no one dared to speak a word as to what had happened that fateful day. They "knew nothing" of the shooting and had "seen no one."

Dominic Resigno lay in a cold, firm bed in the hospital, his face illuminated by the harsh white light of the recovery room. Doctors had delicately extracted one bullet from his abdomen the day before. Deputy Chief of Police John Fleming, Lieutenant Raymond Gallagher, and Sergeant John Cleary bombarded him with questions, but he remained silent. He refused to give any information about the gunmen, no matter how hard they pressed him. His face was set and his expression unreadable, and the three officers had no choice but to end the interrogation.

The detectives continued to scour the crime scene for days, searching for any sign of the hitmen. But as the hours dragged on, the evidence seemed to grow ever more elusive. The officers worked tirelessly, but with each passing minute, the chances of finding something seemed to slip further and further away. The stale air of the investigation was thick with doubt. The detectives exchanged weary glances and grumbled words of frustration. The only chance of finding something useful was a lucky break, something to give them a clue to the murderers' identity.

The headlines screamed from the front page of *The Waterbury Democrat* as the newspaper crinkled in the morning breeze. "Racketeer 'Put On Spot' As Barber Was Cutting Hair." People hurried past, their eyes skimming the black and white print as they rushed to work. The paper rustled in the hands of a man in a crisp suit as he read the shocking news that had been reported. His brow furrowed as he took in the details, his mouth forming a grim line as he realized the story's impact, the words depicting a vivid image of the events that had taken place.

"Michael Fiori, 37, of 1234 Columbus Avenue, alleged racketeer and companion of Mrs. Pasqualina Siniscalchi Miranda, was brutally murdered at a barber shop at 1182 Columbus Avenue. He was met by two members of a gangland execution squad and was shot multiple times in the head and body as he sat in the barber's chair getting a haircut. Fiori met death as he frantically crawled along the floor on his hands and knees in an unsuccessful attempt to escape.

"A friend, Dominic Resigno, 36, also of Springfield, was perhaps fatally wounded. The double shooting was engineered by two unmasked men who escaped, unrecognized, in an automobile.

The Evening Gazette of Worcester reported, "Bootlegger Slain In Barber Chair."

"Michael Fiore, leader of local bootleggers, was shot to death, and Dominic Resigno was probably fatally wounded today by two gunmen who escaped. Resigno was shot when he made a move to interfere with the gunmen."

The news spread like wildfire through the bustling streets of Boston, causing an uproar of conversation. People were buzzing with interest everywhere, discussing the headlines of *The Boston Herald* that had taken the city by storm. Storefronts were filled with people, and it seemed like the city was alive with energy. Conversations were filled with questions and speculations, and the atmosphere was electric. Even the birds seemed to be chirping louder than usual, as if they were part of the excitement.

In my view, I believe this is what happened. Many could have pulled this hit off. Michael Fiore was far from popular - both around here and back in New York. It was clear that Michael Fiore was a man who commanded respect but got it from very few.

Some had the potential to take over Pasqualina's bootlegging operation, but only Anthony Miranda had the support of the notorious Vito Genovese and his brother, Genovese consigliere Michael Miranda. Michael's presence alone was enough to strike fear in the heart of any adversary, as his reputation for mercilessness preceded him. The mere mention of his name was enough to send shivers down the spine of any who dared cross him. Not only that, but his loyalty to Genovese was unwavering, creating an ironclad bond that could withstand any opposition. Together, they formed a force to be reckoned with.

Anthony and Michael Miranda stood before me years prior, their words like a solemn promise. If I kept my operations on this side of the Connecticut River and left Springfield to the Genovese Family, no harm would ever come to the Parisi family again. I had already lost a brother-in-law, Joseph Marvici, and almost my wife and four-year-old nephew, so I was eager to agree. We shook hands, our eyes locked in a silent understanding. The air seemed to linger with the solemnity of the agreement, and a chill ran through me. I knew I had to keep my word; I was sure they would, too.

Pasqualina was dead and out of their way. She had been warned to keep out of the liquor racket, but following Fiore's advice, she became too active and knew too much. What Miranda didn't expect was Michael Fiore slipping his way in and trying to take control. He was spared as he wasn't the target when she was riddled with bullets when he lingered on the porch of the Giannini house while she sat in the car. He was approaching the vehicle when the attack happened. Her death did not scare Fiore. The Italian community knew he was a marked man. Even the police knew and tried to give him a heads up and advised him to take the deportation and enjoy life in Italy. It was thought in both mob and police circles that Fiore knew too much about underworld activities and was in a position to identify the assassins of Mrs. Miranda if he so chose.

Fiore had been told more than once that he would be "put on the spot" and was in constant fear of being "taken for a ride." When plans were made to put Fiore on a boat bound for Italy, he received a message while in the hospital. If he followed through with his plans, he would never make it to the dock.

Michael Fiore strutted around as if he was invincible and untouchable. His life revolved around the criminal world, and he had only known prison life in the United States. But his bravado came to a crashing halt when he decided to take on the New York Mob. He had no idea what he was getting himself into. The ominous energy of the city seemed to close in around him. He could feel the danger and fear in the air and almost hear the mob's silent threats. In the darkness of the night, he could see flashes of violence and hear the sound of cracking bones. He trembled at thinking about what he had gotten into and knew he would never be the same.

District Attorney Moriarty stood before the reporters, his face grim. "It is merely an aftermath of the killing of Mrs. Miranda and was generally anticipated in police circles." He paused, making direct eye contact with each reporter in turn. "The police say that 'more than 300 motives could be advanced for the dual murders.'

"We have questioned the two barbers who were in the shop at the time but noted a reluctance on their part to talk. They said that they failed to notice certain details which might provide a clue in the confusion." He could feel the tension in the room rise as the journalists scribbled down his words.

The reporters asked about the killers with deep curiosity. "We've positively identified that both assailants had guns," Moriarty said, "The bullets found in the premises indicated that they were from two different .38 caliber revolvers."

The reporters then asked about Dominic Resigno. "Resigno's condition is reported as 'fairly good' at Wesson Memorial Hospital, and it was said his name is not on the danger list. Police spent time with him to get some information, which might aid them in their search for the killers, but found him in a reticent mood. He could not recall ever having seen the gunmen before and did not know much of the details that led up to the actual shooting. Neither could he tell how he happened to be wounded."

The reporter's voice echoed in the air as they inquired, "What is the motive behind the shooting of Dominic Resigno?"

"Detectives had managed to piece together the events; Resigno had tried to intervene on Fiore's behalf when he was fired upon. Resigno had been sitting outside of the range of fire, yet more shots had been fired, and it was believed that they were aimed deliberately at Resigno." The room was tense, the air thick with anticipation, as everyone wanted to hear the answer.

When reporters probed Moriarty about Fiore's shady past, he clenched his jaw. He spat, "Michael Fiore has a long criminal record, giving the police and immigration authorities a reason to deem Fiore a 'public enemy' and take him to the county jail. There, a flurry of hearings took place, only for him to be released on $5,000 bail until the immigration authorities in Washington, D.C., could review the proceedings. Fiore was unwilling to return to Italy for the rest of his life although relatives have tried to convince him rather than chance meeting the same fate as Paqualina Miranda," he said.

The district attorney continued, his voice rising with determination as he spoke. "Fiore was adamant about not being deported and had enlisted the help of a New Haven lawyer to fight his case, and it was said that decision was to be made in favor of Fiore. He had been in the United States for about 21 years, and 17 years of this time he spent in correctional institutions, with his last stint in Wethersfield State Prison. But thanks to Mrs. Miranda's generous financial contribution, he was granted a pardon last July and finally freed." He paused, his knuckles turning white, adding, "Fiore had many enemies due to his activities in the South End. He probably knew his killers, believing them to be his friends."

The reporters crowded around Associate Medical Examiner Schillander as he took the podium, their eyes wide with anticipation. "After viewing Fiore's body at the scene, we followed it to the W. H. Graham undertaking rooms for a more thorough examination." Schillander cleared his throat and continued to speak, the journalists leaning in to catch his every word. "I've examined the body," he said, "and I can confirm that the victim suffered two gunshot wounds. The first was to the neck, and the second to the right chest." He held up a hand to silence the noise that had broken out and continued. "The bullet wounds indicate that the shots were fired from a very close range, and the evidence of burn and powder marks on the clothing and skin supports that theory."

The reporters scribbled frantically, capturing every detail of Schillander's findings. After a few more moments, the examiner stepped away from the podium, leaving the journalists buzzing with newfound information.

The morning sun shone brightly through the window of the police station in Connecticut. Inside, officers gravely looked over the mugshot of 37-year-old Michael Fiore, notorious "muscle man" and racketeer, a relic of the night before when he was brutally gunned down in Springfield. After years of feuding, Fiore was the latest victim in the New England underworld feud. The photo, placed among the other mugshots of the "Known Mafia" gallery adorning the wall, the words "Dead" now written boldly across it in red ink. Outside, the birds sang, unaware of the tragedy that had taken place. In the office, however, the atmosphere was heavy. The only sound that could be heard was the rhythmic clack of typewriters, their keys like a chorus of a thousand tiny drumsticks, pounding out a chaotic yet mesmerizing melody. Every clack of the keys sent a ripple through the office, stirring the emotions of those within and reminding them of the importance of the task at hand.

Only that Fiore remained undercover while in Waterbury, Connecticut, the police were sure that he would have been brutally "bumped off" here. Members of the vice squad, alerted by the Springfield police that Fiore had intended to spend a few days in Waterbury, kept a watchful eye on him. The notorious mobster, who was free on bail pending a verdict from the immigration officials, who had plans of expelling him to Italy as an "undesirable" citizen, withdrew into seclusion while here and abstained from making a public appearance. Some of his cohorts had a lavish apartment in the Willow Street section and were living in the lap of luxury. The atmosphere was tense and filled with anxiety as the authorities were sure that Fiore would be targeted for assassination.

Fiore moved into Waterbury with a mission: to act as a strong-arm man in starting a policy game. Rumors quickly spread that he was one of the several suspected promoters of the "Springfield game," which was to include several Waterburians. But when two of the leaders were apprehended, the partnership fell apart. He walked the streets, his heavy footsteps echoing off the walls, his presence alone enough to strike fear into anyone who crossed his path. He heard whispers of his involvement everywhere he went until the whole town was talking. He soon found himself in the middle of a police investigation, and all hopes of his numbers racket were dashed. He had no choice but to pack his bags and leave, leaving behind a legacy of broken dreams.

Police frantically scoured through Fiore's personal effects, finding a letter written in Italian and postmarked from New Haven, Connecticut. They hoped it would provide a significant lead, yet their hopes were dashed when the investigators concluded that the letter was worthless. The only clue that could have shed light on the identity of the slayers had petered out, leaving the police in the same dark abyss they started in.

State Detective Joseph Ferrara of Boston and members of the local department's criminal investigation squad combed the dark alleys of Springfield, desperate to unearth a glimmer of hope that would illuminate the mystery of the recent murder. Detective Ferrara has a reputation for being the cleverest member of the state detective force in solving gangland killings. Their footsteps echoed through the streets, the only sound in an otherwise eerie silence. The officers combed through every nook and cranny they could find, their eyes darting from one corner to the next in search of a clue. Detective Ferrara sighed heavily, his brow furrowed, as he surveyed the scene. "This case is going cold," he murmured, "we need to find anything that can help us move forward." The team worked tirelessly for hours, becoming increasingly frustrated with each passing minute.

"We're not getting anywhere," one of the officers grumbled, "we're just chasing our tails here."

The Italian funeral director gingerly lifted Fiore's body from the stretcher, cradling it as if it were a beloved child. The room fell silent, all eyes trained on the director as he reverently carried the body away. The director's face was grim as he wordlessly made his way down the hallway, a reminder of the finality of death. The mourners watched him go, hearts heavy with grief, until he disappeared around the corner. No one spoke, aware that the arrangements for Fiore's burial had yet to be made. All that was left was the thick air of sorrow that lingered in the wake of the director's departure.

Hundreds of onlookers, many of them moved by curiosity, gathered around the home of Michael Fiore's brother, the slain gangster and racketeer, as a dozen uniformed police silently mingled alongside. They bore the body of the man who had been denied admission to Our Lady of Mount Carmel Church due to the atheistic remarks he'd made while a hospital patient.

The dusty lot was filled with thirty vehicles, each more worn-down than the last. Only one out-of-state car from New Jersey was noticed. The people in attendance were mainly of the poorer class, evident from their tattered clothing and hollowed faces. Not a single notorious figure of the underworld could be seen, not even to the watchful eye of the police. The air was thick with the smell of motor oil and sweat. Conversations between the attendees were hushed and strained, their looks constantly shifting to the police officers nearby. No one wanted to be the one to draw attention to themselves. The police officers walked the lot on the lookout for suspects in connection with the murder of Fiore, surveying the vehicles and the people. They did not see any persons who gave signs of knowing anything of the shooting and ensured no underworld activities were taking place.

The procession formed at his brother's home on Union Street. It proceeded easterly to Main Street, York Street, Columbus Avenue, State Street, and its final resting place in St. Michael's Cemetery, where it was laid to rest in unconsecrated ground. The mourners held their breath as the coffin was slowly placed on the ground, the only sound of the rustling of leaves around them. As the police stepped back, the silence was deafening, the faces of the crowd reflecting the solemnity of the moment. The grief in the air was evident and lingered even after the procession had gone, leaving the cemetery cloaked in a heavy blanket of sadness.

Outside the imposing walls of police headquarters, Deputy Chief of Police John Fleming paced back and forth, eyes sharp and alert. He had been tasked with the investigation into the cold-blooded shooting of Fiore, a known underworld figure, which had taken place in a Columbus Avenue barbershop. The deputy police chief stopped in front of a crowd of reporters, the clattering of cameras and the shouted questions filling the air. "I assure you," he said, in a voice that brooked no nonsense, "we are doing everything possible to clear up the murder of Michael Fiore, as well as that of his companion, Mrs. Pasqualina Siniscalchi-Miranda, and there will be positively no letup until every available clue and motive is thoroughly investigated."

Deputy Chief Fleming appealed to the public, his voice carrying an unspoken urgency that could not be denied. "We are urgently calling on anyone who may have been passing by the scene of the shooting either on foot or in automobiles who must have witnessed some part of it or obtained a glimpse of the killers as they made their getaway to come forward with any information they may have," he said, his voice heavy with conviction. If anyone who possesses any information that might be of some assistance will communicate with me personally, I can promise them that the source of their information will never be divulged. We are looking for and need all the information we can get." His eyes scanned the crowd, their intensity burning with a mission to solve the crime.

The Deputy Chief gestured emphatically as he detailed the dire warnings he and his fellow Criminal Investigation Squad members had issued to Mrs. Miranda and Fiore: Quit their questionable activities, or they would meet their inevitable fate. He had been in close contact with Fiore since the time of his release from Wethersfield State Prison, urging him to "go straight" and even suggesting he return to Italy to escape what appeared to be his destiny, put "on the spot."

Deputy Chief of Police John Fleming and State Detective Joseph Ferrara returned to Springfield with a powerful announcement: they knew the perpetrators responsible for the murder of Michael Fiore, a notorious racketeer and ex-convict. The air was heavy with anticipation as the Deputy Chief spoke, revealing the details of the investigation that had been conducted in Fiore's slaying. With a solemn nod, the detectives made clear their commitment to finding justice and upholding the law. As Ferrara and Fleming left the scene, the community of Springfield was left wondering just who was responsible for the death of Michael Fiore.

Authorities are now in possession of evidence linking the two gunmen to Fiore's murder. Police are satisfied that the Fiore slayers are the same ones who riddled Mrs. Pasqualina Siniscalchi Miranda, reputed "queen" of the local underworld, with bullets while at the wheel of her car on upper Worthington Street. The grand jury will be presented with the evidence so that secret indictments may be returned against the killers.

Police revealed that fear had been clawing its way into Fiore's life, constantly reminding him that at any moment, he would be "put on the spot" and "taken for a ride." The only way he could escape such a fate was to call off his sailing plans and remain in the hospital under the pretense of complications arising from his wound. But then, when New Haven connections supplied him with lawyers, his plans completely shifted, and he served notice that he would oppose any move to deport him from this country back to Italy.

Still looking to solve the murders of Pasqualina and Fiore, Springfield authorities now looked to New York, where detectives had just captured a known mob hitman with connections to Springfield.

The net of justice slowly tightened around Leonard Scarnici, formerly of Springfield, on September 22, 1933, as a New York police commissioner listed him as a "killer" wanted for murder by both New York state and Connecticut. Local law enforcement was on high alert, waiting for a signal from New York City on whether Scarnici had broken under the pressure and confessed to several Springfield area murders. At last, the notorious band of racketeers and kidnappers were apprehended in Mt. Kisco, New York, with their leader, Leonard Scarnici, in tow.

Springfield Deputy Chief of Police John Fleming stood firmly, arms crossed, as he addressed Scarnici. He had been defiantly silent throughout the questioning on the Mrs. Pasqualina Siniscalchi-Miranda and Michael Fiore murders and the Trimboli and "Jazz" Wilson cases. Fleming could feel the tension in the air as he regarded the man who was believed to be responsible for four murders. He noted the sweat dripping from Scarnici's forehead and how his fingers twitched. He saw the fear in his eyes and how his body language shifted uneasily. Fleming's voice was stern as he said, "Scarnici, you are at your rope's end."

State police questioned Scarnici in connection with the murder of Frank "Jazz" Wilson, local Springfield bootlegger, who was slain April 7, 1927, and whose skeleton was dug up in Feeding Hills, Massachusetts, three years later, without being able to obtain any admissions from him.

The police in New York held a press conference, announcing that Scarnici had confessed to five murders. The Springfield police confidently declared that it would be a simple task for their New York counterparts to get the former local man to admit guilt in the Wilson case. Reporters scribbled furiously as the officers continued talking, capturing every story detail. The police chief spoke up, his voice stern and unwavering. "We believe it's only a matter of time before Scarnici confesses to the Springfield murders," he said. The reporters looked at each other wide-eyed. It seemed like justice would finally be served.

Scarnici's lips remained firmly shut, refusing to utter a single word in the admission of the gruesome murders of Pasqualina and Fiore.

MICHAEL FIORE SLAIN, CUSTOMER SHOT IN BARBER SHOP ON COLUMBUS AVENUE

MICHAEL FIORE

BOOTLEGGER SLAIN IN BARBER CHAIR

Springfield Man Killed and Another Wounded—Two Gunmen Escape

The Family Becomes "Organized"

"Gentlemen," he began, "it's time to make history."

-JOHNNY TORRIO, CHICAGO BOSS AND AL CAPONE'S MENTOR

14

The salty air hung heavily in the air as bootleggers from across the United States descended upon Atlantic City for a meeting of the National Crime Syndicate on May 13, 1929. As they gathered on the boardwalk, the smell of the ocean and the sound of the seagulls carried an aura of danger.

The crowded room was stifling with the presence of Italian and Jewish organized crime figures, and the atmosphere filled with a sense of power. Nervous looks were traded as the representatives waited for the proceedings to start, the mood in the room changing as the leaders stepped in. All eyes were locked on them, everyone watching as they confidently walked to the front of the room and began to discuss their strategies. The bootleggers paid close attention, the faint glow of the dimly lit room adding emphasis to their anxious faces.

Johnny Torrio's idea had become a reality, an underground gathering of the most notorious underworld figures. Lucky Luciano, Al Capone, Benjamin "Bugsy" Siegel, Frank Costello, Joe Adonis, Dutch Shultz, Abner "Longie" Zwillman, Louis "Lepke" Buchalter, Gambino crime family head Vincent Mangano, Atlantic City Crime Syndicate boss Enoch "Nucky" Johnson, gambler Frank Erickson, Frank Scalise, and Albert "the Mad Hatter" Anastasia had all made their way to the meeting. The room was filled with the smell of cigars and whiskey. Johnny Torrio stood at the head of the room, commanding the group's attention. A hush descended over the room as America's earliest organized crime summit began.

"Gentlemen," he began, "it's time to make history."

A buzz of agreement went through the room, and a few men nodded in unison. The figures in the room discussed their plans, their voices growing louder and louder as the ideas began to form. Men in pinstripe suits and fedoras shifted in their chairs, their eyes flickering around the room, wary and observant. The discussion centered on the violent bootleg wars and how to prevent them in the future. Ideas of diversifying and investing in liquor ventures, expanding illegal operations to make up for potential losses from repealing Prohibition, and reorganizing and consolidating the underworld into a National Crime Syndicate were tossed around the room. Gangsters, mafiosos, and criminals of every kind exchanged heated words, some strongly opposing any change while others argued for a different way of life. The tension in the air was overt.

Charles Soloman represented New England, the Boston Jewish Mob Boss; Frank "Cheeseman" Cucchiara, the North End Gang/Buccola Family Lieutenant; and Frank "Bootsy" Morelli, the Providence/Morelli Gang Boss. The streets of Boston and Providence buzzed with the power and influence these men wielded. The smell of cigar smoke, the glint of gold rings, and the reverberation of amusement that followed them seemed to echo in the shadows of each city.

Giuseppe "Joe the Boss" Masseria and Salvatore Maranzano, two of the most influential figures of the underworld, were not invited to the gathering. The atmosphere of the room was tense and oppressive. Everyone knew the "Mustache Petes" were excluded, and the silence was almost deafening. The old guard adhered to their traditional old-world ideals and business practices, which made it impossible for them to collaborate with gangs of other ethnicities.

"What we need is collaboration, not competition," Torrio declared. He looked around the room, his gaze slowly taking in the nodding heads and murmured agreement. It was clear that the future of organized crime was at stake, and it would be up to this group of men to decide its fate.

The conference is the earliest organized crime summit held in America.

The Castellammarese War began nine months later, on February 26, 1930, in New York City, resulting in the organization's massive reorganization and expansion. To achieve this, larger Families were created by assimilating smaller gangs and factions, all based on geographical locations.

Rumor has it that Joe Masseria had ordered the killing of Gaetano Reina in the Bronx, believing that Reina was aligning himself with his arch-rival Salvatore Maranzano in Brooklyn. Vito Genovese's face was stone-cold as he pulled the trigger, and the impact of the bullet sent a shockwave through the city. In the streets of New York City, the sound of gunfire echoed through the night as the war raged on, and the smell of smoke and destruction lingered in the air. Genovese and Michele Miranda were arrested for the murder but were eventually acquitted.

Filippo Buccola's Boston crew and Frank Morelli's Providence crew united to form a powerful crime syndicate, the New England Crime Family. With Buccola ruling as boss from East Boston, he had a stronghold on all areas east of the Connecticut River, as well as strong ties to the Profaci/Columbo family in Brooklyn and Staten Island. Meanwhile, the Genovese family maintained its influence on the western side of the river in Springfield, Mass, and New Haven, Connecticut. The new crime families were formidable, their influence spreading far and wide. Respect was commanded, and fear was instilled through their iron-fisted rule. From their base of operations, they ran their criminal empires with a network of trusted connections. The new organizations were a force to be reckoned with, their power and reach undeniable.

The bootlegging business came to a crashing halt on Dec. 5, 1933, when Prohibition was repealed, evaporating the mafia's lifeblood. The Springfield Crew refused to give up their stranglehold on the city, and members were forced to find other ways of earning money. They capitalized on the lack of a real lottery and created their own, known as "the numbers," where citizens could bet as much as they wanted or as little as a penny. This generated a consistent and lucrative income for the Mafia until the state introduced its own lottery. The mob also began running "junkets," bringing high rollers from Springfield to Atlantic City and eventually Las Vegas, confident that these travelers would spend large sums of money, more than making up for the cost of the trip and accommodations. Additionally, the mob had a firm grip on boxing, which was immensely popular in the 1930s. Other less savory sources of revenue included loan sharking, prostitution, narcotics, and pornography.

It's unclear who the first boss of Springfield was after the Prohibition period; however, some people believe Carlo Sarno assumed control from 1932 to 1940. His wife, Josephine Albano, is the sister of Pasqualina Siniscalchi-Miranda. When Pasqualina was killed in 1932, her children went to live with Carlo and Josephine.

The Genovese family has had a longstanding grip on the criminal underworld of Springfield, Massachusetts. The Springfield Crew kept control over Hartford and other parts of

Connecticut, while the New England Crime Family controlled other regions of the state.

Salvatore "Big Nose Sam" Cufari became the first "official" boss of post-prohibition Springfield around 1940. Born in 1901 in Bianco, Reggio di Calabria, Cufari set up what is currently known as the "Springfield Crew" of New York's Genovese Crime Family. To fill the void caused by the death of Antonio Miranda, Sam Cufari was inducted into the Luciano/Genovese Family ranks and was named the official "Capo" over the city of Springfield and its surrounding towns and territories. He ran the Springfield Family from his restaurant, Ciro's, on Main Street in the South End of Springfield. In 1957, he attended the renowned "Little Apalachin" summit of leading U.S. Mafia figures in upstate New York.

Filippo "Phil" Buccola was the head of organized crime in Boston and most of New England from 1932 to 1954, when he eventually had to flee to Sicily to prevent being prosecuted for tax evasion.

During this time, Michael Miranda, brother of Pasqualina's late husband, Antonio Miranda, routinely sent his New York City hitmen to Springfield to "lam it" until the heat that was sure to come had cooled down. On one occasion, two button-men were driven to Springfield, Massachusetts, by another future "made" member, Salvatore "Little Sally" Celembrino, in order to lay low. They were placed under the protection of Nicholas Camerota, a "made" soldier in the Springfield faction of the Genovese family. More than 30 years later, at the U.S. Senate crime hearings, Salvatore "Little Sally" Celembrino was identified as the main executioner in the Michael Miranda regime of the Genovese family. The same Salvatore Celembrino who was found in a Springfield hotel with four other New York Italians the day Pasqualina Siniscalchi was gunned down.

The unsolved murders of Giuseppe "Joe" Marvici, Pasqualina Siniscalchi-Miranda, and Michael Fiore hang over the town like a dark cloud, casting a pall of fear and despair over the inhabitants. No one knows who committed these heinous crimes, and all the evidence has been exhausted.

Giuseppe "Joseph" Parisi lived a long and happy life until he died of natural causes on February 27, 1976, at the age of 81. Joseph's friends and family remember him fondly, his life a testament to living life to its fullest. He embraced every moment, never taking a single day for granted. Though he is gone, his memory lives on in the hearts of all those he touched.

La Fine

Antonio Miranda, Pasqualina's 2ⁿᵈ Husband

Michele Miranda, Genovese Family Consigliere

Filippo Buccola, New England Boss

"Big Nose" "Sam" Cufari

Citations

"The Italians in Springfield." *THE SUNDAY UNION* (Springfield, MA) 7 September 1913, p 5.

"Prominent Italian Resident is Dead." *THE SPRINGFIELD UNION* (Springfield, MA) 24 June 1915, p 7

Cascio, Justin. "What is a Padrone?" 5 June 2023. http://www.mafiagenealogy.com/2023/06/15/what-is-a-padrone/Accessed 15 June 2023.

"Death of John Albano." *Springfield Republican.* (Springfield, MA) 24 June 1915, p 2.

"Chief Gets Statements from Shooting Victims." *Springfield Daily News.* (Springfield, MA) 8 May 1911, p 9.

"Slash Policeman." *Springfield Republican.* (Springfield, MA) 5 August 1915, pp 1, 4.

"Siniscalchi and Fiore on Trial." *Springfield Daily News.* (Springfield, MA) 15 May 1916, pp 1, 9.

"All are Guilty Jurys' Verdict." *THE SPRINGFIELD UNION* (Springfield, MA) 18 May 1916, p 8.

"Knife Strikes Deep." *Springfield Republican.* (Springfield, MA) 23 July 1917, p 4.

"Fiore Held in $1000 Bail in Slashing Case." *Springfield Daily News.* (Springfield, MA) 23 July 1917, p 2.

"Fiore a Free Man." *Springfield Republican.* (Springfield, MA) 27 July 1917, p 4.

"Prohibition in Effect Tonight." *Springfield Republican.* (Springfield, MA) 16 January 1920, p 11.

"Federal Raiders Net 11 City Saloonmen." *Springfield Republican.* (Springfield, MA) 6 June 1920, p 1.

"Scramble Follows Liquor Crash." *Springfield Republican.* (Springfield, MA) 17 September 1920, p 5.

"Siniscalchi Under Arrests For Threats." *Springfield Daily News.* (Springfield, MA) 17 October 1921, p 6.

"Siniscalchi Given Four Months, Suspended." *Springfield Daily News.* (Springfield, MA) 7 November 1921, pp 1, 8.

"Piemontese Gun Player to Concord." *Springfield Daily News.* (Springfield, MA) 17 October 1921, p 2.

"Carlo Siniscalchi Fatally Shot." *Springfield Daily News.* (Springfield, MA) 20 December 1921, p 1.

"Carlo Siniscalchi Murder Victim of Giuseppe Parisi in Main Street Shooting." *Springfield Republican.* (Springfield, MA) 21 December 1921, p 1.

"Murder in Springfield." *The Brattleboro Daily Reformer.* (Brattleboro, VT) 21 December 1921, p 3.

"Liquor Deal Ends in Murder." *THE BOSTON HERALD.* (Boston, MA) 21 December 1921, p 15.

"Parisi Indicted for Killing Siniscalchi." *Springfield Daily News.* (Springfield, MA) 21 December 1921, pp 1, 13.

"Indict Parisi for First Degree Murder." *Daily Kennebec journal. [microfilm reel]* (Augusta, ME) 22 December 1921, pg. 4.

"District Attorney Hints Siniscalchi Murder Work of Individuals Higher Up." *Springfield Republican.* (Springfield, MA) 22 December 1921, pp 1, 2.

"Seeks Big Fellows Among Rum Runners." *THE BOSTON HERALD.* (Boston, MA) 23 December 1921, p 7.

"Funeral of Siniscalchi Under Careful Watch of Local Authorities." *Springfield Republican.* (Springfield, MA) 23 December 1921, pp 1, 2.

"Great Throng Attends Funeral of Siniscalchi but No Demonstration Ensues." *Springfield Daily News.* (Springfield, MA) 23 December 1921, pp 1, 8.

"State Further Probe in Siniscalchi Murder." *Springfield Republican.* (Springfield, MA) 28 December 1921, pp 1, 13.

"Parisi to be Arraigned for the Murder of Siniscalchi." *Springfield Daily News.* (Springfield, MA) 4 January 1922, page 2.

"Four Arraigned for Murder, Making Record for Court Day; All Enter Non-Guilty Pleas." *Springfield Daily News.* (Springfield, MA) 5 January 1922, page 2.

"Inquest Report Shows that Parisi Was Also in Commission of Murder of Siniscalchi." *Springfield Daily News.* (Springfield, MA) 19 January 1922, pp 1, 2.

"No Fear for Parisi on Account of Wright's County Jail Dictaphone." *Springfield Republican.* (Springfield, MA) 13 May 1922, p 1.

"Parisi to be Arraigned for the Murder of Siniscalchi." *Springfield Daily News.* (Springfield, MA) 30 December 1921, pp 1, 20.

"District Attorney Wright Said to Be About to Probe Belmer Incident." *Springfield Daily News.* (Springfield, MA) 19 May 1922, pp 1, 21.

"Belmer Quiz Made Public by Attorney." *Springfield Daily News.* (Springfield, MA) 20 May 1922, pp 1, 2.

"Believe Shooting was Done from Siniscalchi Car." *Springfield Republican*. (Springfield, MA) 4 July 1922, p 1, 2. "Siniscalchi's Nephew Held in Connection With Murder Attempt." *Springfield Republican*. (Springfield, MA) 4 July 1922, p 1.

"Vona and Guerriero Held in Heavy Bonds." *Springfield Republican*. (Springfield, MA) 5 July 1922, p 1.

"Two Men are Held for Firing on Automobile." *THE BOSTON HERALD*. (Boston, MA) 5 July 1922, p 6.

"Hearing Ordered for 25th in Cases Growing Out of Attack by Gunmen in Italian Feud." *Springfield Daily News*. (Springfield, MA) 5 July 1922, p 1.

"To Investigate Parisi Shooting." *Springfield Republican*. (Springfield, MA) 6 July 1922, p 1.

"Parisi Shooting Aired in Court." *Springfield Republican*. (Springfield, MA) 7 September 1922, p15.

"Witnesses Unable to Identify Vona as the Marksman Who Fired Shots at Parisi Party." *Springfield Daily News*. (Springfield, MA) 6 September 1922, pp 1, 11.

"Vona is Freed on Shooting Complaint." *Springfield Daily News*. (Springfield, MA) 7 September 1922, p 1.

"Italian Shot Seriously Hurt May Lose Life." *Springfield Republican*. (Springfield, MA) 17 August 1922, pp 1, 2.

"Would Link Springfield Rum Runners in Murder on Connecticut Road." *Springfield Republican*. (Springfield, MA) 12 September 1922, pp 1, 2.

"Rigid Probe into Rum and Murder at North Haven." *The Bridgeport Times and Evening Farmer*. (Bridgeport, CT) 12 September 1922, p 5.

"One Man Killed in Running Fight." *The Brattleboro Daily Reformer*. (Brattleboro, VT) 12 September 1922, p 6.

"West Side Automobile Believed To Have Been Employed in the Murder of Waterbury Man." *Springfield Daily News*. (Springfield, MA) 12 September 1922, p12.

"Theodore Vona, Nephew of Murdered Siniscalchi, and Salvatore Guriero Are Questioned About Connecticut Murder by Police." *Springfield Republican*. (Springfield, MA) 13 September 1922, p 5.

"Police Think Professional Gunmen Employed by Local People Killed Marvici." *Springfield Republican*. (Springfield, MA) 16 September 1922, p 4.

"Murder Case Held Over Another Term." *Springfield Republican*. (Springfield, MA) 2 January 1923, p 4.

"Parisi and Scibelli to be Tried for Murder." *Springfield Republican.* (Springfield, MA) 30 January 1923, p 5. *Find a Grave*, database and images (https://www.findagrave.com/memorial/180117774/giuseppe-marvici: accessed 07 May 2023), memorial page for Giuseppe Marvici (1888–11 Sep 1922), Find a Grave Memorial ID 180117774, citing Calvary Cemetery, Waterbury, New Haven County, Connecticut, USA; Maintained by Cheryl (contributor 49100113).

"Corruption in Office of District Attorney Wright is New Charge of Talbot." *Springfield Republican.* (Springfield, MA) 2 September 1922, pp 1, 2.

"Siniscalchi's Widow Attacks Talbot." *Springfield Daily News.* (Springfield, MA) 2 September 1922, pp 1, 2.

"Wright Answers Talbot's Charges." *Springfield Republican.* (Springfield, MA) 3 September 1922, p 6.

"Used Siniscalchi Auto in Gathering Evidence." *Springfield Republican.* (Springfield, MA) 25 January 1923, pp 1, 11.

"Fielding Said Daniels was Being Made 'The Goat'." *Springfield Republican.* (Springfield, MA) 26 January 1923, pp 1, 2.

"' Red' Daniels Testifies in His Own Defense." *Springfield Republican.* (Springfield, MA) 27 January 1923, pp 1,3.

"Expect Daniels-Tomlin Trial Will End Today." *Springfield Republican.* (Springfield, MA) 2 March 1923, pp 1, 2.

"Acquit Daniels; Tomlin Guilty." *Springfield Republican.* (Springfield, MA) 3 March 1923, pp 1, 11.

Britannica, The Editors of Encyclopedia. "Calabria". *Encyclopedia Britannica*, 1 Mar. 2023.

The origins of the 'Ndrangheta of Calabria: Italy's most powerful mafia. By Carly Schnabl, on 14 March 2011.

Britannica, The Editors of Encyclopedia. "Messina earthquake and tsunami of 1908". *Encyclopedia Britannica*, 21 Dec. 2022.

Year: 1920; Census Place: West Springfield, Hampden, Massachusetts; Roll: T625_699; Page: 10A; Enumeration District: 188; Image: 995

Year: 2010; New York, Passenger Lists, 1820-1957. Ancesrty.com

Atto di nascita, Giuseppe Antonio Parisi. (1894, May 23). Record no. 23. Archivio di Stato di Reggio Calabria > Stato civile italiano > Caraffa del Bianco > 1894 https://antenati.cultura.gov.it/ark:/12657/an_ua16388283/0JRlJv6 Img 10 of 24.

(1918, December 11). Record no. 1174. Springfield. "Massachusetts State Vital Records, 1841-1920", database with images, FamilySearch. (https://www.familysearch.org/ark:/61903/1:1:Q2ZM-PJZB : 24 November 2022), Joseph Parisi and Raffaela Mezzarino, 1918.

"Jury Summoned For Two Murder Trials." *Springfield Republican.* (Springfield, MA) 18 March 1923, p 7.

"Parisi Placed On Trial For Murder." *Springfield Daily News.* (Springfield, MA) 19 March 1923, p 1, 6.

"Jury Chosen For Murder Trial Of Joseph Parisi." *Springfield Republican.* (Springfield, MA) 20 March 1923, pp 1, 4.

"Jury Visits Seen Of Siniscalchi Murder." *Springfield Republican.* (Springfield, MA) 21 March 1923, pp 1, 8.

"2 Fail To Identify Parisi As Slayer." *THE BOSTON HERALD.* (Boston, MA) 21 March 1923, p 25.

"Parisi Identified As Man Running With Revolver After Killing." *Springfield Republican.* (Springfield, MA) 22 March 1923, pp 1, 6.

"Slain Man's Widow To Tell Of Killing." *THE BOSTON HERALD.* (Boston, MA) 22 March 1923, p 6.

"Both Sides Expect To Benefit By Statements in Parisi 'Confession'." *Springfield Republican.* (Springfield, MA) 23 March 1923, pp 1, 6.

"News Of The Day Told In Pictures." *Springfield Republican.* (Springfield, MA) 23 March 1923, p 20.

"District Attorney Hints Siniscalchi Murder Work of Individuals Higher Up." *Springfield Republican.* (Springfield, MA) 22 December 1921, p 1, 2.

"Defense Opens In Parisi Murder Trial." *Springfield Daily News.* (Springfield, MA) 23 March 1923, pp 1, 24.

"Testifies Parisi Admitted Killing." *THE BOSTON HERALD.* (Boston, MA) 23 March 1923, p 17.

"Both Sides Expect To Benefit By Statements in Parisi 'Confession'." *Springfield Republican.* (Springfield, MA) 23 March 1923, pp 1, 6.

"Shooting Justifiable States Parisi's Counsel In Opening For Defense." *Springfield Republican.* (Springfield, MA) 24 March 1923, pp 1, 2.

"Defense Opens In Parisi Murder Trial." *Springfield Daily News.* (Springfield, MA) 23 March 1923, p 1, 24.

"Parisi Says Siniscalchi Was Armed." *Springfield Daily News.* (Springfield, MA) 24 March 1923, pp 1, 2.

"His Life Or Mine' Is Parisi's Dramatic Self Defense Plea On Stand." *Springfield Republican.* (Springfield, MA) 25 March 1923, pp 1, 3.

"Parisi To Know His Fate Tomorrow." *Springfield Daily News.* (Springfield, MA) 26 March 1923, pp 1, 9.

"Judge Gives Parisi Case to Jury." *Springfield Daily News.* (Springfield, MA) 27 March 1923, pp 1, 12.

"Verdict Expected Today In Parisi Murder Trial." *Springfield Republican.* (Springfield, MA) 27 March 1923, pp 1, 7.

"Judge Gives Parisi Case To Jury." *Springfield Daily News.* (Springfield, MA) 27 March 1923, pp 1, 12.

"Judges Answer Seems Favorable to the Defense." *Springfield Republican.* (Springfield, MA) 28 March 1923, p 1.

"Parisi Found Guilty of Manslaughter." *Springfield Republican.* (Springfield, MA) 28 March 1923, pp 1, 7.

"Request By Parisi's Lawyer Postpones Sentence." *Springfield Daily News.* (Springfield, MA) 28 March 1923, pp 1, 4.

"Sentence Today in Parisi Case." *Springfield Republican.* (Springfield, MA) 29 March 1923, p 1.

"Parisi Is Given 7 To 10 Years." *Springfield Daily News.* (Springfield, MA) 29 March 1923, p 1, 11.

"Seven to Ten Years for Joseph Parisi." *Springfield Republican.* (Springfield, MA) 30 March 1923, p 1, 6.

"Parisi Says He is "Victim of a Cruel Circumstance" *Springfield Republican.* (Springfield, MA) 31 March 1923, p 6.

"Busted Hoodlum Conclave Made N.Y. Hamlet a 'Crime Shrine". *Los Angeles Times.* November 19, 2000.

"Waterbury Man Murdered And Police Say Killing Is Result Of Bootlegger War." *New Britain Herald.* (New Britain, CT) 25 September 1924, p 2.

"Officers Disagree; Case Thrown Out." *Springfield Republican.* (Springfield, MA) 1 July 1924, p 4.

"Lone Bottle Of Bootleg Causes More Trouble For Mrs. Marvici." *Springfield Republican.* (Springfield, MA) 26 September 1924, p 6.

"Accused Of Threat To Shoot Belmer." *Springfield Republican.* (Springfield, MA) 28 April 1925, p 1.

"McKechnie Tells Of Opposition To Move By Belmer." *Springfield Republican.* (Springfield, MA) 26 May 1925, p 1.

"Selectmen Find Belmer Acted In Good Faith." *Springfield Republican*. (Springfield, MA) 27 May 1925, p 1.

"Pardon For Parisi Asked By Eleven Of Jurors Who Convicted Him Of Slaying." *Springfield Republican*. (Springfield, MA) 16 September 1925, p 1.

"Mrs. Parisi Taken On Liquor Charge." *Springfield Republican*. (Springfield, MA) 4 April 1926, p 10.

"Pugliano is Up in Two Counts." *Springfield Republican*. (Springfield, MA) 25 December 1921, p 5.

"Hurley to Testify in Pugliano Case." *Springfield Republican*. (Springfield, MA) 17 March 1922, p 3.

"Fifth Raid on Same House Brings Results." *Springfield Republican*. (Springfield, MA) 1 February 1923, p 6.

"Parisi's Brother-In-Law Raided by "Dry" Agents." *Springfield Republican*. (Springfield, MA) 30 March 1923, p 11.

"Police Get Three Victims in Three Afternoon Jumps." *Springfield Republican*. (Springfield, MA) 28 August 1924, p 4.

"One Shot, 5 Held in Rum Convoy." *THE BOSTON HERALD*. (Boston, MA) 29 March 1926, p 6.

"West-Side Resident Fined $300 for Booze." *Springfield Republican*. (Springfield, MA) 14 May 1926, p 6.

"Five Men Arrested on Gambling Charge." *Springfield Republican*. (Springfield, MA) 12 December 1927, p 4.

"Four Men Arrested on Gambling Charge." *Springfield Republican*. (Springfield, MA) 24 September 1928, p 6.

"West Side Police Stage Rum Raid." *Springfield Republican*. (Springfield, MA) 10 February 1929, p 1.

"Selvatico Denies Liquor Charges." *Springfield Republican*. (Springfield, MA) 28 May 1930, p 7.

"Whiskey Runners Having a Feud." *Norwich bulletin*. (Norwich, CT) 16 June 1920, p 2.

Atti di nascita, Pasqua Albano. (1891, April 15). Record no. 46. https://www.antenati.san.beniculturali.it/ark:/12657/an_ua244328/w9EA9PW/ Retrieved 22 May 2023.

"United States Census, 1900," database with images, FamilySearch (https://familysearch.org/ark:/61903/1:1:M9RL-7JG : accessed 22 May 2023), Louis Albano, Springfield city Ward 6, Hampden, Massachusetts, United States; citing enumeration district (ED) 588, sheet 9A, family 185, NARA microfilm publication T623 (Washington, D.C.: National Archives and Records Administration, 1972.); FHL microfilm 1,240,652

Massachusetts Marriages, 1841-1915," database with images, FamilySearch (https://familysearch.org/ark:/61903/1:1:N4XP-Y13 : 17 February 2016), Carluccio Siniscalchi and Pasqualina Albano, 26 Sep 1912; citing Springfield, , Massachusetts, United States, State Archives, Boston; FHL microfilm 2,409,943.

"Flowers For Dead Amount to $20,000: Elaborate Funeral Planned for 'Little Italy' Chief Mirando of Springfield To Be Buried in $7500 Casket--Hundreds Mourn." Published 10 February 1930 in the Daily Boston Globe. pp 1, 9.

"Woman Is Slain By Machine Gun: Companion in Parked Car at Springfield Wounded Mrs. Miranda's Husband Killed in Same Manner 10 Years Ago." Daily Boston Globe. pp 1, 19. 12 November 1932.

"Gang Machine Gunners Slay Woman And Wound Companion." *The San Diego Union AND DAILY BEE.* (San Diego, CA) 13 November 1932, p 19.

"Woman Put On Spot And Slain By Gunmen." *THE HOUSTON CHRONICLE* (Houston, TX) 12 November 1932, p 7.

"Gangster's Bullets Murder Woman." *THE DENVER POST* (Denver, CO) 12 November 1932, p 20.

"Woman 'Put On Spot' In Parked Machine." *DETROIT TIMES EXTRA* (Detroit, MI) 12 November 1932, p 7.

"Gangster Bullets Kill Massachusetts Woman Companion Wounded." *Wichita Daily Times* (Wichita Falls, TX) 12 November 1932, p 1.

"Bay State Woman Slain By Gunners." *THE BAY CITY DAILY TIMES* (Bay City, MI) 12 November 1932, p 2.

"Gangland Queen 'Taken For Ride'." *Journal Dispatch* (Columbus, OH) 13 November 1932, p 8.

"Mrs. P. S. Miranda Shot In Auto ON Worthington St." *Springfield Republican.* (Springfield, MA) 12 November 1932, pp 1 and 2.

"Massachusetts Woman 'Put On Spot,' Slain." *ROCKFORD Register-Republic* (Rockford, IL) 12 November 1932, page 3.

"Say Same Gang As Slew Mate Killed Woman." *The Evening Gazette* (Worcester, MA) 12 November 1932, p 3.

"Funeral Is Held For Mrs. Miranda." *Springfield Republican.* (Springfield, MA) 16 November 1932, p 4.

"Bullets Removed From Fiore's Arm." *Springfield Republican.* (Springfield, MA) 19 November 1932, p 4.

"Springfield Woman Killed, Man Dying As Machine Guns Rake Motor Car."
THE BOSTON HERALD. (Boston, MA) 12 November 1932, p 1.

"Murder Probe And Man Hunt At Standstill." *Springfield Republican*. (Springfield, MA) 13 November 1932, pp 1, 2.

"Liquor Queen 'Put On Spot,' Partner Shot." *TIMES UNION* (Albany, NY) 13 November 1932, p 6.

"Police To Attend Funeral Today Of Mrs. P. S. Miranda." *Springfield Republican*. (Springfield, MA) 15 November 1932, p 4.

"Refuses To Talk About The Murder Of Local Woman." *Springfield Republican*. (Springfield, MA) 13 November 1932, pp 1, 2.

"Ballistic Expert Studies Death Car and Bullets In It." *Springfield Republican*. (Springfield, MA) 14 November 1932, pp 1. 2.

"Racketeer Put on "Spot" as Barber Was Cutting Hair." *The Waterbury Democrat. [volume]* (Waterbury, CT) 12 April 1933, p 2.

"Bootlegger Slain in Barber Chair." *The Evening Gazette* (Worcester, MA) 12 April 1933, p 2.

"Police Unable to Find Clue in Fiore Crime." *Springfield Republican*. (Springfield, MA) 13 April 1933, pp 1, 2.

"Fiore Killing is Called Part of Feud." *The Waterbury Democrat. [volume]* (Waterbury, CT) 13 April 1933, p 8.

"Gangsters Murder Springfield Man." *THE BOSTON HERALD*. (Boston, MA) 13 April 1933, p 4.

"Important Clue in Fiore Murder Probe Worthless." *Springfield Republican*. (Springfield, MA) 14 April 1933, p 8.

"Gangster is Denied Consecrated Burial." *The Evening Bulletin* (Providence, RI) 15 April 1933, p 2.

"State Detective Busy Probing Fiore Murder." *Springfield Republican*. (Springfield, MA) 15 April 1933, p 4.

"Fiore is Buried Without Services." *Springfield Republican*. (Springfield, MA) 16 April 1933, pp 3, 5.

"Ask Cooperation in Fiore Murder." *Springfield Republican*. (Springfield, MA) 16 April 1933, p 7.

"Slayers of Fiore Known to Police." *Springfield Republican*. (Springfield, MA) 22 April 1933, p 4.

"Murdered Man is Linked With Big Still, Seized By Raiders at Suffield, CT." *Springfield Republican*. (Springfield, MA) 31 August 1933, p 1.

"Scarnici Termed 'Killer' By N.Y. Police Official." *Springfield Republican.* (Springfield, MA) 22 September 1933, p 3.

"Slayer That Ely Defended is Given Pardon by State." *Springfield Republican* (Springfield, MA) 30 March 1933, p 7.

Garvey, Richard C. "When Mob Violence Took a Bloody Grip on Springfield." *Springfield Daily News.* (Springfield, MA) 29 April 1985, p 7.

"Attempt to Shake Down Carnival." *Springfield Republican.* (Springfield, MA) 28 May 1932, pp 1, 3.

"Racketeer Put on Spot as Barber Cuts Hair." *The Waterbury Democrat. [volume]* (Waterbury, CT) 12 April 1933, p 2.

Barry, Stephanie. "Organized crime in Springfield evolved through death and money." Published Dec. 11, 2011 in *The Republican.*

Capeci, Jerry (2002). The Complete Idiot's Guide to the Mafia Penguin. ISBN 978-0-02-864225-3.

Puleo, Stephen (2007). The Boston Italians : a story of pride, perseverance, and paesani, from the years of the great immigration to the present day. Internet Archive. Boston : Beacon Press. ISBN 978-0-8070-5036-1.

Devico, Peter J. (2007). The Mafia Made Easy: The Anatomy and Culture of La Cosa Nostra. Tate Pub & Enterprises Llc. ISBN 978-1-60247-254-9.

"Rogue Mobster: The Untold Story of Mark Silverman and the New England Mafia Crime Magazine". crimemagazine.com. Retrieved July 1, 2023.

Ford p. 38 Archived February 3, 2016, at the Wayback Machine

Hoffman, Chris. (May 31, 2013).

"The History of the Mafia in Connecticut." *CONNECTICUT MAGAZINE.*

Ford, pp. 59-60 Archived May 7, 2016, at the Wayback Machine

Feather, Bill. "Springfield + Worcester factions." 16 March 2018. https://mafiamembershipcharts.blogspot.com/2018/03/springfield-worcester-factions.html

Critchley, David (November 19, 2008). The Origin of Organized Crime in America: The New York City Mafia, 1891 1931. Taylor & Francis. ISBN 978-0-203-88907-7.

Ford, pp.50-51 Archived February 19, 2016, at the Wayback Machine

Babick, Lisa. "The Scibelli Regime Leadership Chart." Button Guys, New York Mafia.

"Jury Quizzes 11 in Crime Probe." *THE SPRINGFIELD UNION* (Springfield, MA) 26 June 1974, pp 1, 13.

"80 years ago, the Mob came to Atlantic City for a little strategic planning". Press of Atlantic City. Retrieved August 13, 2023.

Tonelli, Bill (2012-08-31). Mob Fest '29: The True Story Behind the Birth of Organized Crime. ISBN 9781614520436

Barry, Stephanie. "Organized crime in Springfield evolved through death and money." 11 December 2011. http://www.masslive.com/news/index.ssf/2011/12/organized_crime_in_springfield.html Accessed 15 June 2023.

About the Author

In his book, MAFIA CONFESSION- "King of Bootleggers" Murder, Author Nicholas Parisi dives deep into the dark, riveting history of his family's notorious past as bootleggers.

Nick was born in West Springfield, Massachusetts, having grown up among "The Families" on both sides of the river, direct descendants of the individuals he portrays in his works. Through his art, he immortalizes the stories of those who have come before, honoring their memory for generations to come.

When he is not writing about the New England Mafia, he can be spotted on the golf course, fly fishing in his favorite river, playing poker, or at a local winery.

Nick, the father of Giovanni, Dominic, and Anthony, resides in Southern California with Renee, his beloved partner.

Contact: nparisi1@msn.com

Follow: www.AuthorNicholasParisi.com

www.Instagram.com/Author_Nicholas_Parisi

www.facebook.com /profile.php?id=61552358322030

Thanks for reading. If you enjoyed this book, please consider leaving an honest review on your favorite store.

- AUTHOR NICHOLAS PARISI

Printed in Poland
by Amazon Fulfillment
Poland Sp. z o.o., Wrocław

33691861R00186